THE YALE MANAGEMENT GUIDE FOR PHYSICIANS

T0324815

THE YALE MANAGEMENT GUIDE FOR PHYSICIANS

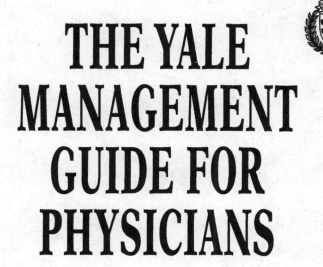

Stephen Rimar

John Wiley & Sons, Inc.

New York • Chichester • Weinheim • Brisbane • Singapore • Toronto

This publication is designed to provide accurate and authoritative information in regard to the subject matter covered. It is sold with the understanding that the publisher is not engaged in rendering legal, accounting, or
other professional services. If legal advice or other expert assistance is
required, the services of a competent professional person should be sought.

ISBN 0-471-38458-5

To my parents, Helen and Steve
Who taught me that if you believe in something
you can make it happen

To my daughters, Liz and Christine
Who gave me a reason to try

And to my wife, Joan
Who showed me how

THE YALE MANAGEMENT PROGRAM FOR PHYSICIANS

FACULTY

- Rick Antle, PhD
  Professor of Accounting and Senior Associate Dean
  Yale School of Management

- Elizabeth H. Bradley, PhD, MBA
  Assistant Professor of Public Health
  Associate Director, Health Management Program
  Yale School of Public Health

- William Gombeski Jr., MBA
  Director of Marketing
  Yale–New Haven Health System

- Theodore Marmor, PhD
  Professor of Public Policy and Political Science
  Yale School of Management

- Christopher McCusker, PhD
  Associate Professor of Organizational Behavior
  Yale School of Management

- A. David Paltiel, PhD
  Associate Professor of Health Policy and Administration
  Yale School of Medicine/Yale School of Management

- Stephen Rimar, MD, MBA
  Director, Yale Management Program for Physicians
  Associate Professor of Anesthesiology & Pediatrics, Yale School
    of Medicine
  Associate Professor, Yale School of Management
  Medical Director, Yale Medical Group

- Victor H. Vroom, PhD
  John G. Searle Professor of Organization and Management,
    Professor of Psychology
  Yale School of Management

- Jeffery T. Wack, PhD
  Lecturer in Epidemiology and Public Health
  Health Management Program, Yale School of Public Health

- William D. White, PhD
  Associate Professor of Epidemiology and Public Health
  Head, Health Management Program, Yale School of Public Health

CONTENTS

SECTION 2: FINANCIAL MANAGEMENT

SECTION 3: ORGANIZATIONAL MANAGEMENT

SECTION 4: ESSENTIAL MANAGEMENT SKILLS

ACKNOWLEDGMENTS

This book would not exist without the Yale Management Program for Physicians, initially developed to increase the number of physician leaders in the Yale School of Medicine. The original steering committee was and remains the force behind this extraordinary Yale program, and I am deeply indebted to its members: Stan Garstka, the deputy dean of the School of Management (SOM), Will White, head of the Health Management Program at the School of Epidemiology and Public Health (EPH), Steven Permut, former Director of Executive Programs at SOM, and Sam Chauncey, the former head of the Health Management Program at EPH.

An educational program is only as good as its faculty, and I've been privileged to work with a truly outstanding group. In addition to the contributing authors of this book who comprise the primary faculty of the Yale Program, several other people have contributed to the development and execution of the curriculum, including Don Hudson, Bruce Carmichael, Ruth Katz, Nancy Keinz, Jason Jennings, and Carolyn Cummings.

In the end, it is the program's graduates that attest to its success, and we've been blessed with an exceptional group of physician-leaders. I am particularly indebted to those who helped develop the case studies used in this book: Douglas Baker, Robert Bernasek, Katherine Biagas, Joshua Copel, John Crowe, Antoni Duleba, Jonathan Goldstein, Howard Haronian, Scott Spector, and Kathleen White.

I owe special thanks to my friend and colleague in the fight for physician leadership in healthcare. David Leffell, the senior associate dean for Clinical Affairs at the School of Medicine, has been essential to the success of the program. The sponsorship of the program by the Yale Medical Group, the Medical School's faculty practice plan which he directs, provided the support to make it happen. And it was he who first suggested I write this book.

Several outstanding editors have contributed to the effort: Renana Myers, who championed the book's concept, Karl Weber, who helped solidify my early ideas, and Karen Hansen, who made it a reality. Finally, I am eternally grateful to my wife Joan, whose in-house editing helped channel my energy and focus my thoughts.

New Haven, CT
September 5, 2000

INTRODUCTION

Physicians and Management

Stephen Rimar

We physicians are in trouble. Having dominated healthcare delivery for nearly a century, we find ourselves floundering in the wake of recent events. Surveys show that unhappiness and a feeling of helplessness continue to grow among both new and experienced practitioners. Managed care, consumerism, expensive technology, and government regulation have altered the landscape of medical practice, and physicians are unequipped to deal with these changes. Indeed, simply pursuing what's in the patient's best interest has become difficult. And the line between the practice of medicine and the business of medicine has grown thin.

We developed the Yale Management Program for Physicians in 1998 to train physicians to cross this line and take a leadership role in the evolution of healthcare. The premise of the program is that traditional medical education fails to provide the knowledge and experience that doctors need to shape the evolving system. The goal of the program at its inception seemed simple: to provide a quality introduction to management. Drawing on the knowledge and experience of the outstanding faculty of the Yale Schools of Management, Medicine, and Epidemiology & Public Health, a curriculum was developed.

But management programs for physicians are a dime a dozen, including at this writing more than 10 MBA programs established just for doctors. We distinguished ourselves from the competition (a theme discussed repeatedly in this book) by incorporating a unique element: a required management project to be completed by participants, often with the help of a management graduate student, during the three-month program. The project consists of developing a plan for the physician's practice that involves either a new business opportunity (e.g., opening a new office, adding a partner) or a reorganization of an existing process (e.g., redesigning office telephone coverage or patient flow). It was the introduction of this project that demonstrated to us the real depth of the helplessness physicians feel, and the profession's failure, despite extensive training, to prepare doctors to be leaders in the healthcare arena.

What's Wrong with Medical Education

The American medical educational system is arguably the best in the world. Its contributions to medical research and practice are unparalleled, and students from around the world come to the United States for medical training at all levels. But while the curriculum and experience offered to trainees have undergone only minor modifications in the past 20 years, the skills required to practice medicine in the real world have changed considerably. The practice of medicine is more than determining the correct diagnosis and overseeing the appropriate therapy. Today it encompasses integrating people, systems, and technologies. It requires working *with* organizations and *within* organizations. And it can no longer be accomplished through a series of doctor's orders.

Our first session of the Yale Program was truly enlightening, and we modified the curriculum, sometimes on the spot, to accommodate what we observed. Physicians had no problem with the traditional course content—indeed, most physicians are outstanding students who have mastered the art of digesting large amounts of material in a short period of time. The projects, however, baffled them. Despite their education and experience (all were midcareer physicians with a management role in their practice group), they had no idea how to approach the organizational project. It was then that we realized the real deficit of medical education: The ability to develop an idea, articulate it, and then convince others to support it, is never addressed. Such management skills have little to do with the practice of medicine as traditionally conceived, but they have everything to do with managing and leading effective medical practices.

This became the primary driver of the Yale Program. Of course, management is about finance, marketing, economics, and the other staples of a business school curriculum; the Yale Program could easily provide this content. But in order for physicians to make a difference in healthcare, for them to assume the leadership roles so many are seeking, this knowledge must be taught in the context of experience. Integrating the lecture content with the experience of the organizational project achieved this. Our experience with physicians has convinced us that learning to develop, articulate, and persuade others to support an idea for an organization by using the tools and concepts of the management disciplines is the key to becoming a successful manager and leader in healthcare.

The Take-Home Version

The Yale Program is extremely interactive, with sessions that are more discussion than lecture. In keeping with our philosophy that pertinent experience fosters skill and knowledge development, it culminates with a Saturday retreat at which each physician gives an oral presentation of his or her project. The presentation is actually a sales pitch. The physicians are given 10 minutes to sell their ideas to the group, which assumes the role of the audience to whom the idea must be sold (e.g., hospital administrators, practice partners, a managed-care organization). This approach is not only effective as a teaching method, but is extremely popular with the physicians. So as we approached the concept of a book based on this highly interactive program, we were challenged to capture its spirit as well as its substance. We needed to incorporate the project experience.

The book is designed to give the reader the unique essence of the Yale Program: that combination of the theoretic and the practical, the perspective of the academic and the practitioner. It accomplishes this by supplementing each lecture (a traditional classroom-style introduction to an essential management discipline) with a case study. The idea for each of the cases came from actual projects by physicians in the Yale Program, although the cases themselves (including names and circumstances) are fictional. Each was written to illustrate the practical application of the concepts outlined in the corresponding lecture and concludes with a How to Do It section, which suggests steps to follow if one is involved in a similar situation.

How to Use This Book

Although each lecture and case is written as a self-contained unit, there is considerable cross-referencing. This is essential because management, like medicine, requires the synthesis of information and thought. References to other sections and overlapping ideas, content, and discussion are necessary to reinforce many critical concepts. Because of this, the book is best read in its entirety, from start to finish. The cases, however, are titled to help locate a specific practical solution to a management problem. The reader, therefore, can quickly find a case that provides concise, practical advice and proceed from it to its associated lecture and to other sections of the book as needed.

But physicians take note. This book, like the program from which it evolved, is simply a primer on management. We hope it stimulates the interest of physicians and provides the impetus for them to delve into other books and articles (many of which are provided as references) for more detailed information. For readers like the physicians in our program, it will surely whet their appetite. And a taste for management, once acquired, can signal the beginning of your transformation from a provider to a healthcare leader. Good luck, doctor!

Healthcare Systems

LECTURE 1

Introduction to Healthcare Policy*

Theodore Marmor

Overview—Where We've Been in Healthcare Policy and Where We're Going

Why should physicians and healthcare managers care about healthcare policy? This serious question deserves careful reflection. The past 10 years have without a doubt produced great changes in the world of healthcare financing, as well as significant changes in the perception of the healthcare professions. Is this a revolution? How are we to make sense of these changes? What do they auger for the future? In answering these questions, I will suggest some ways of understanding the volatile context within which you will be practicing your profession. This requires a step back, to think about American healthcare as a whole.

To begin, we need to describe the arrangement of financing, delivering, organizing, and overseeing healthcare in the United States, what some people ambiguously call the healthcare system.

---

*The phrase "healthcare policy," while in common usage to designate policies affecting the financing, delivery, quality, cost, and regulation of medical care services, is actually misleading. In this lecture we discuss the policies that shape the world doctors, nurses, administrators, and payers face with medical care. Healthcare is a euphemism and is a much broader concept than medical care. Hence the lecture uses "medical care" to refer to the policies cited above.

Figure 1.1 The American healthcare system.

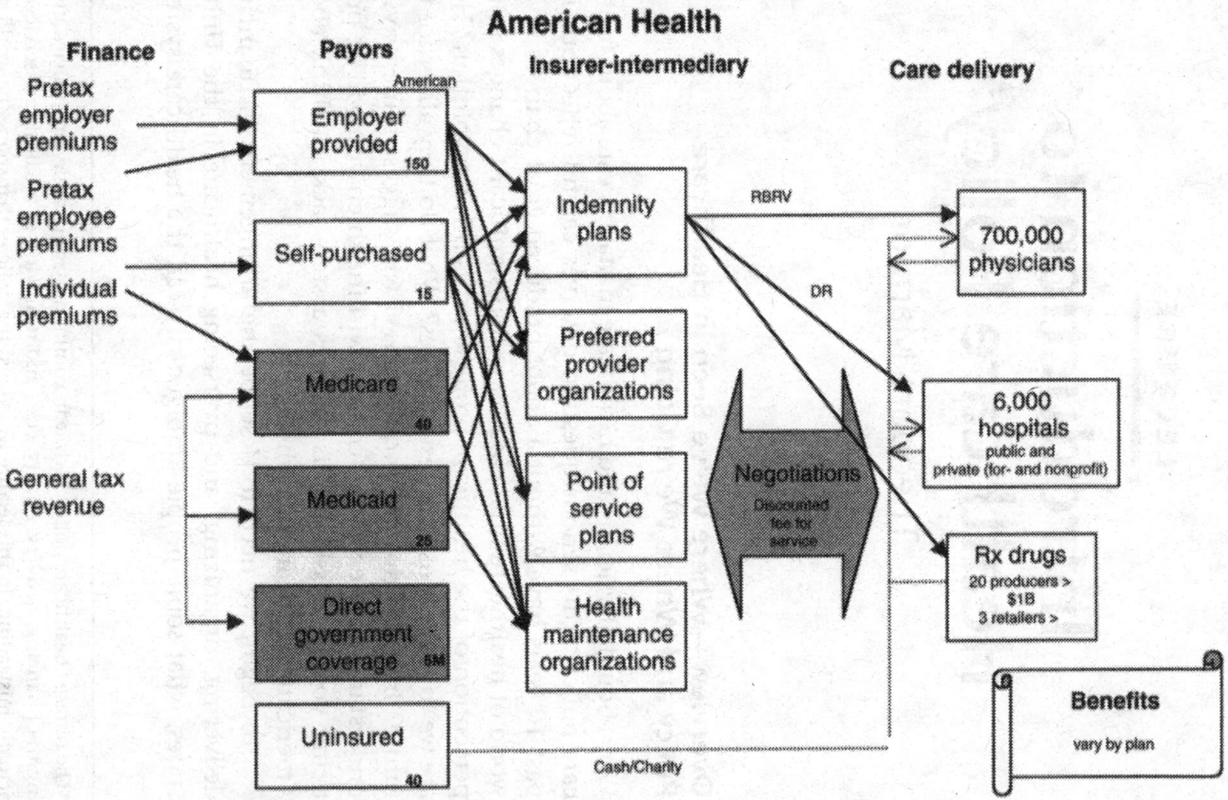

American Health

Finance | Payors | Insurer-intermediary | Care delivery

American

Pretax employer premiums

Pretax employee premiums

Individual premiums

General tax revenue

Employer provided 150

Self-purchased 15

Medicare 40

Medicaid 25

Direct government coverage 6M

Uninsured 40

Indemnity plans

Preferred provider organizations

Point of service plans

Health maintenance organizations

RBRV

DR

Negotiations
Discounted fee for service

Cash/Charity

700,000 physicians

6,000 hospitals
public and private (for- and nonprofit)

Rx drugs
20 producers >
$1B
3 retailers >

Benefits
vary by plan

4

Because of significant changes in the past two decades, we must examine not only the different elements, but also how they relate to each other (Figure 1.1). As this diagram shows, American healthcare is an amalgamation of public, for-profit, and nonprofit institutions, operating with private and public finance, and marked by both competition and regulation. One way to think about this complex mix is to consider separately the sources of finance, the payment methods for services, the structure of insurance intermediaries, and how care is organized and delivered.

Sources of Finance

From where do the resources originate that ultimately finance healthcare? The first thing to notice in answering this question is that, contrary to popular shorthand, the American system is not one of private sector, free enterprise. Rather there exist enormously significant public, as well as private, sources of financing. General tax revenues provide the lion's share of financing for over 70 million Americans in Medicare (40 million), Medicaid (25 million), and the Veteran's Administration/Department of Defense (5 million). Combine this direct public funding for 70 million individuals with the tax treatment of medical insurance premiums for the 150 million Americans covered by employment-related plans (where the premiums are nontaxable to the recipient and tax-deductible to the employer) to see that public funding comprises a large share of American healthcare. (You surely knew this before, but probably not the magnitude of public funding.) Turning to the private sources of finance, we find self-purchased plans, individual Medicare premiums, employee premiums, and pretax employer premiums. Looking at the complex and varied sources of funding, you can describe the U.S. system as a fragmented mix of public and private sources. Or you can say America has a balance between public and private finance. (Note the difference in connotation.)

Not only is there a complex mix of funding sources, but also a diversity of institutions operate between those sources of finance and the delivery of care. This category—all too familiar to medical professionals and administrators—includes indemnity plans, HMOs, PPOs, POSs, and still other acronyms.[1] When analyzing any insurance plan, it helps to think in terms of three important dimensions. One dimension is the location of financial risk. The second dimension comprises the degree of regulation in services provided—from zero or neutral (no interference for services provided that are not prone to fraud) to 10 (the plan evaluates whether the activity should have been done and at what price the activity should have been done).

The third dimension categorizes the organizational form, ranging from prepaid, group practice to solo practice and so on. All three dimensions together characterize the fundamental ways in which healthcare insurance operates. This does not, I should emphasize, constitute a full description of health insurance; it is rather an initial guide to understanding.

Modes of Payment

Much controversy in recent years involves changes in how medical professionals are paid for their services. For all the controversy, there are really only three ways to pay for professional work. One can be paid by the act (fee for service). One can be paid based on the person for whose care (or organ system) one is responsible (capitation), or paid by time (salary or sessional). Most important, every form of payment has distinctive virtues and concomitant vices. This is essential, especially now when there are so many false or misleading claims about payment. (By that I mean false or misleading in the representation of the advantages of any one method of payment.)

A closer examination of each payment method reveals the potential vice that accompanies its virtue. Fee for service payment, for instance, rewards those who work hard. However, that very virtue simultaneously creates an incentive to produce more actions than necessary. The method that rewards energy can reward the possible misapplication of that energy as well.

What of capitation? This payment method disconnects the professional's treatment decision from immediate financial awards. It permits the professional to focus on the medical necessities—for an individual or a group of patients—independent of the immediate reward structure. What is the vice of this payment virtue? The more patients on your list, the better you do financially. It is not simply: The better care you provide those patients, the more you earn.

Let me dwell on the positive side of capitation for a moment. Current disputes (related more to the level of reimbursement and particularly the structure of bonus payments) can obscure capitation's positive incentives. When I visit my physicians at a prepaid, group practice financed by per capita payments, they and I have no obvious and direct monetary connection. Nor is there any connection between their providing more or less medical service to me and a financial reward to them. This permits my doctors to decide, given other constraints, what is most important among the competing claims of their patients. The vice of this virtue is its inherent incentive to take on too many patients, each of whom gets less and less time with physicians, and to do (i.e., spend) less on each patient in the way of tests and procedures. By its nature, capitation creates a tension between independence to allocate care among patients and the flip-side incentive to take on too many patients. That is why in parts of the world where capitation is widespread (e.g., the United Kingdom and Holland) those institutions financing care pay less per capita as the number of patients increases. This is precisely to avoid the risk of the economic incentive just discussed.

What of payment by salary? Take my situation as a professor. Receiving a salary has the great professional merit of keeping my financial well-being independent of my efforts to assist my students. This means dealing with students can be guided by my own conception of appropriate professional conduct. This seems like the professional ideal: The core of the professional's duty is to identify the interests of the client (or patient) and act as their agent. That, in principle, justifies professional autonomy, licensure, and substantial professional rewards. However, salary payment neither rewards doing the right thing (providing more and better care for patients) nor penalizes doing the wrong thing (providing less and worse care). Both behaviors are compatible with payment by salary. Salary systems assume a large set of nonfinancial social and/or occupational constraints to ensure adequate professional performance— doing nothing and doing the right thing are equally compensated with salaries. As I hope this discussion has shown, no one method of payment is self-regulating. Each has vices as well as virtues and that, incidentally, helps to explain the mix of payment methods we increasingly find used in contemporary industrial democracies.

Figure 1.2   U.S. health spending as percent of GDP (1960–1997).

Source: OECD Health Data 1998.

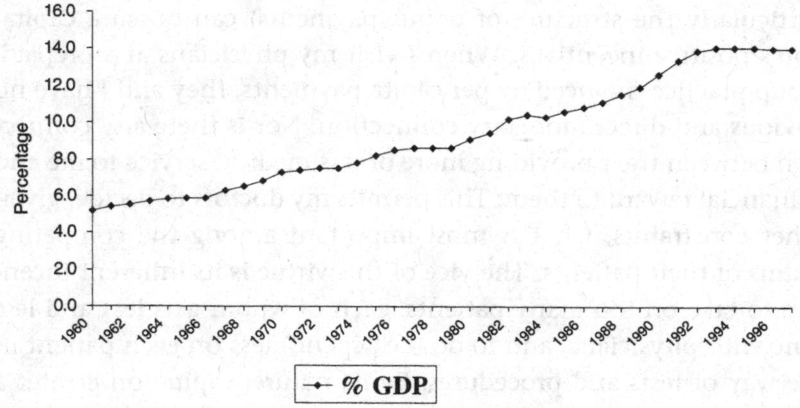

The American Healthcare System—Facts and Figures

As Figure 1.2 illustrates, U.S. spending on healthcare as a percentage of gross domestic product (GDP) has climbed rapidly over the last 40 years, from somewhat over 5 percent to the present 14 percent level. What does this chart mean? Does it indicate the United States spends too much? Not necessarily. As the next chart shows (Figure 1.3), one must also consider the impact of inflation. The inflation in healthcare costs has largely tracked the movement of general changes in the consumer price index (CPI). Periods of high relative inflation in the CPI are also periods of high relative inflation for healthcare. What is important to remember here is to be attentive to the difference between real and nominal increases—real increases deflate the effect of general inflation.

Another point worth noting about U.S. health spending over the last 40 years is the extent to which public spending increased as a percentage of the total, from approximately 25 percent of total spending in 1960 to over 40 percent today. Over that same time period, the federal government assumed a larger role in the payment for medical services. The Health Care Financing Administration (HCFA) became the dominant public actor, creating Diagnostic Related Group (DRG) and Resource Based Relative Value System (RBRVS) payment methods in the 1980s, which in turn were adopted and modified by private insurers. In private-health spend-

Figure 1.3 U.S. healthcare versus CPI (1960–1998).

Source: United States Health Care Financing Agency, Department of Labor.

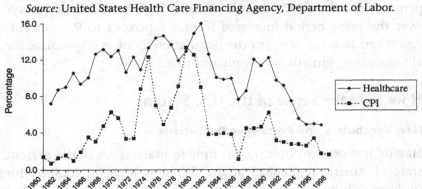

ing, we witnessed a shift from out-of-pocket spending to prepaid insurance. In 1960, over 65 percent of private spending was out-of-pocket, compared with under 40 percent today. Where have these healthcare dollars gone? Since 1960, the physician's share of the healthcare dollar has remained fairly constant, while hospitals have been pressured to reduce costs and length of stays over the past two decades, and nursing homes have received a larger percentage of the healthcare spending pie (Figure 1.4).

One final note about what the facts and figures do not show: Contrary to assertions in the press and by some politicians, demography is not destiny. From 1970 to 1990, Canada and the United

Figure 1.4 U.S. health spending by major components (1960–1997).

Source: United States Health Care Financing Agency.

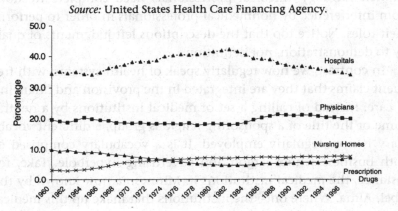

States aged identically. During that time, U.S. outlays rose from 7 percent of GDP in 1970 to 11.5 percent in 1990. Canadian outlays over the same period increased from 7.1 percent to 9.3 percent. Assertions that the aging of the population alone is responsible for U.S. spending growth are simply not true.[2]

How to Make Sense of the U.S. System

New Vocabulary and Persuasive Definitions

Having framed the context, it is time to make sense of the present state of American medical affairs. What is a useful toolbox for understanding where we are? First, I want to discuss standard ways of characterizing medical care and whether those descriptive labels are useful. There have been undeniably dramatic changes in American medicine over the last 30 years. But one major change has been the transformation of the vocabulary with which healthcare is described. Thirty years ago there was a common way of describing medical institutions, one that did not imply a judgment about the quality of the care provided. So, for example, one would describe medical arrangements by the type of patient (e.g., Boston Children's Hospital), the hospital's (often religious) ownership (e.g., St. Vincent's, Mt. Sinai, St. Barnabas), or by a specialty area (e.g., Menlo Park Orthopedic Center). Such descriptions would not, however, convey any overall conclusion. They would not allude to modes of payment, nor necessarily point to anything about the quality of the medical providers. That mode of description in part represented an implicit ideology—medical professionals need complete freedom from interference by nonmedical professionals in order to perform their roles. Notice too that the descriptions left judgments of quality to demonstration, not definition.

In contrast, we now regularly speak of health systems, with frequent claims that they are integrated in the provision and financing of care. Instead of calling a set of medical institutions by a neutral name or the title of a sponsoring religious group, a different vocabulary is now regularly employed. It is a vocabulary comprised of both business school jargon and advertising hyperbole. Take, for instance, the medical institutions in Minnesota now known by the label, Alina. Where once the institutions that make up this medical conglomerate were known by names like Group Health, or Abbott-Northwestern Hospital, the marketing teams devise terms that suggest rather than name. So, to take this particular example another step, Alina is not only to be thought of as an integrated health delivery system, but also one where the incentives of the units are supposedly aligned with those of the patients (or potential customers).

This illustrates a persuasive definition. How do you know an integrated system works well? What can one say about whether incentives are compatible on the basis of a label? The name supposedly says it all—surely you wouldn't want a fragmented system, a nonaligned one! Would you want *un*managed care? One needs to be alert to this associational thinking so as not to be blindly persuaded by labels. Calling something a health maintenance organization does not, in and of itself, mean the organization is in fact operating (or is even designed to operate) to promote health.[3]

The Fallacy of Financial and Professional Independence

The traditional ideal of the learned professional holds that doctors can properly perform their jobs only if they are completely independent financially and professionally. According to this older view, dominant in North America and Western Europe before the Second World War, there should be no intermediaries between physicians and their patients. The ideal presupposes that professionals, certified as competent by self-regulation or by the state, offer their services to patients, who typically spend their own money out-of-pocket. The threat of patient exit (finding another doctor) is supposed to serve as an additional discipline on the professional. This ideal of financial autonomy (charge whatever you decide) and professional autonomy (do whatever you think is right) simply cannot be achieved in the contemporary world of modern democracies, where it is widely believed access to care ought to be available and largely independent of ability to pay. These are the foundational principles of, for example, the Canada Health Act, the legislation setting up the National Health Service, and the statutes governing national health insurance in general. What is incompatible between the traditional professional ideal and contemporary ideas about fair access to healthcare? Access under the traditional model depends on ability and willingness to pay for healthcare, which necessarily conflicts with responding to medical need as defined by ability to benefit. For all its appeal, the traditional professional vision of complete independence in its pure form is simply not viable in any modern democracy, including the United States.

Medical Care—Like Food in a Restaurant?

In recent years, many enthusiastically applied the lessons of free markets to new areas, including medical care.[4] In formal theory and in much practice, free markets allocate capital efficiently because well-informed consumers demand that suppliers produce desired goods or services of high quality at acceptable cost. Transactions between willing buyers and sellers produce an allocation of goods and services that beats the alternatives. Is this way of thinking applicable to medical care? Is it useful in some areas and not others? To answer those questions, we must clarify the presumptions behind free markets, and critically examine them in terms of medical care as the economic good. As I detail in the following, such an examination reveals that healthcare markets do not generally meet these ideal conditions. Market incentives, to be sure, affect the distribution of medical services. But medical care differs in so many ways from the typical market good, wariness is the appropriate stance.

A common free market analogy for medical care is food. Food, the argument goes, is at least as much a necessity as medical services. Yet no patron dictates to restaurants what they must serve, how much they can charge for their meals, or limits the number of restaurants allowed to do business. Nor does anyone sensibly suggest there should be any regulation of where, when, and how often people should be allowed to go to restaurants. (We do, of course, assume some public-health regulation of restaurant conditions is necessary because ordinary customers are not in a position to know a restaurant's hygienic status.) Individuals know when they are hungry, what food they like, and how much they are willing to pay relative to other claims on their budgets. This, according to standard defenses of markets, allows for an efficient allocation of food, so why not use the same type of market for medical care?

The analogy is provocative, but incomplete. There are three important ways in which the analogy breaks down, and the response to each difference underscores the ways in which medical care is not comparable to other economic goods and services.

Certainty of Need   The first difference is that although you know when you're hungry, you don't always know when you are in medical danger. Everyone knows they will experience hunger and they must eat regularly. For health, one does not necessarily know in advance what one's needs are or will be.

Completeness and Symmetry of Information   The second difference that undermines the analogy of medical care to other goods and services involves the distribution of crucial health information. In the case of the restaurant, individuals are uniquely knowledgeable about food preferences and can gather comprehensible information on restaurant alternatives (e.g., read restaurant reviews and ask acquaintances with similar tastes). Note, however, that even if a citizen knowingly requires medical care, he is unlikely to know the specific kind and amount. There is an expected asymmetry of knowledge between the patient (consumer) and the medical professional (provider). By definition, the professional possesses greater knowledge of symptoms, diagnoses, options, and consequences. This imbalance creates a subordinate position for the patient; it requires an element of trust in the physician's application of superior knowledge to the patient's circumstances. The doctor-patient relationship is qualitatively different from that between even the best chef and the most uninformed restaurant patron. This difference in information is significant in identifying why medical care should not be allocated by market principles.

Private versus Community Interest   There is a third way in which the analogy to ordinary economic goods and services is flawed, and that concerns the degree to which community interests are implicated in medical services allocation. One's choices about where and what to eat have little or no affect on others. There is no reason why I should worry or care if someone eats at a restaurant three times a week or once a month. But I should worry if they have a contagious disease and don't get treatment. This direct impact on others of communicable diseases (e.g., tuberculosis) has no counterpart in food, clothing, or housing, essential as those may be. Community interest illustrates yet another way in which the analogy of medical care as a standard economic good is flawed. But the public-health rationale does not begin to exhaust the grounds for policy interventions in the medical world. For a wide variety of reasons—ranging from charitable concerns for the poor, to utilitarian concerns for healthy societies, to egalitarian notions advocating equal access as crucial to medicine— every modern democracy (and most nondemocracies) provides for medical care to be available on some other basis than willingness and ability to pay. Although views range widely in the United States about what care people should receive if they are sick and on what precise terms, the long-standing support for the provision of some medical services regardless of ability to pay (charity care at hospitals, free clinics, prenatal care, vaccinations, etc.) underscores the conviction that medical care is different from a classic economic good.

How Is Medical Care Different?

Modern societies have all responded to these differences in ways that illustrate just how unique medical care actually is economically. The response to the patient's uncertainty of need for medical services has been health insurance. To address the issues about completeness and asymmetry of knowledge, there exist professional standards, licensing, malpractice law, and reimbursement policies. To address community interests in public health and the allocation of care, American policy makers legislated health departments locally, public health-insurance programs (e.g., Medicare and Medicaid), and subsidies. However, like the virtues and vices of payment methods, the responses to medicine's distinctive features can create their own problems.

Health insurance, which correctly recognizes that sick people are not shoppers, at the same time *does* reduce a typical consumer's caution about outlays. Professional standards and sanctions recognize the asymmetry of information between patient and physician. But the high barriers to entry into the medical profession (the long years of training for professionals and the high cost of creating medical facilities) mean that response to change is slow. Public programs and subsidies designed to address the community's interest in a basic level of medical care also creates free rider problems and issues of unequal access (e.g., someone on disability gets Medicare coverage, while many workers in low-income jobs have no health coverage of any kind).

Some regard the nonprofit form of medical care delivery (in hospitals especially) as a response to market failures, in particular the limited access to care that rationing by income entails. Could a nonprofit provide free or subsidized care to meet the needs of those not served under the current medical system? The categories nonprofit and for-profit are easily subject to distortion and misrepresentation. The technical definition of a nonprofit institution is simply that ownership cannot convey an equity interest in the assets of the institution. So, for example, the Ford Foundation cannot issue stock or sell its assets and distribute them to shareholders. That undeniable restriction on a form of wealth acquisition does not, however, mean that nonprofits can ignore the laws of economics. For any institution to survive, it must have resources available roughly equal to its expenditures or claims on its activities. Thus it is not surprising to find that in the 1970s and 1980s, although for-profits provided less free care, on average, than nonprofits, *both* offered less free care in response to increasing financial pressures than they had in earlier decades. The nonprofit organizational form cannot, in and of itself, meet the demand for free care in the face of pressures to hold down expenditures.

Medical Care As Political Football—Explaining the Past and Predicting the Future

We might ask whether there is anything in the broader world of public-policy analysis that might enlighten our analysis of medical care. Are there useful guides on how to characterize, explain, predict, and evaluate the actions of actors whose decisions have a major impact on our lives, whether Medicare, Medicaid, insurance carriers, or professional review boards? Over the last 25 years, analysts of public policy have developed a variety of models to help understand and explain decision making by large organizations. One model is particularly useful.[5]

The Rational Unitary Actor

Graham Allison's model of decision making suggests three ways to analyze a particular course of action taken (or to be taken).[6] The first model, called the rational unitary actor, treats large organizations as unitary and rational. According to it, actors choose policies and actions because they offer the best alternative for the given problem. This model focuses on an action—say, the decision to build a children's hospital—and asks why it made sense.

This model is useful in characterizing problems and establishing potential policy responses. It helps make sense of arguments by analysts who use cost-benefit approaches to evaluation. However, the model is misleading in suggesting that most decisions are made in a unitary, rational way (it is descriptively inaccurate). It also fails to explain the timing of most decisions or provide an adequate account of decisions not taken. Anyone involved in the building of a new medical facility understands how the unitary, rational model fails to capture the diversity of agendas and efforts within an organization, as well as the nonrational elements that come into play.

Organizational Politics

This model focuses on an organization's past behavior as the best predictor of its future behavior. According to this view, organizations do similar things in time $t + 1$ as in time t because routines and standard operating procedures drive day-to-day life. It is not simply that inertia is at work or there are organizational stakes at play (for example, bureaucracies like to grow). In most organizations, the method of decision making involves articulating standard operating procedures. The very nature of this approach implies big organizations don't change rapidly, and knowing the habits and routines of the organization you work for is crucial in predicting what will happen tomorrow and beyond.

This model provides only part of the answer about why a given policy action is taken or not. For some decisions, the model provides a very accurate description of the present and prediction for the future. However, it fails to provide explanations for radically new policies that appear to conflict with the routines of the organizations involved. Moreover, it ignores the role of misunderstandings and personalities in the making and unmaking of policy decisions.

Bureaucratic Politics

The third approach described by Allison is the bureaucratic politics (or micropolitics) model. This model emphasizes determining who gets what, when and how. It is similar to a journalist's account of an event or decision. Several individuals or groups have conflicting desires; they bargain and/or fight, and the outcome is the result of their tactics, intensity, and influence (as well as luck). The model examines the individual players and each person's stakes and interests. This can be quite useful in understanding any decision, particularly when the question is the timing of a policy choice or the way in which a decision emerged.

For example, in order to understand Medicare policy, one needs to consider the role of the House Ways and Means and the Senate Finance Committees. Since its inception, these committees have been directly involved in overseeing Medicare. Even with fairly stable membership on both committees, however, their decisions have varied considerably. The organizational politics model alone can't explain this. And while the rational unitary actor model might set the parameters of actions the committee could have taken, the bureaucratic politics model is more likely to provide the best explanation (for example, the inclusion of the Medicare provisions in the Balanced Budget Act of 1997).[7]

Again, this third model is incomplete. Not all actions can be explained by the behavior of particular parties, unaffected by either an assessment of what is possible, or by the standard orientation of the relevant organizations. To use the Balanced Budget Act of 1997 as an example, the inclusion of HMO provisions for Medicare was in part a reflection of a persistent intellectual movement for over 20 years touting the benefits of market mechanisms in medical care. Simply examining the rise of Newt Gingrich as Speaker of the House and the shift in the partisan control of House committees would not fully explain those dramatic 1997 changes.[8]

Overall, these three models provide a variety of lenses through which to view the world. The type of lens determines the level of detail one can see, and it shapes the patterns of description (what one finds) of explanation (what relieves puzzlement). By extension, it shapes one's anticipation. Because each model suggests different ways of understanding outcomes, they ought to have some impact on how one views a particular situation. In this sense, they can shape our view of the nation's leaders.

Change in the Public Image of Physicians

Of all the changes over the last 30 years, perhaps the most striking in health policy has been the public image of physicians.[9] The traditional conception is that physicians are instruments of improvement in their patients' lives, whether they cure patients of illness or mitigate the consequences of their ailments.[10] The rising, new conception views physicians as simply professionals who treat sick people.[11] According to this view, physicians' claims to superiority and independence demonstrate a conspiracy against laymen. This view holds that much of what physicians do can be duplicated by a computer. Attempts to convince the layman otherwise are simply efforts to protect the economic interests of the physicians' guild.

These two conceptions now exist side by side. Several changes are, however, quite clear. These are charges against all professionals, not just physicians. It exemplifies a view of professional organizations as groups seeking special privileges under guild status, trying to confuse ordinary people about their alleged superior knowledge.

Within the medical field, the growth of medical knowledge has become so rapid, no physician can know all pertinent information in his or her field, let alone relevant developments outside that field. As a result, the traditional notion of a sole practitioner or independent professional and the individual patient in a sealed doctor-patient relationship with no interaction with anyone or anything else is increasingly unrealistic.

In perhaps the most striking change of the last 25 years, the traditional ally of the medical world—big business—has in many instances turned against physicians. Business, driven in part by the rising real and relative cost of care (remember, 150 million Americans are covered in part by employer health plans), has joined the attack on physicians as a cottage industry. They pose this guildlike arrangement is archaic and has insufficiently responded to the industrialization of the possibilities of medical care, the world of computerization and information technology. This breakdown of a solid coalition opposed, for example, to national health insurance, is really quite important.

The combination of these factors has led to a striking shift in public perception of the medical professions. Surprisingly, the medical community has been largely unresponsive to this dramatic shift in public opinion. Consider, for example, the reaction of the medical community to Clinton's health-reform proposal. In the course of that frustrating fight, enormous changes took place outside national politics, especially among private insurers misleadingly called managed-care firms. As a result, there was a great deal of public talk about choice, but no policy change occurred in the end. At the same time, a great deal of change was implemented without choice (consolidation of insurers, reductions and restrictions in benefits, changes in compensation methods).[12]

Challenge of the Future

There has been little, if any, response in the past few years by actors in the public arena to the complaints and concerns of the American medical establishment. Why is this so? I believe it relates in large part to a failure by the medical community to understand the impact of the constant attack on (1) guildlike behavior, (2) the claim of medical competence to do things uniquely that others arguably could do, and (3) the profession's apparent opposition to any type of reform. Without understanding the impact of these attacks, it is difficult to understand how both professional and financial autonomy—so central to the traditional concept of the decent professional—have both become so threatened.

As physicians go forward, they need to hear the critiques of their profession from the media and others and not be defensive. As a society, we have shifted from adulation to skepticism without reflection. You, as doctors, must take part in righting that balance and achieving that reflection.

Acknowledgments

Professor Marmor would like to acknowledge the assistance of Elizabeth Esty, John Pakutka, and Camille Costelli in producing the final draft.

Notes

1. Kongstvedt, P. R. *The Managed Health Care Handbook*. Gaithersburg, MD: Aspen Publications, 1996.

2. Klein, R. "Learning from Others: Shall the First Be Last?" *Journal of Health Politics, Policy and Law* 22 (1997): 1267–1278; Marmor, T. R. "Global Health Policy Reform: Misleading Mythology or Learning Opportunity." *Health Policy Reform, National Variations and Globalization.* New York: Macmillan, 1997.

3. Hacker J., and T. R. Marmor. "How Not to Think About Managed Care." *University of Michigan Journal of Law Reform* (1999): 32.

4. Epstein, R. A. *Mortal Peril: Our Inalienable Right to Health Care?* Reading, MA: Addison Wesley, 1997; Marmor, T. R. "The Procompetitive Movement in American Medical Politics." In *Markets and Health Care: A Comparative Analysis,* edited by W. Ranade, 54–78. New York: Addison Wesley Longman, 1998; Marmor, T. R. "Market Failure." *The Washington Monthly* (2000): 52–56.

5. Allison, G., and P. Zelikow. *Essence of Decision: Explaining the Cuban Missile Crisis.* New York: Addison Wesley Longman, 1999; Marmor, T. R. *The Politics of Medicare.* New York: Aldine de Gruyter, 2000.

6. Allison, G. and P. Zelikow. *Essence of Decision: Explaining the Cuban Missile Crisis.* New York: Addison Wesley Longman, 1999.

7. Marmor, T. R., and M. L. Barer. "The Politics of Universal Health Insurance: Lessons for and from the 1990's." In *Health Politics and Policy,* edited by T. J. Litman and L. S. Robins, 306–322. Albany, NY: Delmar Publishers, 1997.

8. Marmor, T. R. *The Politics of Medicare.* New York: Aldine de Gruyter, 2000.

9. Stone, D. A. "The Doctor as Businessman: The Changing Politics of a Cultural Icon." *Journal of Health Politics, Policy and Law* 22 (1997): 533–556.

10. Relman, A. S. "Physicians and Business Managers: A Clash of Cultures." *Health Management Quarterly* 16 (1994): 11–14.

11. Reinhardt, U. "The Economist's Model of Physician Behavior." *Journal of the American Medical Association* 281 (1999): 462–465.

12. Hacker, J. S. *The Road to Nowhere: The Genesis of President Clinton's Plan for Health Security.* Princeton, NJ: Princeton University Press, 1997.

CASE 1

How to Change Healthcare Policy from the Office

Stephen Rimar

You read it in the newspaper every day: A panel of health policy experts recommends legislative action. Or a managed-care organization adopts a new policy based on a study by health policy experts designed to save costs and improve care. Without reading any further, doctors know it's unlikely their perspective will be represented in the proposals. But what can they do? After all, doctors are not health policy experts—or are they?

Dr. David Gersoff heard constant complaints from his office staff about the amount of time and effort required for obtaining preauthorization from managed-care payers for routine procedures. He decided to perform a simple study to explore the issue.

How Much Does Preauthorization Cost?

Dr. Gersoff wanted to know the administrative cost of preauthorization and whether it varied by managed-care payer. His office staff was convinced they regularly wasted time getting preauthorizations and that some managed-care payers demanded more time than others. To determine this cost, he undertook a simple study in his practice. He investigated the process of securing preauthorization from payers for MRI, surgery, and physical therapy. The data collection procedure was simple. Office staff entered four pieces of information in a log for each preauthorization: the patient's name, the managed-care company, the procedure, and the amount of time spent on the telephone. This log was compiled during two consecutive months. The findings were surprising.

For all payers combined, the average time to obtain a preauthorization for an MRI was 8 minutes; for surgery, 8.5 minutes; and for physical therapy, 10 minutes. The average time to obtain a preauthorization for these procedures, however, varied greatly by payer. On average, payer A provided preauthorization after 10 minutes on the telephone; payer B, 6 minutes; payer C, 14 minutes; and payer D, only 4 minutes. The average time to obtain a preauthorization from all payers was 8.5 minutes.

Dr. Gersoff's office spent significantly more time obtaining preauthorizations from payers A and C, and the total amount of time was staggering—especially given that only three procedures were examined. In addition, when he reviewed the results of this preauthorization process, he discovered *not one preauthorization had been denied*. His staff was right.

In order to approximate the cost of the preauthorization effort to his practice, Dr. Gersoff divided the time spent on the preauthorizations by the salary of his staff members employed in this activity. He knew this would be a conservative estimate of the total cost, since he also spent time obtaining preauthorization, as did his partners, their patients, and their families. The analysis also neglected the opportunity costs associated with preauthorization time—the equally or more beneficial activities that might otherwise have been accomplished using this time.

Dr. Gersoff calculated the average cost to his practice of a preauthorization was $7.50 for payer A, $4.30 for payer B, $11.75 for payer C, and $2.59 for payer D. For all payers, the average was $6.50 per preauthorization. The average time spent on obtaining a preauthorization was 8.5 minutes, and the average cost was $6.50. By multiplying this average time and cost by the total number of preauthorizations for the procedures tracked in the two-month study (168), Dr. Gersoff discovered it cost his practice $6.50 × 168 = $1,092 and 8.5 minutes × 168 = 1,428 minutes (which is 23.8 hours or approximately a day). When he extrapolated this data from two months to an entire year, he realized preauthorizations cost the practice $6,552 ($1,092 × 6) and 6 days (1 day × 6)—more than one workweek a year. And this was only for the most common forms of preauthorizations in the practice!

This simple study powerfully illustrates the impact of preauthorization policies and processes on an office's productivity. Better use of time and money is certainly possible, particularly when one considers not a single preauthorization was denied.

Dr. Gersoff presented his findings to both the managed-care payers and his IPA. In response, each began to examine its policies more closely. Propelled by his findings and the response the data received, Dr. Gersoff committed to studying the situation again in six months. He plans to look for trends within and across payers. In addition, he will examine the steps of the preauthorization process in his own office. While Dr. Gersoff has limited control over payers and the IPA, he does have power to institute changes that make his office processes more efficient and effective.

How to Do It

1. *Learn which organizations interact with your practice the most.* It goes without saying that every good businessperson knows his key customers and suppliers. But customers and suppliers—or patients and referring physicians, in the case of most physicians—are not doctors' only business partners. Physicians rely on a variety of organizations to pay them for services. Managed-care organizations, insurance payers, as well as the state and federal government comprise the group that funds medical practices. Yet many physicians in the Yale Program cannot name the top payer in their practice. Physicians often complain about the impact government or managed care has on their practices, but few make a serious effort to understand or get involved in influencing or changing the system.

The best way to learn about the organizations critical to your practice is to ask your staff which organizations they call the most or whose manuals or materials they consult regularly. Also inquire as to the reasons for the calls and consultations. Write down the responses. This will help you understand the relationship you and your partners have with the organizations. But you need to know more than the name of an organization. After all, you don't call the federal government or an agency; you call a person.

2. *Establish a contact at each one of these organizations.* Establishing a relationship with a human being is the key to a successful relationship with an organization. Ask your staff the name, title, and role of the person they most frequently contact at each important organization. Assess the value of cultivating a relationship with this person. Consider the individual's role in decision making related to medical policy. He or she may be your best contact too. Sometimes, however, a provider relations representative is the key decision maker. More often than not, a case manager or medical director is the real policy maker, and thus the one to know.

One of the most difficult realities of managing contacts in payer organizations is the high turnover of personnel; this makes it particularly difficult to develop long-term relationships. Therefore, know both the name of a contact in the organization and the individual's title and role. Armed with this information, you will be better able to find a new contact if your current one leaves. In addition, people in the managed-care industry often move from organization to organization, following opportunities and organizational restructuring. Your contact person may become a valuable contact in several organizations over the years.

3. *Spend time to learn what's going on.* Contrary to common practice, the best time to cultivate a contact relationship is *not* during a crisis. Establishing a good relationship is rarely a priority in the midst of an emotional shouting match. The key for most physicians is to understand that when they choose to participate in a managed-care plan or enter into a contract with a payer, they are forming a business partnership. And in a partnership, you must know the other person's name.

Once you have identified a contact, the best way to develop a business relationship is to exchange visits. Initiate the exchange by inviting this person to your office. During the visit, introduce the contact to staff members (faces and names are put together) and encourage observation of staff at work. This is a perfect opportunity to discuss your interaction with their organization—perhaps by describing some of the obstacles, and asking for suggestions about solutions. Take this opportunity to arrange a visit to their organization.

This is especially important with regard to your major payer. Many physicians view such a sojourn as a waste of time, citing repeated refusals by payers to listen to them. Successful business-people, however, understand that a good relationship with business partners is critical to success. Because some organizations' employees are more willing or able than others to visit physicians' offices, it is possible you will receive a negative response to your initial invitation. If this occurs, make an effort to visit critical organizations. When disagreements arise, firsthand knowledge of pertinent people and processes is so important to successful resolutions.

4. *Don't forget organized medicine.* Medicine has an extremely large and powerful organization network designed to advance the profession and patient care. Surveys, however, continue to indicate that most doctors are uninvolved. An oft-cited reason for physicians' inability or lack of desire for collaboration is that they are trained to be independent practitioners and have little interest in working as a group. If you are serious about taking back the control of your medical practice, investigate these organizations and get involved. Also remember that policy, like politics, is often a local issue. Organized medicine (e.g., state and county societies, practice associations, etc.) can often exert more leverage than individual physicians or practices. Many societies also form political action committees that are proactive as well as reactive, and they need support. Local PACs often work on issues of direct importance to physicians. Find out what they're dealing with and join forces with them.

5. *Keep up with national and local issues.* By now you may be thinking, "Great, I understand what I need to do, and I want to get involved, but how do I find out what's going on?" In the Yale Program, we encourage physicians to make a habit of reading one source of health policy information on a regular basis. For most, a daily newspaper is a convenient choice. In addition, each society has a newsletter, and there are a variety of professional journals and magazines dedicated, at least in part, to policy issues. The *AMA News*, which is available online, is an excellent single source on issues of interest to doctors. But begin by looking in your home and office at the professional and news publications you already receive. Most physicians say that until they specifically looked for it, they did not realize how much health policy news was already in their hands. By adding just five or 10 minutes a week to your reading, you'll pick up a significant amount of information. Finally, surf the Internet. It is an incredible source of policy information. Bookmark the sites that deliver the information to you with the right amount of detail; the volume and depth of offerings can be overwhelming.

And don't forget your community. Why do so many business-people spend time in charity work or chamber of commerce activities? Often it is to learn what is happening locally and secure a position to influence events. Physicians, particularly those who complain the public does not understand our issues, should consider spending time with nonphysicians. Is community involvement a waste of time or an alternative to income-producing activity? If you're reading this book, you believe the old ways no longer work. Consider doing something different.

6. *Study something in your practice.* As most business professionals understand, cultivating and establishing good relationships with contacts does little for your business if you have nothing substantive to address. Adequate preparation for meetings is crucial. The more specifically you outline the issue and the more compelling the data, the more likely something will happen.

Dr. Gersoff studied a specific office activity for two months to obtain data. Was it pure scientific research? Hardly. But was his methodology acceptable given his goal? Absolutely! Many physicians, particularly those with academic affiliations, say there is no point to such studies; they have so many methodological flaws, they will never hold up to scrutiny. The point they miss, however, is that the data will not be presented to scientists, but to managed-care companies. These companies expect and accept data obtained using a commonsense approach rather than the scientific method. If the purpose of science is to find truth, then the purpose of these studies is to argue for change.

Dr. Gersoff's study was powerful. He persuaded at least two managed-care organizations to research ways to improve their preauthorization processes. His study was simple, focused, required minimal resources, and addressed an issue that affected the care of his patients and the satisfaction of his staff. These are the characteristics of a study worth emulating.

7. *Make data, not opinion, the issue.* Many physicians have a difficult time speaking with managed-care organization representatives because of the emotions elicited by the payers. I have heard doctors refer to payers as Satan's agents (and worse) and criticize them for profiting from the hard work of others while contributing nothing of value. This viewpoint can predispose one to emotional outbursts over such issues as obstruction of care. But business relationships are, after all, people relationships. And people are better able to talk about facts than opinion, especially in an adversarial situation.

If you are angry or confused—get the facts. Study the situation as Dr. Gersoff did and discuss the results with each of your contacts. If possible, couch the problem in the context of other local or national issues to bolster its chance for attention. For example, determine if there is a patient privacy dimension to the problem. And work with your business partners to resolve issues, if not operationally, then contractually. With the right data in your hands, you'll persuade people as effectively as any health policy expert.

LECTURE 2

Management Strategy and Health Economics

William D. White

Economics, Management, and the Allocation of Scarce Resources

The Economic Problem

At the heart of economics is what many economists term the *economic problem—the allocation of scarce resources*. By scarce, economists mean resources for which demand exceeds supply at a zero price (i.e., when a resource is free). Resources that are not scarce may still be very valuable. The air we breathe is an example. Air is essential for life, but (absent problems such as pollution or being locked in a sealed room) there is more than enough to go around. Accordingly, allocating air is not a problem—whoever wants a breath of air can do so without impinging on the ability of others who wish to do so as well.

For most goods and services, there are competing wants. As a result, there is an *opportunity cost* to using resources, which means employing a resource for one use implies foregoing another use. Consequently, demand typically exceeds supply for land, labor, and capital at zero price. Thus a mechanism is required to determine how these resources will be used (e.g., to produce medical care, autos, or housing) and for whom.

There are a number of possible ways society can allocate its resources. One is through markets and the *price system*, defined as the rationing of resources among competing uses based on the ability to pay for them in the marketplace. Another mechanism is through administrative systems such as bureaucratic command-and-control systems. Government regulation is one example. Administrative systems within private firms are another.

Economics provides a powerful framework for examining the interactions of consumers and firms in a market environment and the potential role of government. Business strategy draws on a similar framework to develop management strategies for an individual business organization. In both cases, important issues exist in adopting standard tools of analysis to a healthcare environment. While healthcare shares many common features with other goods and services, there are important differences.

Chapter Overview

This chapter draws from economic theory and business strategy literature to consider generic management challenges firms face when coordinating the production of goods and services and interacting with their external environments. It then considers specific issues involved in applying these frameworks to healthcare. The discussion begins by comparing market systems and public and private administrative systems of allocation—government and private firms. In our system, the firm's basic challenge is to pursue its organizational objectives in the context of a market environment and government oversight.

Then the economic theory of the firm is considered as a basis of the firm's problem from a managerial perspective. This problem can be broken down into two components. First is the analysis of the firm's costs of production and the optimal method of producing any given level and combination of outputs given available technology, organizational capacity, and input prices in light of the firm's objectives. Based on this analysis, the second component is to consider the optimal level and scope of operations given the firm's external environment.

The chapter then considers the firm's costs. It illustrates how economic models can be used to examine the firm's market environments, which may range from highly competitive to monopolistic. The development of business strategies by individual firms to maximize their organizational objectives in the context of their external environments and internal capacities is then discussed. A discussion of what makes the healthcare management environment different and some of the implications of this for business strategies ensues. The chapter closes with a discussion of how the different types of management tools considered in this book, including accounting, marketing, leadership, cost-effectiveness analysis, and decision science, may assist in developing and implementing business strategies.

Allocating Resources—Markets versus Administrative Systems

Market Allocation

One powerful mechanism for coordinating resource allocation is the *market,* defined as the allocation of resources through supply and demand and *the price system.* Commodity markets are an example of price-based allocation. Commodities like beef, corn, heating oil, or gold are allocated to the highest bidder. Price is determined by supply and demand, reflecting consumer demand and the amount sellers are willing to supply at various prices. Adjustments in allocation occur through changes in prices. An increase in the demand for beef will drive up beef prices. This leads to two kinds of adjustments.

First, a higher price will reduce the effective demand for beef. Second, a higher price will lead suppliers to increase production and shift resources (e.g., land, labor, and feed) into raising cattle and away from activities that offer less opportunity for reward. Eventually, barring further changes, a new equilibrium will be reached in which the amount of beef supplied is just equal to the amount demanded at the market price. The market will clear, and anyone wishing to buy (or sell) beef can do so at the market price. The market will balance competing wants and ration resources through the price mechanism. Who gets what will depend on their willingness and ability to pay.

Administrative Allocation

An alternative means of coordinating the production and distribution of goods and services is to allocate resources through bureaucratic command-and-control systems. In command-and-control systems, resources are rationed through administrative decisions. Managers, not markets, ultimately decide allocation within these organizations.

Administrative Allocation and the Role of Government For many, the concept of a command-and-control bureaucracy conjures up images of state-run systems, like the former Soviet Union, in which the entire economy is controlled by the government. Although allocation decisions are primarily made by the private sector in the United States, government does play a central role in the economy. The first role is umpire or arbitrator in the marketplace. The government sets the underlying rules, which enforce contracts and maintain property rights, and, when deemed necessary, rewrites the rules (e.g., introducing environmental regulations due to growing pollution problems). A second important government function is paying for and sometimes producing goods and services in areas where society feels the private market fails to produce an adequate level. Important examples include education, defense, and, as will be discussed in more detail, healthcare.

Private Firms as Command-and-Control Systems Government planning is one example of the bureaucratic allocation of resources, but administrative systems are far from the province of government alone. Vast private systems of administrative allocation exist in our economy in the form of private sector for-profit and nonprofit *firms*. Large for-profit firms like GM, Microsoft, and IBM generate sales that exceed the entire national product of many smaller nations. In healthcare, the budget of a big academic medical system can approach a billion dollars a year. For-profit managed-care organizations (MCOs) like Aetna, CIGNA Healthcare, and drug firms are even larger. Each of these firms has a well-developed administrative system of allocation that coordinates the production of goods and services.

Consider the delivery of inpatient hospital care. Suppose a patient needs hospitalization, and a hospital is selected, typically through a market decision. Once the patient is admitted, this triggers a cascade of internal bureaucratic decisions within the hospital. The admission office assigns the patient to a bed. On the floor, working with the patient's physician, hospital administrators and nursing staff coordinate the delivery of diagnostic, therapeutic, and housekeeping services.

More broadly, hospital managers engage in strategic decisions about what services the hospital or health system should provide and how to market them. Similarly, in the medical services market, physicians who are owners and managers of medical groups routinely make internal administrative decisions about the allocation of resources such as support staff, space, and backup services, while mapping overall strategies for their organizations.

Transaction Costs and the Choice of Allocation Systems

The underlying logic for setting up firms, be they hospitals, group practices, drug firms, or steel companies, is similar. The *transaction costs* of administratively coordinating the production of goods and services within a firm must be lower than attempting to coordinate their production through market exchange. In other words, firms use internal command-and-control systems to coordinate production process for particular goods and services at lower cost than the market could. By the same logic, if markets were more efficient than firms, other things being equal, we would expect buyers to turn to the market rather than firms. A counterexample in the hospital, although less common now, is the use of private-duty nurses. A more extreme version would be a system in which patients and their doctors simply rent bed space in a hospital and then coordinate themselves the provision of nursing care, diagnostics services, drugs, housekeeping, and so on from separate, independent vendors.

Note that while we are aware of the costs, monetary and otherwise, of relying on bureaucracies to perform tasks, using markets can also have substantial costs. For example, consider selling a house and the role of real-estate agents. The typical real-estate commission is 6 percent of the home's purchase price. This means there is a commission of $18,000 for selling a $300,000 home. This is a substantial amount to pay considering the primary product of Realtors is to link buyers and sellers, not add anything to the inherent value of a home.

In this context, the key practical issue from a management perspective is not whether firms do some things better than markets, but exactly where to set the boundary between a firm and the marketplace. One such issue concerns whether the firm should seek to expand or contract the range of goods and services it produces. Should, for example, a single-specialty medical group consider turning itself into a multispecialty group? Or should a multispecialty group consider breaking up into separate single-specialty groups? A closely related issue is the *make or buy decision*. For instance, should a medical group produce its own record keeping and billing services internally? Or should it rely on an external vendor? The economic theory of the firm provides a useful framework for addressing these issues and more broadly exploring its strategic options.

The Economic Theory of the Firm

Economists usually divide the field of economics into two parts: macroeconomics and microeconomics. Macroeconomics deals with the economy at an aggregate level: the national and global economy, international trade, and variables such as consumer spending, the savings rate, inflation, unemployment, and the level of economic growth. Microeconomics deals with the behavior of individual consumers and firms. The basic building blocks of microeconomics are the theory of the consumer and the theory of the firm. Microeconomic models combine these building blocks to examine interaction between buyers and sellers in the marketplace and the implications for social welfare. In this section, we focus on the microeconomic theory of the firm and the supply-side of the market.[1]

The Firm's Problem

In theory of the firm, the basic unit of analysis is an independent business organization—a firm. The underlying challenge for any firm is to select the optimal combination and level of production of outputs to maximize its organizational objectives. For simplicity, we can begin by considering the case of a firm whose sole goal is to maximize its profits from producing a single output, Q. Formally, the firm's problem in this case is to select Q to maximize

$$\Pi = TR(Q) - TC(Q)$$

where we define Π as the firm's profit, let $TR(Q)$ be the *total revenue* the firm receives from selling Q units of output in the marketplace, and let $TC(Q)$ be the *total cost* of producing Q units of output.

Drawing on this framework, the firm's problem can be broken into two parts. The first is to internally examine the firm's cost structure and determine its least-cost way of producing any given level of output Q, $TC(Q)$, given the technology available to the firm and input prices. The second part is to assess the possible revenue the firm may obtain for various levels of output, $TR(Q)$, given the external market conditions it faces. These two analyses can then be combined to determine the level of output that will maximize profits, Π.

In practice, firms typically produce multiple products. They may also have multiple objectives (e.g., a physician practice whose members are concerned about not only income, but also patient welfare), and in healthcare, many firms are nonprofit organizations (i.e., organizations that cannot distribute profits to their owners). Moreover, most firms operate in a dynamic environment. Conditions constantly change and firms need to continuously reassess their problem because of these changes.

While more complex, the same basic analysis presented here can be extended to consider the production of combinations of outputs for a multiproduct firm over time. In particular, breaking up the firm's problem into two components and looking separately at the cost side and revenue side provides a useful starting point.

Terminology and Economics

Before moving on to this analysis, a brief discussion of terminology is useful. Accountants usually define profits as the difference between a firm's receipts and its outlays. They also usually cost inputs at their purchase price. Economic definitions differ from these standard accounting definitions in two important respects. Economists define *economic* profits as a firm's return on investment net the *opportunity cost* of tying up this investment in the firm. This opportunity cost is usually defined as equal to the *market rate of return,* which is the return the firm could obtain from its assets in a representative investment portfolio. An implication of this definition is that a firm will only have profits in this sense if it earns *supernormal* rates of return above market rates—for a firm just earning the market rate, profits will be zero. Likewise on capital assets, economists view the cost of using these assets as their *opportunity cost* based on the return that could be obtained from them at current market rates versus their historical purchase price. This is because values may change substantially over time and no longer reflect the scarcity of the resources involved. For example, a building bought cheap years ago may now be prime real estate.

This terminology is important for two reasons. First, a key premise in economic theory is that competition will drive economic profits to zero. At first blush, this seems puzzling. Profit is supposed to motivate firms. But by this, economists do not mean firms will earn nothing. Rather they mean that under competition, opportunities for *supernormal* profits will be eliminated. Second, *opportunity cost* focuses attention on the need to look at the current value of assets to avoid possible distortions that may arise from relying on historical cost information.

Analyzing the Firm's Costs

The Firm and Its Technology

The firm's cost of producing any given level of an output will depend on the technology of the firm and the cost of inputs. A firm's *technology* can be described as a set of choices between different possible ways of producing output. In some cases, only one technology may be available. In others, there may be a broad range of choices. A key issue is the degree to which it is technologically feasible to substitute alternative inputs. For example, is it possible to substitute physician extenders for physicians, or more generally, to substitute capital for labor? *Input prices* mean the costs to the firm of using inputs. Examples are the costs to a medical practice of hiring personnel, paying for supplies, and leasing equipment and office space.

In a narrow sense, technology may be thought of as physical technology. For example, it may encompass various alternative methods of performing a surgical procedure or diagnostic test, or obtaining a patient history utilizing various combinations of physician time, nonphysician support personnel, and capital equipment and supplies. More broadly, technology may be thought of as encompassing not only physical technology, but also what may be described as organizational technology—choices about how delivery is organized.

From an organizational perspective, an underlying issue is the appropriate choice of incentives to motivate workers. Economists like to describe workers as *agents*—individuals acting on behalf of others. This approach offers a useful framework not only for examining traditional employment relationships, but also relationships between patients and their physicians. We begin by considering generic tools for examining a firm's costs and then discuss agency issues.

The Firm's Costs

Given the range of feasible technologies available, a manager's problem is to assess the costs of alternative methods of producing various levels of output. That is, to cost out these various alternatives and determine the least-cost option for each possible level of output. In this way, the manager can arrive at a *cost function* for the firm.

We have already defined *total cost,* $(TC = TC(Q))$ as the total cost of producing a given level of output Q. Two additional cost concepts are *average cost* and *marginal cost. Average cost* (AC) is defined as the average cost per unit of producing a given level of output, $AC = TC/Q$. *Marginal cost* (MC) is the change in total cost as the result of producing an additional unit of output, $MC = \Delta TC/\Delta Q$. These concepts provide a useful basis for evaluating relations between volume, the range of products produced, and a firm's unit costs due to *economies of scale* and *economies of scope* (see the following). In addition, it is important to consider the time period over which costs are being considered.

Short- and Long-run Costs Not all inputs used by a firm can be readily varied. In the *short run,* the possible level of some inputs may be *fixed.* Consider for example a 300-bed hospital. Suppose the hospital faces a falling census. In the *short run,* it may be feasible to cut nursing staff and other personnel. Staff thus represent a *variable* cost. But the hospital cannot readily downsize capital plant (the buildings) and equipment. In the interim, there may be *fixed* costs associated with these capital investments that cannot be avoided such as maintenance and debt service. Conversely in the *short run,* because a hospital cannot readily expand its number of beds as it approaches full capacity, its costs may be higher than in the long run when it can build new facilities.

Economists define the *long run* as the period in which it is possible to vary all a firm's inputs. The time period encompassed by the short run will, of course, depend on the particular aspect of production being considered. For example, it may be possible to rapidly expand MRI imaging capacity through the use of mobile units. However, adding a new permanent MRI unit or a new operating suite may take years.

Economies of Scale   *Economies of scale* exist when a firm's average cost of producing a unit of output decreases as total volume increases. This implies that at the margin, the cost of an additional unit of output is falling, $MC < AC$ (marginal cost < average cost—see previous material). Conversely, *diseconomies of scale* exist when a firm's average costs are increasing and $MC > AC$. Finally, *constant returns to scale* exist when the cost of an additional unit of output is identical to the cost of producing the previous one.

Economies of scale may arise in two ways. First, if there are substantial setup costs involving fixed-capital investments, but the marginal cost of providing services once these investments are made is constant or decreasing, total average cost may fall as fixed costs are spread over more and more units of output. For instance, setting up a new operating suite requires substantial fixed costs. Once it is established, however, the marginal costs of providing additional services (e.g., the variable costs of increasing the level of services) may be quite low until the suite reaches capacity. Second, there may be economies in the production process itself. For instance, an operating suite staff may be more efficient when they regularly perform open-heart operations than when they do them infrequently. Conversely, *diseconomies of scale* may arise if a firm's costs increase with volume. As a firm grows larger, it may, for example, become less effective in coordinating production than when it was a smaller and more nimble organization.

Economies of scale provide a potential rationale for *horizontal integration,* combining two or more smaller firms to form a large one. Thus, if there are economies of scale in open-heart surgery, it may make sense to combine programs at two hospitals into one to realize the benefits of higher volume at a single site. Conversely, if there are diseconomies of scale, this may provide a rationale for breaking up a large firm into several smaller ones. For example, if there are costly coordination problems in a large group practice, efficiency gains may be realized by breaking it into several smaller groups.

Economies of Scope Another important concept is *economies of scope.* Economies of scope exist when costs are reduced by jointly producing two or more outputs within the same firm. For example, there may be economies of scope from providing medical and surgical services within the same hospital, versus having separate hospitals specializing in each. Patients may, for instance, benefit from increased coordination if both types of services are needed.

Economies of scope are particularly important as a rationale for *vertical integration.* The underlying notion of vertical integration is that firms may be able to realize efficiencies by performing multiple activities in the vertical chain of production. Staff and group health maintenance organizations (HMOs) like Kaiser and the Henry Ford Health System that integrate the provision of care and health insurance are examples. More generally, vertical integration involves decisions by a firm to produce a service or good itself rather than buy from the external market (called *make or buy decisions*). For example, depending on the relative costs, a physician practice may decide to staff its own internal billing department or clinical laboratory or obtain these services from outside vendors. Issues are not limited to the unit costs of services per se, but also consider the implications for coordinating care. For instance, an outside laboratory that is less expensive, but slow, may result in delays that increase overall costs and reduce quality of care.

Agency Issues and Firm Organization

Agency Problems There are obvious gains from the use of agents. Patients can greatly benefit from delegating oversight of their care to a knowledgeable physician, rather than attempting to coordinate it themselves. Firms routinely delegate tasks among employees. However, the interests of agents may not necessarily be aligned with those they serve. This creates the potential for agency problems—abuse by agents of their trust at the expense of those they serve. A provider may, for example, fail to assure the quality of care, provide unnecessary services to inflate a bill, or claim skills they don't actually have.

A major management challenge is to successfully motivate agents. Economists focus on the use of incentive schemes. In broad terms, part of the technology of a firm includes the choice of organizational structure and the types of incentive schemes embedded in these structures. The economic theory of agency provides a useful framework for considering some key dimensions of such schemes and their implications.

In the context of medical care, the basic notion in the theory of agency is that incentives can be created through the use of contingent contracts in which an agent is rewarded (or punished) on the basis of their performance.[2] A useful baseline is a perfect agent who always acts as directed by the employer. In cases where it is easy to observe performance, devising appropriate incentive schemes to replicate perfect agency is trivial. The wage is set at the minimum level, and the agent agrees to deliver a specified level of performance. If they perform as promised, they receive the payment. If not, they are not paid. An example is hiring someone on the spot to shovel snow off a sidewalk. Monitoring whether the job was done correctly is simple. A quick inspection is sufficient—either the snow is off the walk, or it is not. With a small investment in monitoring, the situation of a perfect agent can be replicated.

In many cases, however, the situation is more complex. Collecting information about performance may be costly and measures may include conditions beyond an agent's control. Medical care, as we will discuss later, is an important example. It is often very costly to gather and evaluate information about physician performance. Hard to observe factors beyond a physician's control may play an important role in determining the costs of care and outcomes. Doctor A's patient costs may be higher than Doctor B's because A has a more costly practice style. Alternatively, A may have a more complex case mix. (Or both may be the case.) Even with the best care, a patient may die, while even with poor care, a patient may recover. So outcomes are not always a reliable guide.

Under these circumstances, replicating the outcome that would result from perfect agency through contingent contracts, if feasible at all, may be very costly. Large investments may be required in monitoring. If the agent is at risk for events beyond their control, they may demand a risk premium. An added problem may be that if measures of performance are difficult to objectively validate, agents may refuse to be subject to contracts based on these measures because they do not trust those employing them. An example is a contract in which a patient pays a physician if the physician successfully alleviates the pain. If the contract is based on the patient's subjective assessment of pain level, there is an incentive for the patient to misrepresent the pain level to avoid payment.

Trade-Offs   A central conclusion of agency theory is that when replicating outcomes under perfect agency is costly, consumers may prefer contracts that yield alternative outcomes at lower cost. An especially important application of agency theory in medicine involves trade-offs between quality and cost, but quality in particular is hard to observe. Suppose there is some ideal standard of quality and cost in the absence of any problems with agency. It may be possible to replicate this ideal standard. Suppose, however, this process requires large investments in gathering and evaluating clinical and financial data that dramatically adds to total cost.

As an alternative, imperfect sets of incentives may be preferred that involve trade-offs between total costs and quality. Consider traditional fee-for-service payment versus capitation in the absence of complete monitoring of the appropriateness of care. Under fee-for-service, the more care provided, the greater the reward to the physician. There is, therefore, an incentive to overprovide services. In contrast, under pure capitation, incentives are reversed. A physician receives a flat per-member-per-month payment to cover patients' care. The more care provided, the greater the expenses that must be charged against these payments and the smaller the reward to the physician. Accordingly, other things equal, the incentive is to underprovide care.

The particular type of incentive scheme selected will depend both on provider responses and consumer preferences. Many complex issues are involved in the design of schemes. Two points are important in the context of this discussion. The first is that problems with agency may affect decisions about what firms produce and how. The second is that changes in conditions under which agents operate may lead to changes in the structure of these relationships. Examples are changes in monitoring costs, the ability to gather information about performance, and changes in technology that affect cost and quality.

Analyzing the Market Environment

The prices a firm can command for its products and how sensitive demand is to changes in these prices reflect the underlying demand for goods. They also reflect competitive conditions in the marketplace. It is therefore important to look not only at factors affecting overall demand, but at market structure as well.

In discussing market structure and its implications, useful revenue concepts are *total revenue (TR)*, *average revenue*, and *marginal revenue*. *Total revenue* was defined as the total revenue a firm receives for an output of Q. If it receives a uniform price P per unit, this will simply be $TR = PQ$. *Average revenue (AR)* is defined as TR/Q, the average price per unit of output received. Assuming uniform pricing, AR equals the price P per unit charged by the firm $TR/Q = P$. *Marginal revenue (MR)* is the change in total revenue as a result of an increase in output. If price is unaffected by a firm's output decisions, then marginal revenue equals price, $MR = P$. But if price depends on the quantity of output offered for sale, more output may result in a lower price. As a result, the marginal revenue of offering additional units of output may be less than average revenue. Indeed, if price is very sensitive to the quantity offered (i.e., a small change in quantity results in a large fall in price), marginal revenue may be negative, and TR may fall.

Underlying Determinants of Demand

Underlying determinants of demand include a variety of factors. For instance, the underlying demand for medical care in a community may reflect population demographics because older people use more care. It may also reflect income, other sociodemographic factors, travel patterns, and social norms about care. One key factor is health-insurance coverage. This in turn may reflect social and economic conditions, for example the employment rate, whether employers offer health insurance as a benefit, and in what form.

In addition to factors that directly affect the demand for a good (e.g., demographics), another important consideration is the availability of complements and substitutes for a firm's product. Economists define two products as *substitutes* if an increase in the price of one leads buyers to purchase more of the other. Conversely, two products are *complements* if a rise in the price of one leads to a fall in purchases of the other.

Consider outpatient surgery. Substitutes for hospital outpatient surgery include freestanding surgery centers and surgery at doctors' offices. Complements include physicians who perform outpatient surgery. The price sensitivity of demand for hospital outpatient services is likely to be greater when substitute sources are available at a lower price. At the same time, overall demand for outpatient surgery may reflect the availability of surgeons, and hospitals may offer incentives to recruit physicians who are likely to generate demand for their facilities.

Market Structure

In economics, the term *market structure* refers to the way competition is organized in the market for a good or service. Economists typically draw on the concept of *perfect competition* as a baseline. There are four key characteristics of a perfectly competitive market as typically defined. The first is the existence of a uniform, standardized product and determination of prices by supply and demand. That is, all firms produce an identical output with no product differentiation with respect to quality, custom features, and so on. The second is large numbers of buyers and sellers, each too small individually to influence price or exercise any market power. The third is free entry into and exit from the marketplace (i.e., there are no barriers to entry or exit). The fourth is perfect information, meaning buyers and sellers are fully informed about prices and the technology required for production, and no uncertainty exists about product characteristics.

In many respects, perfect competition represents an ideal market, rarely seen in actual practice. However, the concept serves as a valuable tool in understanding how markets operate and the implications of different types of market structure for prices and quantities and for consumer welfare. We can first consider the properties of a perfectly competitive market and then explore the possible scenarios caused by affecting the number of competitors, the type of product offered, and information available about quality and price.

A central feature of a perfectly competitive market is that competition is impersonal. Because individual buyers and sellers are too small to influence price in any significant way by their behavior, it is rational for them to accept the market price as given (i.e., assume $MR = P$). Under these circumstances, a profit-maximizing firm will expand its output to the point where the marginal cost of an additional unit of output just equals the market price. Below this level of output, it will forego opportunities to increase profits. Above this level, assuming it is operating in the realm where marginal cost is increasing, further increases will diminish profits.

Under these circumstances, competition acting as price takers will drive price down to the level of the minimum price at which firms can operate and just cover their costs and make the market rate of return. This means that in equilibrium in a perfectly competitive market, consumers obtain output at the lowest possible price at which firms will provide it and stay in business. It also means for firms there will be no supernormal economic profits in the sense profits that exceed the market rate for return. Finally, price will just be equal to the marginal cost of producing an additional unit of output—the value of the resources necessary to bid away from other uses to produce this unit of output.

Monopoly—A Single Seller   At the other end of the spectrum from perfect competition is monopoly. By definition, a monopoly exists when a single firm controls the entire market. With total output depending on the amount produced by the firm, output decisions of a firm clearly influence price. The more output a firm attempts to sell, the lower the price it will command, implying $MR < AR$. As a result, it makes sense for a monopolist to act as a price setter and take into account effects on price in selecting the optimal level of output. Therefore, in contrast to perfect competition, assessing buyer responsiveness to price becomes critical for the firm seeking to maximize profits. In particular, economic theory predicts that a profit-maximizing firm will set output at the level at which marginal revenue from selling an additional unit of output is just equal to the marginal cost of producing it ($MR = MC$). Because $AR > MR$, output will be priced above the marginal cost of production. From society's perspective, too few resources will go into producing the monopolized product (i.e., price will be too high and output too low under monopoly).

Monopolies exist because of barriers to entry that prevent competition. There are several possible barriers to entry. One is control over critical resources and/or knowledge. A second is government regulation, like an exclusive franchise. A third is a *natural monopoly*—the existence of economies of scale sufficiently large enough to allow only a single firm to operate efficiently. Natural monopoly is, for example, common with public utilities like electricity and gas.

In the face of barriers to entry, monopolies are in a position to make *supernormal profits,* which are rates of return above the market level. As a result, other firms will have a strong incentive to enter a monopoly's market. Indeed, pressures may be such that monopolies end up dissipating some (and possibly all) of their supernormal returns in defending their markets and maintaining barriers to entry. Examples are expenditures on lobbying to maintain regulatory barriers to entry and expenditures to ensure control of key resources. By implication, this suggests the line between monopoly and more competitive market structures is not always a rigid one and depends on political, economic, and technological factors, which may change over time.

Oligopoly—Competition among a Few In practice, most markets fall in a gray area between perfect competition and perfect monopoly. There are almost always competitors. But competition is among a few rather than many. That is, in the language of economists, production is concentrated among a relatively small number of firms. Under these circumstances, it makes sense for firms to act *strategically* toward each other. The price of output and the quantity produced will depend on how firms interact. Consider a city with three hospitals. The outcome of any action taken by one hospital will depend on the response of its rivals. Accordingly, there will be strong incentives for them to game each other. Sharply different outcomes may arise depending on the way this game plays out. For instance, hospitals could aggressively compete, adopt a live-and-let-live policy, or seek to collude to obtain maximum profits. An important and growing area of microeconomics uses what is known as game theory to explore factors that may lead to these alternative types of outcomes.[3]

The picture may be further complicated if there are concentrated buyers of services and/or concentrated sellers of key inputs. Thus, on the demand side, a hospital may have to deal with managed-care plans that control substantial market share. On the supply-side, a hospital may face concentrated provider groups. One example is a group practice that contains the majority of the physicians in a given specialty in a hospital's market. Another is a nurses' union.

Product Differentiation   Another characteristic of perfect competition that typically does not hold in markets like healthcare is a uniform standardized product. Competition between firms occurs not only on the basis of a product's price, but also its attributes. Important attributes in healthcare include perceived technical quality, the range of services available, location, and amenities. Indeed, a provider's reputation, service offerings, and location may be far more important to consumers in selecting doctors and hospitals than price. This is especially true if consumers are insulated from the full cost of care by insurance. The result is the incentive for providers to differentiate themselves in ways that make them more attractive to consumers. This may include investments in advertising to project an attractive image as well as investments in tangible attributes.

Imperfect Information   Clearly, industries like healthcare do not satisfy the assumption of perfect information. There are large uncertainties about when healthcare is needed and what type of care is required when illness occurs. It is also difficult to evaluate the quality and appropriateness of care. As will be discussed in the final section of this chapter, the presence of these kinds of uncertainties pose major problems for the effective operation of market competition. Responses to these problems help explain many of the unique institutional features of the healthcare industry. Problems with uncertainty may also help explain continuing reservations that exist about market-oriented strategies in healthcare.

Developing a Business Strategy

The heart of *business strategy* is the analysis of complex business environments that deviate from perfect competition. One focus is improving overall market performance from a societal perspective. But a second, our focus here, is assisting individual firms to successfully interact with their external environments to maximize their organizational objectives.

There are three important steps in developing a successful business strategy. The first step is to assess the strengths and weaknesses of the firm's position in the marketplace. The second is to evaluate alternative options for defending against competitive threats faced by the firm and exploiting its strengths. The third is to select among these options to develop a coherent and consistent business strategy to promote the firm's objectives.

In his seminal work on business strategy, Michael Porter observes that business strategy is often thought of primarily in terms of interacting with a firm's existing competitors.[4] In order to be truly successful, however, he argues that the firm needs a much broader perspective. In particular, he identifies five key market forces that are essential for a firm to address in developing a successful business plan:

- Threat of entry
- Bargaining power of customers
- Bargaining power of suppliers
- Threat of substitute products
- Jockeying among current contestants

Porter's framework offers a powerful tool not only for assessing a firm's competitive position at a given point in time, but for evaluation on an ongoing basis. Underpinning this framework are many of the microeconomic concepts we have just discussed.

Threat of Entry

Understanding the barriers to market entry can allow a firm to successfully exploit them. At the same time, however secure a firm is with its current environment, it must be alert to the threat of entry of new competitors. Failing to do so can be fatal. One key factor to assess is the presence of economies of scale. For example, opening a new academic teaching hospital involves enormous costs, not only in building a facility, but also in finding and hiring medical staff. Potential entrants must be prepared to make a very large front-end investment and have adequate sources of capital to finance this investment.

A second issue is product differentiation. A firm may be much more difficult to challenge if it offers a product that is unique in the market. Automobiles like Volvo, BMW, and Mercedes created their own market niches. Their high quality and special features insulate them from the competition of auto companies producing low-cost, generic autos. However, they may still need to compete with well-established rivals seeking to enter the market with a new product line. Lexus is an interesting story. The Toyota Corporation, after securing itself as a leader in low-cost vehicles, pursued the high-quality, high-price end of the auto market. The result has been significant trouble for the likes of Cadillac, Lincoln, and even Mercedes. Medical practices may pursue a similar strategy of product differentiation, but need to be prepared for the potential threat that rivals will introduce new, competing product lines.

A third source of barriers to entry is distribution channels. Lack of access to distribution channels can sharply limit the ability of new firms to enter the market. For instance, access to physician referral networks has traditionally been critical to establish a new medical practice. Entry for physicians lacking such access has frequently been very difficult. Conversely, if changes occur in the organization of distribution channels, this may open access, in turn easing entry and threatening established firms. An interesting example is the emergence of Internet-based marketplaces for a variety of goods and services. Although still a new area, the future may bring significant changes in distribution channels for medical equipment and supplies and possibly even physician services.

A final important source of barriers to entry is government regulation. Patent laws and federal drug-testing requirements create major regulatory barriers to entry in the drug industry. In the hospital industry, a potential barrier is the requirement for a Certificate-of-Need (CON) for those states where they are still in force. Such laws may enable established hospitals to make it quite difficult for competitors to build new facilities in their markets. Conversely, changes in CON laws may increase the threat of entry.

Bargaining Power of Customers

Firms also need to assess customers' bargaining power. The emergence of a powerful buyer can have a major impact on a firm. The growing role of MCOs has substantially altered the market position of physicians in many areas of the country. Under managed care, the ability of practices to bear financial risk and exert market power has become much more important. Both factors offer a rationale for moving from solo to group practices and even horizontal integration. Likewise, market power may offer a powerful incentive for hospital mergers independent of any efficiency gains, raising the concerns of antitrust regulators. Finally, the presence of powerful concentrated buyers may offer a rationale for new institutional forms such as Independent Practice Associations (IPAs), which bring together individual physician practices to bargain as a group with MCOs, again raising antitrust concerns.

Bargaining Power of Suppliers

The bargaining power of suppliers is critical to a firm. For example, physician practices must pay close attention to their relationships with hospitals. Cultivating a relationship with a particular hospital may strengthen a practice's position with respect to its rivals. But it also makes the practice more vulnerable to problems with a hospital. For example, the hospital can exercise market power, knowing the physician practice cannot use another. This is a particular concern for practices that have exclusive contracts with a hospital in areas like radiology, pathology, and emergency services.

Threat of Substitute Products

Some firms focus myopically on their particular products and fail to consider trends in substitute products—a potentially lethal error. For example, many hospitals failed to embrace outpatient surgery, holding fast to their traditional inpatient services. As payment and consumer preferences changed, however, hospitals scrambled to catch up with the competition of freestanding outpatient surgery centers. A similar situation is happening again, in which many hospitals find themselves competing with office-based surgery. Unless the hospital can develop a strategy to address these threats, the result may be a rapid decline in business.

Jockeying with Current Contestants

A firm must also examine the threats and opportunities in jockeying for position with existing competitors. One important consideration is whether the firm is operating in a growth area, a mature market, or a declining industry. The hospital industry in the United States enjoyed rapid growth in the post–World War II era in an environment of generous fee-for-service reimbursement. Since the mid-1980s, however, it has experienced excess capacity in inpatient beds, a shift towards outpatient services and hospital closings. This has dramatically altered the strategic environment in which hospitals operate.

Selecting a Strategy

Once a firm assesses its position, it needs to map out options and select among them to develop a strategy. In developing a strategy, it is important that the individual components make sense and are consistent. Beyond this, Porter notes two broad types of strategic approaches.[5] The first is to work within the constraints of the existing marketplace, considered a reactive strategy. The second is to change the structure of the marketplace, which he calls proactive. Exploiting a firm's relationship with an existing distribution channel is an example of a reactive strategy. Creating a new distribution channel would be a proactive approach.

What Makes Healthcare Different?

Distinctive Features

In typical consumer industries like automobile, soft drink, or soap manufacturing, consumers pay for goods and services directly out-of-pocket. Firms in these industries are for-profit, and the roles of professionals and public subsidies are minimal. Healthcare is very different. Distinctive institutional features of the healthcare industry as traditionally organized are discussed in the following.

Large Public Subsidies of Care Federal, state, and local governments pay directly for over 45 percent of all healthcare in the United States. This includes public insurance programs, particularly Medicare and Medicaid, and direct provision of care, through public hospitals and public subsidies for indigent care. In addition, the federal tax indirectly subsidizes private health-insurance premiums by allowing firms to provide insurance on a tax-free basis.

Heavy Reliance on Insurance to Pay for Care Insurance is the primary method of paying for care. Combining public and private sources, insurance accounts for the bulk of total expenditures. Consumers pay for less than 20 percent of care out-of-pocket.

Extensive Reliance on Self-Regulating Professionals to Provide and Coordinate Care Medical professionals play a key role in producing this care. Physicians are the primary coordinators of care, and the practice of medicine is regulated under state licensure laws and a complex web of voluntary certification standards and insurance rules regarding reimbursement for services.

A Major Role for Nonprofit Institutions in Delivering Care Although there are some for-profit hospitals, the hospital industry, which accounts for about a third of all health expenditures, is dominated by nonprofit voluntary and public institutions. In 1997, for-profit hospitals accounted for only 13 percent of all hospitals and 9 percent of all hospital beds.[6]

Underlying Reasons

What explains these unusual features of the industry? At least two factors appear critical. First, there are strong public preferences for ensuring access to healthcare. Second, as noted earlier, there are major problems with uncertainty in healthcare markets. In particular, consumers are frequently uncertain about their future demand for care, which may be very expensive. They are also uncertain about exactly what care they will need if they fall ill. Finally, they are uncertain about the quality and appropriateness of the care they receive. It is often difficult for patients to evaluate whether care was good or bad.

The traditional features of the healthcare industry are, in many ways, a response to these issues. But while they solve some important underlying problems, they have generated new ones. This is particularly true in the case of managed care—an attempt to satisfy both the need for access and the demand for quality. In attempting to do so, however, a new set of problems has arisen.

Assuring Access There are two aspects to assuring access. One involves public health and concerns about issues that go beyond a particular individual. Untreated, infectious diseases like tuberculosis can pose risks for the entire population. Children's health can determine the future quality of the workforce. Clearly, the government has a responsibility to assure access to protect the general population. Most public dollars, however, go to groups like the elderly and the disabled, for whom the benefits are largely at the individual level.

The other aspect of assuring access involves equity and fairness. An important vehicle for access to care has been public insurance. Public insurance, however, is far from comprehensive. Some 44 million people lack any form of health insurance. Many without coverage obtain care through charity by hospitals and provider groups. But as the healthcare system becomes increasingly subject to tight financial constraints, charity care is diminishing. Many healthcare managers are reassessing their role in providing charity care.

Uncertainty The uncertain nature of demand for healthcare coupled with the high cost of care created the initial demand for health insurance. Healthcare expenditures are highly concentrated, and difficult to predict. In 1999, the top 4 percent of spenders in the United States accounted for $450 billion, more than half the U.S. total expenditures on patient care. The top 10 percent of spenders accounted for $613 billion, almost three-quarters of total U.S. expenditures on patient care.[7]

In exchange for a relatively small payment of an insurance premium, health insurance offers a relatively certain way for consumers to protect themselves from potentially ruinous expenditures. In addition, public tax subsidies of private insurance create an added incentive even where expenditures are relatively predictable (e.g., routine preventive services).

Once illness occurs, however, consumer uncertainty about what care is needed generates obvious incentives to employ sophisticated professionals, particularly physicians, as agents. Patients need agents not only to provide services, but also to coordinate the services. Thus patients rely on their physicians not only to directly provide specific diagnostic services and treatments, but also to develop and oversee treatment plans. Reliance on agents, combined with uncertainty about the quality and appropriateness, in turn opens patients to agency problems that generate a demand for quality-assurance mechanisms. Examples include public standards and professional self-regulation.

Managed Care

One striking feature of the healthcare system since the early 1980s has been a major restructuring of the insurance system and the rise of managed care. Until the early 1980s, public and private insurance in the United States was on a fee-for-service basis.[8] Shopping decisions about what care to buy and from what providers were made by patients and their doctors. There was little or no effort by insurers to evaluate appropriateness and neither patients nor providers had much incentive to control costs. Under fee-for-service payment, the more care doctors and hospitals provided patients, the more they were paid. Meanwhile, individual patients were largely insulated from the cost of services, paying only a small portion of the bill.

Many have argued that this system created incentives to overprovide care. In any case, coupled with rapid technological change, this system led to a rapid growth in healthcare spending that pushed healthcare expenditures up from around 6 percent of national income in the 1970s to 10 percent in the late 1980s and today's level of approximately 13.5 percent.[9]

Managed care may be seen as a response to this situation. The thrust of managed care has been to shift the control from patients and their doctors to payers. In contrast to individual patients, payers stand to reap the full benefits of reductions in expenditures from more competitive shopping and reductions in the use of services. They have sought to realize these gains by selectively contracting with providers and then using payment incentives to steer patients to these groups. Through use of administrative controls and new types of payment schemes, they have further attempted to modify provider behavior. Examples include precertification requirements for hospital admissions, utilization review, and capitated payment schemes.

These changes have been associated with a marked decrease in the growth of healthcare costs in the private sector. The future, however, is unclear.[10] Regardless of what lies ahead, the advent of managed care has dramatically changed the business environment in which physicians operate. For example, physician practices historically marketed to individual patients and referring physicians. In the new business environment, however, contracting with MCOs has become critical for physicians to keep their patient base. Cost pressures by MCOs in turn have contributed to hospital mergers and a shift away from traditional solo physician practices.

At the same time, managed care has led to mounting consumer and provider concerns about controls on the use of services and choice of providers. The effect of this on quality is unclear.[11] But concerns about the adverse effects of managed care on quality are reflected in a shift in patterns of growth in MCO enrollments toward plans that are less restrictive. In addition, they have led to legislative proposals for a patient bill of rights and legal actions against MCOs.

Management Tools and Implementing Business Strategies

This book provides the reader with an introduction to the field of management science and a range of tools that can assist managers in developing and implementing business strategies. A critical aspect of management involves successfully coordinating and motivating employees. This raises issues beyond the underlying economics of incentive system design. Organizational culture, communication, and coordination are essential to success. The fields of organizational behavior and leadership science provide a powerful framework for considering these issues (Lecture 6).

Externally, the field of marketing offers a basis not only for developing strategies to sell a firm's product, but to assess underlying market conditions. Key tools include techniques for evaluating consumer preferences and price sensitivity and identifying potential market segmentation that offer opportunities for niche products (Lectures 8, 9, and 10). The field of finance likewise offers tools for facilitating firm interactions with financial markets and capital sources (Lectures 3 and 4).

The economic tools describe relationships between the firm and its external environment in largely impersonal terms. But building relationships with customers and suppliers often involves developing close relationships. Tools for facilitating negotiation can be critical in building these relationships (Lecture 7).

Finally, accounting tools are critical both for supporting internal decision making and for a firm's interactions with its external environment (Lectures 3, 4, and 5). Cost accounting systems provide the firm's eyes and ears in evaluating internal performance; without an adequate assessment of costs and sources of value within the firm, managers can find themselves flying blind. Economic models typically take accounting information as given. But failure to develop high-quality accounting systems led to problems at several healthcare organizations, including Oxford Health Plans and Harvard Pilgrim.

Notes

1. Mansfield, E. *Microeconomics*. New York: Norton, 1997.

2. Dranove, D, and W. D. White. "Agency and the Organization of Health Care Delivery." *Inquiry* 24 (1987): 405–415.

3. Brandenburger, A. M, and B. J. Nalebuff. *Co-opetition: 1. A Revolutionary Mindset That Redefines Competition and Cooperation: 2. The Game Theory Strategy That's Changing the Game of Business*. New York: Doubleday, 1997.

4. Porter, M. E. "How Competitive Forces Shape Strategy." *Harvard Business Review* (March/April 1979): 137–145.

5. Ibid.

6. *Statistics NCHS. Health United States*. Hyattsville, MD: U.S. Government, 1999.

7. *Research AHRQ. The Distribution of Projected Health Care Expenditures, 1999*. Division of Modeling and Simulation, Center for Cost and Financing, 1999.

8. Dranove, D., and W. D. White. "The Changing Nature of Health Care Competition." *Journal of Medical Practice Management* 8 (1993): 233–236.

9. See note 6 above.

10. Chernew, M, R. Hirth, and S. S. Sonnad. "Managed Care, Medical Technology, and Health Care Cost Growth: A Review of the Evidence." *Medical Care Research and Review* 55 (1998): 259–415.

11. Miller, R., and H. Luft. "Does Managed Care Lead to Better or Worse Quality of Care?" *Health Affairs* (September/October 1997): 7–25.

For additional information on business strategy: Besanko, D, D. Dranove, and M. Shanely. *The Economics of Strategy.* New York: Wiley, 1996.

2

How to Expand a Practice and Retain Control

Stephen Rimar

Simple ideas often spawn complex organizations. Thus controlling while growing is a common problem for successful businesses. As a business grows, the rules must change. To sustain the vision of the founder, large organizations also need the right people and systems in place. The larger the organization, however, the harder it becomes to manage people and processes.

The growth of medical practices from mom-and-pop operations to multi-office, multiple-provider businesses has been commonplace in the last decade. The way in which practices grow, however, often predicts their success or failure. The secret to a positive outcome lies largely in how the organization is structured.

Opening New Offices

Dr. Phillip Harvey opened two additional offices and hired an associate in the past year. In his words, "The growth and expansion of my practice has led to nothing but confusion. Despite our best intentions, it seems impossible to standardize operations at the three offices. The problem is that this business is used to having one decision maker. And since I can't be in all places at all times, each office does what it wants." Dr. Harvey needed a way to command and control his growing business because he could no longer oversee everything himself. Finding the right balance between standardizing and individualizing and between centralizing and decentralizing activities was a major challenge.

Dr. Harvey began the overhaul of his practice by reviewing the workflow process in each office. By asking staff, "What needs to be done and how do we currently do it?" he developed a list of common tasks. From this list, he identified processes suitable for standardization (scheduling, patient and referring physician communication, payment, and medical record keeping) and those better left to the discretion of the individual office staff (physical layout and upkeep, hours of operation, dress code). He then determined the role of each employee in these processes and formalized it with the development of a job description that reflected the workflow. More importantly, he designated a leader in each location to oversee office operations. He met with these office managers individually and as a group to review and record standardized policies as well as job descriptions.

While Dr. Harvey was quite sure his employees and patients would prefer a small-office environment to a corporate, franchised look, he wanted some of the advantages enjoyed by franchises because of centralization, such as economies of scale. Buying in larger quantities to realize cost savings could be achieved only through centralizing the purchasing process. Also, using a single employee to schedule visits at all three offices would improve efficiency and possibly patient satisfaction. In addition, Dr. Harvey hoped to create new staffing options by cross-training employees to work at all offices. This would be more easily accomplished if office processes were the same. Other aspects he easily determined must be centralized included strategic planning, financial control, and marketing.

Monitoring performance at each office was critical. When the practice comprised a single physician in a single office, it was easy to know how things were going. But how could Dr. Harvey know about an office's performance if he was only there part-time? The answer was to set up a performance monitoring system for the practice. First, he needed to decide what measures were critical. Tracking the number of office visits was important, but so was monitoring things that he used to have a feel for simply because he was present, such as patient waiting time. He decided on the following list of performance measures:

CLINICAL OPERATIONS

Total patient visits

Number of new patients

Visits and procedures by type

Consultations

Time between patient check-in and checkout

FINANCIAL OPERATIONS

Billings

Deposits

Expenses

Having chosen his measures, Dr. Harvey then developed a system for collecting data and reporting results. With the help of his office managers, he established standardized reports (and their frequency) and made their production and review one of the managers' primary responsibilities. Furthermore, he engaged his accountant as an internal auditor to review the performance system data and verify its accuracy. In this way he had centralized oversight of the office managers' reports.

Dr. Harvey's plan to manage his growing practice was reasonable and practical given the nature and size of his organization. But how closely does his experience represent that of slightly different organizations?

What Is an Organization?

Traditionally, economists speak of the firm as an owner/entrepreneur-directed entity. The simplest organization consists of a freelance worker, contracted independently for services. This individual knows everything about his business and controls it completely because he *is* the business. Even if he hires two or three assistants, as long as the service he provides is the direct result of his actions, and he is in direct contact with his customer, he remains the firm. His individual spirit and energy is a major attraction to customers and often the reason they seek his help. So it is with an individual physician in practice.

As a business grows, however, it becomes difficult for one individual, no matter how energetic or spirited, to control a firm. The business takes on the characteristics of an organization—a collection of people who must function as a group to succeed. For the owner/entrepreneur, it's no longer sufficient that *he* alone achieves his goals. He must now see that *his organization* achieves its goals.

This is a difficult concept for many physicians. Medical training focuses on the individual, an independent practitioner. While doctors are taught to seek the advice of others, they are told repeatedly that a good doctor must be capable of making his own decisions. Furthermore, they are not trained to work in organizations. This schooling can produce great owner/entrepreneurs, but leaves physicians totally unprepared to be organizational leaders, or chief executive officers as they're called today.

How to Do It

1. *Articulate processes and develop procedures.* What does your organization do, and how? If this is not clearly articulated by management, then employees will decide for themselves. So begin by writing down, in broad terms, everything you and your employees do. From this list, certain critical processes should become obvious. When Dr. Harvey provided oversight of the scheduling process, there was little need to write the steps down. The more people involved in an activity, however, the greater the need to develop standard operating procedures. Physicians generally hate the idea of standardized processes (remember clinical pathways?). But operating procedures and process articulation enable employees to do things in the same way. Standard procedures consist of steps intentionally designed to optimize the process. They allow the physician to ensure that what he (the owner/entrepreneur) would do by himself, is done by others.

2. *Develop job descriptions.* Once you list what is done in your organization and how, you need to assign the work. You need to consider the types of skills necessary for each employee. This exercise results in job descriptions, a difficult but essential ingredient of a successful organization. Securing examples of descriptions from colleagues in other offices or hospitals or via the Internet can ease the task. The trick is to develop job descriptions that are detailed enough to describe the work that must be done, but not so detailed that they stifle talented employees willing to take initiative.

3. *Design a reporting structure.* Procedures and job descriptions delineate who does what. However, they do not necessarily address who will be responsible for ensuring the work is done. Since Dr. Harvey could no longer personally oversee the work of each employee, he needed a management group to help. He structured reporting relationships such that each employee answered to an office manager (there was one in each office), who, in turn, reported to Dr. Harvey. The owner/entrepreneur of an expanding business must learn to run his organization through his managers.

4. *Select performance measures.* If the owner/entrepreneur cannot directly oversee an organization's work, it is unlikely that he can accurately assess its performance without some assistance. This help comes in the form of organizational performance measures. Like Dr. Harvey, each owner/entrepreneur must identify measures that best answer the question, "How well are we doing?" But the answer to this question must be expressed in terms that reflect the organization's purpose and goals. For example, a practice that is primarily interested in maximizing profit for its shareholders may have quite different measures than one devoted to providing excellent affordable healthcare. The definition of success, as well as its measurement, must come from the organization's purpose and goals.

5. *Establish a reporting system.* Simply selecting performance measures is not enough to ensure they will be collected and distributed. Delineating a means of reporting these results—and a reasonable frequency of reporting—is essential. It did not take Dr. Harvey long to realize that the collecting and reporting of performance measures was a valuable new activity for his practice. He made it his number one priority, convinced that it was the key to his organization's success.

6. *Control the flow of information.* Dr. Harvey's employees knew how important the performance data was because he told them their salaries depended on this information. For this reason, he needed some way to ensure its accuracy. This was already being done with financial reports; Dr. Harvey's accountant served as an outside auditor and all the offices used a single entry system. Handling of operational data (patient visits, etc.), however, needed to be done similarly. Dr. Harvey, therefore, purchased a software program that tracked both operational and financial data. His accountant, in his external auditing role, audited all performance information twice a year, the results of which were announced to the employees.

7. *Be the leader.* No matter the size or complexity of an organization, success does not come without leadership. As his practice grew, Dr. Harvey invested more time on the leadership of his practice and less on the practice of medicine. Many physicians are unwilling to make this commitment, but the legacy of an inactive leader is often a failed enterprise. Some physicians abrogate their leadership role and unofficially transfer power to competent office managers. Their practices may continue to succeed by most measures, but, if examined closely, they will primarily reflect the priorities of the office manager.

8. *Get help.* A leader needs a management team. This was clear to Dr. Harvey. He developed the office manager position and expanded his accountant's responsibilities. He relied on these people to command-and-control while he led the organization. Dr. Harvey realized the practice had become too big for everyone to report directly to him.

9. *Avoid creating a bureaucracy.* Ineffective, inefficient, rigid, and unresponsive—that is how people often describe a bureaucracy (the positive aspects of a bureaucracy are seldom considered). Many people blame command-and-control systems for the loss of enthusiasm and spirit in a growing organization. While it is difficult to compete with start-up businesses for seemingly endless supplies of energy, it is possible to secure a responsive and productive working environment by carefully developing and implementing what are often viewed as the stifling force—the business systems themselves. Review your systems on a regular basis and change them if necessary. The hallmark of a great organization is its ability to change. Signs of an unhealthy environment may be subtle (e.g., fewer patient referrals) or blatant (e.g., increased staff turnover). Watch for them.

10. *This is not just for start-ups.* The process Dr. Harvey underwent is helpful for growing businesses and businesses that are failing. How better to cure an organization than to assess it from the ground up? In many ways, the process is analogous to a physical examination. If you suspect an aspect of your practice is not functioning as it should, thoroughly examine it. If you think the entire organization requires attention, try Dr. Harvey's approach. In either case, you are bound to find something you can heal.

Financial Management

3
LECTURE

Introduction to Accounting

Rick Antle

In the film *RKO 281,* Orson Welles and Herman Mankiewicz have a shouting match about William Randolph Hearst's attempts to prevent the release of *Citizen Kane,* which portrayed a thinly disguised Mr. Hearst in a manner he found disagreeable. Mr. Mankiewicz, the coauthor of the *Citizen Kane* script, is concerned that the heads of the major movie studios will succumb to Mr. Hearst's threats and destroy the movie. At one point, Mr. Welles screams at Mr. Mankiewicz: "Who are they, Mank? Who are these men that you are so afraid of? Who are these tiny, little, f***ing men? They're accountants!"

Mr. Mankiewicz was unmoved by Welles's argument. Perhaps he thought the studio heads were not accountants, or that being accountants was irrelevant. Or perhaps Mr. Mankiewicz knew that accountants *could* be very dangerous, especially to those who are ignorant of the fundamentals of their profession.

Experienced managers have learned, sometimes the hard way, that it pays to know something about accounting. This lesson is often repeated, most recently in the managed-care industry. Attempts to bring more management into healthcare have unleashed the accountants, and caused more than a little anxiety.

One way people combat their anxiety is by acquiring knowledge. This works particularly well for accounting anxiety, since the fundamentals of the discipline are quite easy to master. And since all accounting is based on these fundamentals, it's well worth the effort. This chapter provides a brief introduction to the fundamentals of accounting. Knowledge of these fundamentals can go a long way to understanding the financial aspects of any business—whether it be a multinational corporation or a solo medical practice.

Overview

The fundamentals of accounting can be grouped into three components: economic concepts, accounting conventions, and accounting mechanics. *Economic concepts* are the ideas that guide the construction of accounting reports. *Accounting conventions* are the rules and customs used to apply economic concepts to practical situations. *Accounting mechanics* are the procedures to ensure the accounting system properly processes the data it receives.

Before going further, the definition of accounting must be addressed. *Accounting is a process of writing a financial history of an organization.* It focuses on the *stocks* of financial resources and obligations at points in time, and the *flows* of financial resources over time. Accounting results in periodic *financial statements,* which depict these stocks and flows. The *balance sheet* is the financial statement that shows financial resources and obligations at a point in time. The *income statement* and the *statement of cash flows* are two financial statements that depict the flows of resources over time. Economic concepts provide overall guidance for the measurement of stocks and flows contained in balance sheets and income statements, and accounting conventions provide more detailed instructions.

The depictions of financial resources and obligations at points in time should fit with the depictions of the flows of resources over time. That is, the balance sheets, income statements, and statements of cash flows should *articulate*. Accounting mechanics work to guarantee that balance sheets actually do balance and that the financial statements articulate properly. Accounting mechanics ensure that the accounting process functions as intended.

The Balance Sheet—Assets, Liabilities, and Equities

Figure 3.1 shows balance sheets for Microsoft Corporation at June 30, 1998 and 1999. A balance sheet lists an entity's *assets, liabilities,* and *equities*. These are the economic concepts that guide the presentation of balance sheets.

In common usage, an *asset* is a resource, which is something that will yield a benefit for its owner. Benefits come in many forms, including enhanced enjoyment of life. However, in economics, we are usually more specific about the benefits. We require them to be *financial*. So an asset in economic terms is something that will yield a financial benefit.

Similarly, in common usage, a *liability* is something that imposes a cost on its owner. In economics, we specify that this cost is financial.

Equity commonly means the value of what the owner owns. We talk about our equity in specific *entities*. For example, a bank might offer you a loan in the amount of your equity in your house and the land on which it sits. The house and land are the specific economic entities at issue in the bank's offer. The value of your equity is the value of your ownership claim on your house and land.

The Microsoft Corporation is the economic entity being depicted in the balance sheet in Figure 3.1. The equity on Microsoft's balance sheet reflects the value of what Microsoft's shareholders own.

It is important to understand exactly what kind of reflection this is. Everything that affects equity is either a plus (an asset) or a minus (a liability). For example, the value of shelter provided by your house is an asset. The fact that its roof needs a costly repair is a liability. We can always separate the things owned into those components that provide benefits and those that impose costs. Equity is then a residual. It is net resources owned, the difference between assets and liabilities. In equation form,

$$\text{Equity} \equiv \text{assets} - \text{liabilities}$$

The symbol "$\equiv$" signifies that we are making a definitional connection between equity, assets, and liabilities. There are many ways

Figure 3.1   Balance sheet.

Microsoft Corporation
BALANCE SHEETS
In millions

June 30	1998	1999
Assets		
Current assets:		
Cash and short-term investments	$13,927	$17,236
Accounts receivable	1,460	2,245
Other	502	752
Total current assets	15,889	20,233
Property and equipment	1,505	1,611
Equity and other investments	4,703	14,372
Other assets	260	940
Total assets	$22,357	$37,156
Liabilities and stockholders' equity		
Current liabilities:		
Accounts payable	$ 759	$ 874
Accrued compensation	359	396
Income taxes payable	915	1,607
Unearned revenue	2,888	4,239
Other	809	1,602
Total current liabilities	5,730	8,718
Commitments and contingencies		
Stockholders' equity:		
Convertible preferred stock—shares authorized 100;		
shares issued and outstanding 13	980	980
Common stock and paid-in capital—		
shares authorized 12,000;		
shares issued and outstanding 4,940 and 5,109	8,025	13,844
Retained earnings, including other		
comprehensive income of $666 and $1,787	7,622	13,614
Total stockholders' equity	16,627	28,438
Total liabilities and stockholders' equity	$22,357	$37,156

we can work with this identity, but two are especially important. We can measure the value of equity and then deduce what the values of assets and liabilities might be. Or we can measure the value of assets and liabilities, and then deduce the value of equity. If all measurements were perfect, both approaches would lead to the same amount. But measurements are not perfect, and we can get radically different answers for the value of equity, assets, and liabilities depending on the approach taken.

A Balanced Sheet?

For example, economists and financial analysts often begin with the *market value* of a company's equity, and seek to understand what assets and liabilities it implies. The *market value* of a corporation's equity is the price of its common stock times the number of its shares outstanding. On June 30, 1999, the closing price of Microsoft common stock was $90.1875 per share. From the stockholders' equity section of Microsoft's balance sheet presented in Figure 3.1, there were 5.109 billion shares of common stock outstanding on June 30, 1999 listed. Therefore, the stock market valued Microsoft's common stock as

Market value = $90.1875 × 5.109 billion = $460.8 billion

Economists and financial analysts may value the equity first, but accountants start from the other direction. Accounting starts with the assets and liabilities and then derives the equity. We can determine the accounting results, called the *book value,* from Figure 3.1.

The book value of a firm is tied to the assets and liabilities recorded on its accounting balance sheet. For simplicity, let's think about a firm with no liabilities, so its book value is equal to its total assets. Where can these total assets come from? There are only two possibilities. One is that the shareholders contributed them (or the cash that was used to purchase them). The other possibility is that the entity generated them by earning a profit. Stated in terms of equity instead of assets, the common shareholders have equity from two sources: what they contributed to the corporation and the earnings of the corporation that have not been distributed to them.

This characterization of equity holds even when a firm has liabilities. Equity is either contributed or generated by earnings.

Therefore, the part of common shareholders' equity in Microsoft that arose from their contributions is listed as common stock and paid-in capital. That amount is $13.844 billion on June 30, 1999. The undistributed income is listed as retained earnings, and that amount is $13.614 billion on June 30, 1999. These combined are approximately $27.4 billion:

Common stock and paid-in capital	$13.8 billion
Retained earnings	13.6 billion
Total book value of common shareholders' equity	$27.4 billion

The difference between the market and book values of Microsoft's common equity is $433.4 billion! In ratio terms, the market value of Microsoft's common stock was 16.8 times its book value on June 30, 1999:[1]

$$\frac{\text{Market value}}{\text{Book value}} = \frac{\$460.8}{\$27.4} = 16.8$$

This difference raises two questions:

- What assets and liabilities does the market think Microsoft has?
- How can Microsoft's balance sheet work when book value is so different from market value?

The Accounting Identity

Let's start with how Microsoft's balance sheet works. The key observation is the *definitional connection* between assets, liabilities, and equities. Whatever assets and liabilities are, or however they are measured, equity is the difference. If accounting leaves out a portion of Microsoft's economic assets, the book value of its equity will be less than the market value of the equity. Skim the list of Microsoft's assets and judge if this is the case. You will see one important item is missing: the value of intellectual property in Windows and Office software.

Balance sheets work because we *define* equity to be the amount that makes them work. The order of items presented on the balance sheet disguises this a bit. Instead of presenting the balance sheet as

$$\text{Equity} \equiv \text{assets} - \text{liabilities}$$

it is arranged as

$$\text{Assets} \equiv \text{liabilities} + \text{equity}$$

This form is commonly called the *accounting identity*, and is used to structure the presentation of balance sheets. For example, Microsoft had total assets of approximately $37 billion, total liabilities of $9 billion, and total equities of $28 billion on June 30, 1999. Therefore, Microsoft's balance sheet on June 30, 1999, is really an identity:

$$\text{Assets} \equiv \text{liabilities} + \text{equities}$$
$$\$37 \text{ billion} = \$9 \text{ billion} + \$28 \text{ billion}$$

Likewise, its balance sheet on June 30, 1998, is an identity:

$$\text{Assets} \equiv \text{liabilities} + \text{equities}$$
$$\$22 \text{ billion} = \$6 \text{ billion} + \$16 \text{ billion}$$

One can now see why a balance sheet always balances: Equity is the amount defined to make it so.

In other words, the accounting identity holds no matter how we measure assets and liabilities. The measurement could be precise and exacting, or it could be inane. For example, one possibility is to say assets and liabilities are always exactly zero. It's not very accurate, and certainly not very useful, but it works in the accounting identity. We would just define equity as always exactly zero, and would get

$$\$0 = \$0 + \$0$$

While Microsoft's balance sheet omits some important economic assets, it reflects more than an inane $0 = 0$ relationship. That is, the balance sheet at least provides some details to define Microsoft's assets and liabilities. The market value of its equity gives us a total value, but it provides no specifics as to Microsoft's individual assets and liabilities.

Accounting would be easier if we could measure asset and liability values exactly. But this is impossible. For example, whenever a physician treats a patient, there is a potential legal liability. Malpractice insurance generally covers the easily measured costs of the attorneys and the award or settlement. However, costs such as lost income from time attending legal proceedings and the potential damage to a physician's reputation (and subsequent impact on future income) cannot be measured. This is also true for the cost to the physician in anxiety and hours of lost sleep. Like determining the chances that a specific patient will suffer a second heart attack within a specific six-month period, these potential costs are impossible to quantify with any precision.

Accounting Conventions—The Balance Sheet

This discussion may seem a bit esoteric, but it illustrates an important accounting principle. Since the accounting identity holds with even an inane measurement system, and since a completely accurate system cannot exist, what matters most in constructing a balance sheet are the *conventions* used for the measurement of assets and liabilities.

Accounting conventions fall into two categories: recognition and measurement. *Recognition* is the act of formally incorporating an item into the accounting identity; recognition conventions guide this process. *Measurement* is the act of assigning numerical values to items; measurement conventions guide these assignments.

Accounting conventions begin with more specific definitions for assets and liabilities than introduced thus far. In accounting

> **An asset is a probable future economic benefit obtained or controlled by an entity as a result of a past transaction or event.[2]**

> **A liability is a probable future sacrifice of economic benefits arising from present obligations of an entity to transfer assets or provide services as a result of a past transaction or event.[3]**

To see how these definitions are applied, let's examine some of the assets and liabilities that Microsoft lists on its balance sheet (Figure 3.1 again). The first asset Microsoft lists is cash and short-term investments. Cash is the item that most directly generates a future economic benefit. Cash can be used to acquire materials, labor, or even an intangible asset like a patent. Cash can be used to settle obligations. Further, there is no great difficulty measuring the financial value of cash: We just count it.

So cash is clearly a probable future economic benefit, and we can presume Microsoft owns or controls the cash listed on its balance sheet. But where did Microsoft get this cash? No doubt, some past transaction like a sale of products or services resulted in Microsoft's cash acquisition. So all the requirements for asset recognition exist.

Microsoft lumps short-term investments in with cash. These investments are highly liquid assets that are almost cash. For example, Microsoft probably owns a few shares of General Motors, mostly as a way to invest surplus cash. If necessary, Microsoft could easily convert a few shares of General Motors into cash by selling them on the New York Stock Exchange. Further, we could estimate what Microsoft would have received for those shares on June 30, 1999, had it sold them. We could just look up the price in the *Wall Street Journal*.

Accounts receivable are amounts owed Microsoft by its customers as a result of goods delivered or services performed. Because accounts receivable are claims to future cash payments, they are assets. Microsoft owns these receivables, and they arose from a past transaction. If there are expected uncollectible amounts, these are deducted from the gross accounts receivable to accurately reflect the amount Microsoft expects to collect.

Property and equipment are the land, buildings, computing equipment, vehicles, and so on that Microsoft owns for use in the business over several periods. They are assets to the extent they will be used to Microsoft's economic advantage. Microsoft owns this property and equipment, and it came into Microsoft's possession from a past purchase transaction.

Property and equipment are shown on the balance sheet at historical cost net of (minus the) accumulated depreciation. The accounting depreciation is simply an allocation of the initial cost of these assets over time. For example, their accounting depreciation in each year may be a constant fraction of their historical cost. These assets are not as liquid as short-term investments, and their economic value is probably not easily obtainable.

Equity and other investments include Microsoft's stakes in other corporations and joint ventures. They are assets because they will result in future profits for Microsoft. Microsoft owns these assets, because they were purchased or created by past transactions. These investments have book values that range from their market values to their historical cost.

Microsoft does not have many liabilities. Accounts payable are the amounts Microsoft owes to suppliers. They will require cash payment, which is a sacrifice of future resources. They arose from Microsoft's purchase of goods and services in past transactions.

Accrued compensation represents amounts owed to Microsoft employees for work they have performed. Microsoft's consumption of their services is the past transaction that gave rise to them, and they will almost surely be settled in cash.

Unearned revenue is one of Microsoft's more interesting liabilities. These are amounts Microsoft has received from customers, but has not yet earned. Microsoft's cash receipt from customers is the past transaction that gave rise to these liabilities. Microsoft's ultimate delivery of the good or service to the customer that will earn these revenues is the future sacrifice that makes these amounts liabilities.

Accounting Mechanics—The Balance Sheet

While these examples provide insight into how accounting conventions translate to the assets and liabilities on balance sheets, a more elementary exploration using some accounting mechanics is necessary to stimulate a deeper understanding. The definitions of assets and liabilities indicate the importance of transactions in accounting conventions. Consider the following hypothetical transactions and how they are recorded and reflected on a balance sheet:

Item 1. Suppose Rick's Company begins operation on January 1, 2001 with an initial public offering (IPO) of 10,000 shares of stock. Suppose the stock fetches $15 per share from investors. How would Rick's Company record this transaction?

Rick's Company receives $150,000 in cash. (To keep things simple, let's ignore financing costs.) This amount represents contributed shareholders' equity. For the balance sheet, we would have the following (amounts in thousands):

Rick's Company Balance Sheet #1

	Assets	=	Liabilities	+	Equities
1	+150 cash	=	0	+	+150 common stock
Total	150	=	0	=	150

Item 2. Now suppose Rick's Company takes out a bank loan for $75,000:

Rick's Company Balance Sheet #2

	Assets	=	Liabilities	+	Equities
1	+150 cash	=	0	+	+150 common stock
2	+75 cash	=	+75 loan	+	
Total	225	=	75	+	150

Item 3. Rick's Company buys supplies for $175,000 in cash:

Rick's Company Balance Sheet #3

	Assets	=	Liabilities	+	Equities
1	+150 cash	=	0	+	+150 common stock
2	+75 cash	=	+75 loan	+	
3	+175 supplies −175 cash	=		+	
Total	225	=	75	+	150

Item 4. Rick's Company performs services for a client and bills it $30,000:

Rick's Company Balance Sheet #4

	Assets	=	Liabilities	+	Equities
1	+150 cash	=	0	+	+150 common stock
2	+75 cash	=	+75 loan	+	
3	+175 supplies −175 cash	=		+	
4	+30 accounts receivable	=		+	+30 retained earnings
Total	255	=	75	+	180

Item 5. Rick's Company counts supplies on hand and finds that there are only $160,000 left:

Rick's Company Balance Sheet #5

	Assets	=	Liabilities	+	Equities
1	+150 cash	=	0	+	+150 common stock
2	+75 cash	=	+75 loan	+	
3	+175 supplies −175 cash	=		+	
4	+30 accounts receivable	=		+	+30 retained earnings
5	−15 supplies	=		+	−15 retained earnings
Total	240	=	75	+	165

Item 6. The employees of Rick's Company earned compensation of $5,000, but it will not be paid until next month:

Rick's Company Balance Sheet #6

	Assets	=	Liabilities	+	Equities
1	+150 cash	=	0	+	+150 common stock
2	+75 cash	=	+75 loan	+	
3	+175 supplies −175 cash	=		+	
4	+30 accounts receivable	=		+	+30 retained earnings
5	−15 supplies	=		+	−15 retained earnings
6		=	+5 accrued compensation	+	−5 retained earnings
Total	**240**	=	**80**	+	**160**

Item 7. A customer calls Rick's Company and promises to buy $50,000 worth of services. It is expected that supplying these services will entail using $17,000 of supplies and incurring $23,000 in labor costs. This event is not recognized in the accounts, so the balance sheet remains as depicted after item 6.

These transactions illustrate several points about accounting conventions and accounting mechanics. First, there are three types of transactions. One type affects the level of the balance sheet equation, which means the amount of total assets. Items 1, 2, 4, and 5 involve increases or decreases in total assets from various sources: issuing equity (Item 1), incurring debt (Item 2), creating assets by performing services (Item 4), and recording the usage of assets (Item 5).

The other types keep the level of the balance sheet the same. One of these reclassifies amounts within a single category (assets, liabilities, *or* equities). The last affects both liabilities *and* equities. Item 3 reclassifies an amount within the general category of assets. Item 6 records a liability and reduces equity.

Another important point is that the need to incorporate a transaction on the balance sheet varies. The issuance of equity and incurrence of debt (Items 1 and 2) clearly call for recognition because they involve the receipt of cash. A cash expenditure for supplies (Item 3) also calls for recognition.

Whether sending a client a bill (Item 4) warrants recognition is another matter. Recording an account receivable and an increase in equity to reflect creation of an asset due to a sale of a good or delivery of a service is called *revenue recognition*. Revenue recognition has long been one of the most difficult areas of accounting. In the case of Rick's Company, how do we know an asset has really been created by the delivery of service to the client? One crucial factor is how likely the client is to actually pay the bill. Another factor is whether Rick's Company has supplied the services for which it has billed. This supply of service is what separates the recognition of revenue in Item 4 from the nonrecognition of a customer's promise to purchase services in Item 7. Accounting conventions require that the earnings process the entity uses be *substantially complete* and that collection be *reasonably likely* before recognizing revenue.

The definitions of substantially complete and reasonably likely are the subjects of many specific accounting rules, and are inherently contextual. Specifics of the industry in which the entity operates, the usual customs and practices of that industry, and step-by-step physical processes involved in providing value to customers all affect the point at which revenue is recognized.

Recording the usage of supplies (Item 5) and the incurrence of liabilities such as accrued compensation (Item 6) are examples of accounting *adjustments*. An *adjustment* is a change to the balance sheet equation that is not prompted by an obvious transaction. For example, from the count of supplies, Rick's Company deduced that an entry should be made to reflect their usage. From an analysis of labor usage, perhaps from employee time sheets, Rick's Company deduced that an entry should be made to reflect the fact that workers were owed compensation. You are probably familiar with many adjustments, including the recording of depreciation on long-lived assets and the allocation of overhead to individual departments in a large entity. Figure 3.2 summarizes the transactions in this example, how they affect the balance sheet equation, and whether the need for an entry is clear or unclear (should it be recognized).

T-accounts—Debits and Credits

Preserving the balance sheet equation, even when different people are involved in different parts of the recognition, is the function of accounting mechanics. The most elementary of these mechanics, *t-accounts* and the *double-entry* system of debits and credits, have been used for over 500 years.

Here's how it works. Instead of listing all items affecting cash in one long column with pluses and minuses intermixed, a t-account separates the items that increase cash from those that decrease cash into different columns.[4] The picture formed is a T:

Cash

| increases | decreases |

For no particular reason, *debits* are in the left-hand column, and items in the right-hand column are called *credits*.

Here's the big trick for how t-accounts work the balance sheet equation. We define debits as increases for assets, but decreases for

Figure 3.2 Classification of transactions.

		Level of total assets	
		Affected	Unaffected
		Reclassification	Record a liability and reduce equity
Need for an entry	Clear	1,2	3	6
	Unclear	4,5,7?		

liabilities and equities. That is, we use the following conventions, where (Dr) stands for debit and (Cr) stands for credit:

Assets		Liabilities and equities	
increases (Dr)	decreases (Cr)	decreases (Dr)	increases (Cr)

Any entry that preserves debits equal credits will also preserve the balance sheet equation. As an exercise, try recording the transactions for Rick's Company using debits and credits in t-accounts1. This should show how the mechanics work to keep the balance sheet equation intact.

The balance sheet equation pertains to a point in time. It gives a snapshot of the stocks of assets and liabilities on that specific date. Income statements are presented to show the flows of resources that arise from an entity's profit-making activities *between* balance sheet dates.

The Income Statement—Revenues and Expenses

Microsoft's income statements for the years ended June 30, 1997, 1998, and 1999 are provided in Figure 3.3. Income statements are driven by three main economic concepts: revenues, expenses, and income. *Revenues* are increases in assets or decreases in liabilities resulting from operations. *Expenses* are the assets used or liabilities incurred in the process of carrying out operations. *Income* is the difference between revenues and expenses. It is the excess (hopefully) of resources brought in (or liabilities extinguished) by operations over resources consumed (or liabilities generated) by operations. Here, the word operations refers to activities other than financing, which is the raising and returning of resources from owners and creditors.

Microsoft's net income for the year ended June 30, 1999, was $7.79 billion. The items that increased income compared to June 30, 1998, were the revenues of $19.75 billion, the investment income of $1.80 billion, and the gain on sale of a subentity of $0.16

Figure 3.3 Income statement.

Microsoft Corporation
INCOME STATEMENTS
In millions

Year Ended June 30	1997	1998	1999
Revenue	$11,936	$15,262	$19,747
Operating expenses:			
Cost of revenue	2,170	2,460	2,814
Research and development	1,863	2,601	2,970
Acquired in-process technology	—	296	—
Sales and marketing	2,411	2,828	3,231
General and administrative	362	433	689
Other expenses	259	230	115
Total operating expenses	7,065	8,848	9,819
Operating income	4,871	6,414	9,928
Investment income	443	703	1,803
Gain on sale of Softimage, Inc.	—	—	160
Income before income taxes	5,314	7,117	11,891
Provision for income taxes	1,860	2,627	4,106
Net income	$ 3,454	$ 4,490	$ 7,785

billion. The items that decreased income compared to June 30, 1998 were operating expenses of $9.82 billion and the provision for income taxes of $4.11 billion.

The interesting detail in Microsoft's income statement is in its operating expenses. Sales and marketing was Microsoft's largest expense, followed by research and development and the cost of revenue. Sales and marketing expenses are all the salaries, commissions, advertising fees, and so on that Microsoft incurs from marketing and selling its products and services. Research and development is a unique item because there is a special accounting rule in the United States that requires almost all research and development costs to be counted as expenses. This is true even if the research leads to valuable intellectual assets. The cost of revenue likely consists of service providers' salaries, expenses incurred in making CD-ROMs, and other costs associated with making products and delivering services.

Accounting Conventions—The Income Statement

We have already discussed the revenue recognition that guides the process of formally counting revenues earned. The guide for recognition of expenses is *matching*. *Matching* is the process of recognizing all expenses incurred in generating the revenue recorded. Although economists are usually given credit for the saying, "There's no such thing as a free lunch," no one takes it more seriously than accountants. Accountants believe, "There's no such thing as free revenue," and whenever revenue is recognized, accounting conventions demand a thorough search for any expenses incurred in generating that revenue. This is the essence of matching: For every revenue, there must be an expense.

Accounting Mechanics—Temporary Accounts and Closing

Income affects the equity of common shareholders, and we usually create a special type of account to record it. Refer to the Rick's Company example. There are three items that affect retained earnings: the recognition of revenue (Item 4), the recognition of the usage of supplies (Item 5), and the recognition of accrued compensation (Item 6). While we could simply use the basic accounting identity (Assets $\equiv$ Liabilities + Equity) to record all items and then analyze the retained earnings account to figure out income, there are better ways to compile income statements. Special t-accounts, called *temporary accounts,* are established to hold revenue and expense amounts between balance sheet dates.

When preparing the balance sheet, these temporary accounts are *closed* by bringing them to a zero balance, and carrying the other side of the entry to retained earnings. While balance sheet accounts are like markers that measure the water level in a lake, temporary accounts are like rain gauges. Closing the temporary account is like emptying the rain gauge.

When the temporary accounts are closed, revenues increase equity and expenses decrease equity. This means that increases in revenues must be credits, and increases in expenses must be debits. Closing a revenue account involves debiting the revenue and crediting equity, thus increasing equity. Closing an expense account involves crediting the expense and debiting equity, thus decreasing equity.

To illustrate the use of these temporary accounts in the preparation of a balance sheet, let's record Items 4, 5, and 6 for Rick's Company and then close these accounts to retained earnings. Item 4 was the recognition of $30,000 in revenue and the creation of accounts receivable. Let's make a temporary t-account called revenues to record the revenues we will list on the income statement. The entry would be

Accounts receivable		Revenues	
30			30

Items 5 and 6, which record the usage of supplies and the accrued compensation, call for the creation of supplies expense and compensation expense accounts. The t-account entries are

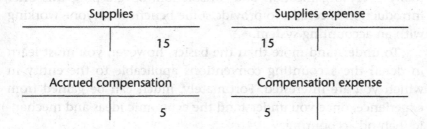

Supplies		Supplies expense	
	15	15	

Accrued compensation		Compensation expense	
	5	5	

It is crucial to refresh your memory about what type of account each of these is. Accounts receivable and supplies are assets. Accrued compensation is a liability. These will be listed on Rick's Company's balance sheet. Revenues is a revenue account. Supplies expense and compensation expense are expense accounts. These are temporary accounts that will be folded into retained earnings through closing entries. The closing entries are

Revenues		Supplies expense	
	30	15	
30			15

Compensation expense		Retained earnings	
			30
5		15	
		5	
	5		

If you tally these accounts, you will find that all the temporary accounts have zero balances, and retained earnings has a balance of 10, as it should. The end product of these temporary t-accounts is $10, which would be reported as retained earnings on the balance sheet of Rick's Company.

Summary

This chapter provided a very brief introduction to basic economic concepts, accounting conventions, and accounting mechanics and how they interact in the accounting process. The mechanics work for any set of conventions. The economic concepts are used in virtually every organization and jurisdiction. So grasping this brief introduction is certain to provide some benefit to anyone working with an accounting system.

To understand more than the basics, however, you must learn in detail the accounting conventions applicable to the entity in which you are interested. Fortunately, much can be gained from experience, once you understand the economic ideas and mechanics behind accounting.

Notes

1. The nature of Microsoft's assets and the way in which it acquired them make assigning a specific accounting value on them very difficult. It has mostly intangible assets (intellectual property) that were self-constructed, not purchased. Such assets provide

few reliable clues as to when they should be recognized and how they should be measured. An entity such as a savings and loan is the opposite, and the book and market values of savings and loans are often very closely aligned.

2. Financial Accounting Standards Board (FASB) Concepts Statement No. 3.

3. FASB Concepts Statement No. 3.

4. Many checkbooks use this representation by providing different columns for withdrawals and deposits.

For a more detailed review of the concepts presented in this chapter: Anthony, R. N. *Essentials of Accounting.* Reading, MA: Addison-Wesley, 2000.

Antle, R., and S. Garstka. *Financial Accounting.* Cincinnati: South-Western, 2002.

CASE 3

How to Talk about Money

Stephen Rimar

When people think of business, they think of money. Many doctors, however, know little about either. They entered medicine to care for people, not manage a business. Today, however, it's increasingly difficult to provide healthcare without attending to the financial conditions under which it's delivered. But many doctors are reluctant to discuss money—perhaps some harbor a fear of exposing what they consider an intellectual weakness. Furthermore, they may view accounting and finance as complicated areas of expertise that take years to master. The basics of accounting, however, are fairly simple to grasp.

The first thing to understand about accounting is that it's completely made up. Unlike medicine, it is not based on evidence or experience, but on convention. It is a contrived procedure for tracking the flow of money into and out of an organization. So expect to understand it only within the framework of this convention; reasoning plays little part in mastering accounting.

Second, an accountant's job is to account for every penny. He must track, in a very detailed and sometimes boring manner, each financial transaction, and subsequently summarize the transactions in reports. This tracking and reporting follows very specific rules (again, the convention). The rules are not intuitive, and though accountants do make some judgments about how data is detailed and aggregated, doctors with the interest and time can easily follow each step of the process. Once the rules are known, understanding accounting is easy. In order to understand the rules, however, one must speak with the accountants.

How Do You Get Financial Information?

As the junior member of a four-person group, Dr. Lauren O'Connor knew little about the business aspects of her practice. Only after the senior partner informed the group that they were looking at another year in the red and another decrease in salary did she recognize the personal and professional jeopardy associated with her financial naiveté. She decided to act.

Dr. O'Connor asked the group's office manager for a financial report that included all the practice's revenue and expenses for the last fiscal year. When she examined the report, however, it made little sense to her; she did not understand a single expense category. In an effort to uncover why the practice was in trouble, she asked the office manager. The reply was simply, "Managed care."

It occurred to Dr. O'Connor that she needed to invest time learning about the practice's finances if she were to play a role in its survival. She began by reviewing every item in the budget, in detail, with the accountant and the office manager. By repeatedly asking "What does this mean?" she was able to understand each entry in the budget spreadsheet. This enabled her to account for every entry. Looking at the whole picture, she formulated an idea that might help the ailing practice.

The Informed Doctor Knows Best

As a cost-cutting measure, Dr. O'Connor's practice closed their office lab a year ago and hired an outside group to perform all routine tests. This move seemed to make sense at the time, although the only information involved in making the decision was the expense of the in-house technician and equipment rental. While it saved some money, the doctors and the office staff still spent a lot of time (non-billable) following up on test results, which they found annoying. In addition, most patients disliked trekking to a second place for tests. It was particularly burdensome to those who required frequent testing, and they complained daily. Dr. O'Connor suspected she could find a way to reestablish the office's lab and restore a desirable patient service while producing a profit (or a least minimizing the loss).

In reviewing the financial performance of the old in-office lab, Dr. O'Connor calculated that the revenue from this service amounted to 70 percent of the cost of the program (including equipment, technician salary, and fringe benefits). By adding just two tests, another 20 percent of the cost could be recovered. This meant the practice needed to recover an additional 10 percent of the total cost to break even.

Dr. O'Connor convinced her partners to reestablish the in-house laboratory service for two years. The new tests were added and the laboratory technician was assigned responsibility for some office work; a staff position was thereby eliminated. The cost savings realized with this final move made the in-house laboratory program a potential revenue producer for the practice.

Is the Managed-Care Contract the Problem?

Despite the prevalence of capitated payment systems in some areas of the country, many physicians continue to be reimbursed via some discounted, fee-for-service arrangement. Depending on its specifics, minor changes to the fee schedule can have major effects on medical practices' revenue. Contracts pass the desks of busy physicians quite frequently, requiring a yes-no decision in short order. But how can one know whether a proposed fee schedule is better or worse than the existing one? Evaluating the financial impact of a proposed contract on a practice can prove critical to a practice's survival.

Dr. Fred Christopher received a proposed fee schedule from a managed-care organization. He had little time to decide whether to continue participation with this payer. The proposed fee schedule consisted of a CPT codes list and the proposed fees associated with each in the new contract. When Dr. Christopher compared the existing fee schedule with the proposed one, he became concerned. Another cut in fees. Then it occurred to him: The financial impact of the proposed fees was a function of both the fee change and the number of times a code was billed to this payer. To calculate the actual financial impact of the proposed fee schedule on his practice revenue and determine whether there was real need for worry, Dr. Christopher developed a simple model.

Like many physicians faced with a new managed-care contract or a renewal of an existing one, he based his decision on a single piece of data—how the fees compared with those of other payers. But Dr. Christopher knew this simplistic approach didn't provide enough information for an informed decision. He needed to consider other variables and analyze options beyond a quick acceptance or rejection of a contract. In particular, he wanted to know if he could afford to refuse the contract. To assess such an action, Dr. Christopher needed to know the full financial value of the contract (how much money it was worth in business) and how the new fee schedule would change that. For this, he needed more than proposed fee-schedule data.

Dr. Christopher's model included

- CPT code frequency (number of times the CPT code was billed)
- Current and proposed fee schedule (by CPT code)
- Current collection ratio (amount collected over contracted amount)
- Withholds or other discounts (current and proposed)

To simplify the calculations, he assumed constant patient volume and service mix for his practice for the next year (i.e., no change in the type or frequency of CPT codes billed). The question to be answered was, If this contract were in place last year, how much money would I have been paid? The calculation for each CPT code then became

$$\text{(CPT code frequency)} \times \text{(change in fee schedule in \$)}$$
$$= \text{change in revenue (\$)}$$

Table C3.1 is a sample of the simple analysis he performed on three of his group's most frequently billed codes.

From this example, one can see that seemingly small changes in a fee schedule can significantly impact the revenue of the practice. And while the change in fee schedule is important, the frequency of the CPT code is critical to the financial calculations as well. For instance, if the frequency of the 99204 code was half that projected

Table C3.1 Fee Schedule Impact Analysis

CPT Code	CPT Code Frequency (#/yr)	Change in Fee	Impact
99213	536	−$5.59	−$2,996.24
99214	382	−$8.07	−$3,082.74
99204	390	−$7.83	−$3,053.70
		Total Revenue Impact	−$9,132.68

in the example (his practice saw fewer new patients), the total revenue impact would be considerably less. This is why changes in fee schedule alone do not accurately predict financial impact.

Dr. Christopher went one more step in his analysis, however. He expected his practice to grow by approximately 3 percent each year. Since this proposed contract was for three years, he calculated the total impact of the proposed changes over that period by assuming a 3 percent increase in all codes. Representative results of this analysis are shown in Table C3.2 for three CPT codes. His complete analysis included all CPT codes billed by the practice.

This analysis demonstrated the total impact of the proposed fee schedule on the revenue of the practice. With little additional effort, however, the analysis can be even more valuable. Multiyear data can reveal increasing and decreasing trends in codes thereby allowing for reasonable predictions of frequencies. By changing the value of variables (i.e., performing a sensitivity analysis), Dr. Christopher could fine-tune his estimates. He could also couple either payment data (e.g., actual payments vs. contracted fees, reasons for denied claims, time from claim submission to payment) or cost data (e.g., office overhead, additional costs associated specifically with a payer), or both, with the fee-schedule data to generate a comprehensive picture of the payer's performance. This kind of comprehensive analysis is essential if a medical practice is to make informed decisions about its business relationship with a payer.

Just a few years ago, performing the analyses described previously would have been nearly impossible for a small practice.

Table C3.2 Fee Schedule Impact Analysis 2

CPT Code	Frequencies (#/yr)				Change in Fee	Impact		
	1999 (actual)	2000 (projected)	2001	2002		2000	2001	2002
99213	536	552	568	584	-$5.59	-$3,085.68	-$3,175.12	-$3,264.56
99214	382	393	405	416	-$8.07	-$3,171.51	-$3,268.35	-$3,357.12
99204	390	402	413	425	-$7.83	-$3,147.66	-$3,233.79	-$3,327.75
Total Revenue Impact						-$9,404.85	-$9,677.26	-$9,949.43

Today's extremely powerful and inexpensive computers and software, however, allow physicians to perform calculations quickly and easily. In addition, once an appropriate template is designed, it can be used repeatedly to assess financial impact. With its use, an informed decision to accept fees or opt out of a contract is possible for any practice, regardless of the size. Dr. Christopher knew exactly how much money this contract would cost the practice.

How to Do It

These cases highlight the use of accounting to manage a physician practice. Both demonstrate the value of a financial analysis before making a decision, even if the analysis is a simple one.

1. *Define terms.* Want to know how much something costs? Begin by defining it. Each service or product requires explicit definition because people often use the same word to describe quite different things. Conversely, accountants, office managers, and doctors might categorize the same things differently. Never assume a term means the same thing to different people. For example, an expense to a bank is a credit to a depositor. What is the difference between supplies and equipment? What expenses are included as benefits, and which are overhead? Dr. O'Connor began by learning about each revenue and expense for her practice in terms she could understand. Knowing this is the first step to controlling finances, rather than allowing finances to control you.

2. *Ask the right question.* An informed decision requires the correct information. In order to obtain this information, one must ask a question that, when answered, best informs the decision. Dr. O'Connor needed to answer her initial question, Should we reopen the lab? in order to make a decision. But that question could not be answered without first answering others. Her final question was more like, "What are the costs and benefits of reopening the lab?"

Dr. Christopher wanted to know whether he should sign a managed-care contract. But in order to make an informed decision, he needed to develop a financial model to examine the impact of the proposed fee changes on his revenue. He therefore began by asking what the total revenue was from the existing contract and compared this result to the revenue that would have occurred had the proposed fees been in effect for the past year.

In both cases, the physicians began with a broad question that needed to be answered in order to make a decision. Neither of their initial questions, however, could be answered without more information. And it was the subsequent questions, and their answers, that provided the information to inform their final decisions.

3. *Drill down, and then build up.* Once you have articulated the question and clearly defined its elements, determine *all* costs and revenue associated with *each* element. With predictive models, base estimates on real data whenever possible—either your own or someone else's. After itemizing everything, reconstruct the elements in a way that makes sense to you rather than your accountant or office manager. Dr. O'Connor could only evaluate the financial impact of her idea after dissecting financial reports and reassembling the data in a way she found meaningful. The most useful financial information comes from data that is collected, assembled, and presented in a way that can be understood by the decision maker who will use it.

4. *Develop a financial model.* The simplest way to create a financial model is to envision a spreadsheet built around the elements of a question. The elements can be items like fee-schedule changes or volume of visits. Each column contains the values associated with each element essential to the equation that will accurately answer a question. In the case of a retrospective analysis, one set of values will be entered (i.e., the actual values) and a single result will be obtained. But because financial analyses designed to predict future cost or revenue provide only approximations, modeling estimates using more than one set of data can be very useful. Altering the values of the elements (e.g., changing one by 10 percent while holding the others constant, or changing all by the same or varying percentages) may provide insight into potential outcomes. When performed systematically, for example, with anticipated high and low values, this is called a sensitivity analysis.

Interactions of elements also can be examined through serial analyses. For example, a practice's loss (or gain) of patients with diabetes may mean a concomitant change in revenue associated with in-office glucose testing. A financial model can be developed that, when populated with varying numbers of patients, will determine the number at which significant revenue changes occur for the better or the worse. Once a model has been developed, adding or changing data is easy. With time and a little help, a physician can construct a library of financial models into which financial data can be fed.

5. *Seek intelligent advice.* Physicians understand medical practices better than anyone. But only when this understanding is combined with a detailed knowledge of the practice's financial aspects can appropriate decisions be made. Developing a good working relationship with a financial expert underlies a physician's ability to capably manage the financial aspects of a practice. So while a doctor may not have time to become an accountant, he should have a good teammate who is.

Only by taking time to understand the finances of her practice (and its particular accounting system) was Dr. O'Connor able to appreciate all aspects of the practice relevant to her plan for in-house lab services. And only after developing a model for evaluating the financial implications of a new managed-care fee schedule was Dr. Christopher able to make an informed decision about signing the contract. Other physicians must follow their lead if they want a successful practice today. It's no longer enough to leave money matters to businesspeople.

LECTURE 4

Healthcare Financial Management

Elizabeth H. Bradley

Accounting and Finance

Definitions

The term *finance* refers to money or funds. The management and study of money and funds are driven by a set of accounting and financial principles and tools. To understand the application of these principles and tools to healthcare, it is useful to distinguish three areas within the broad field of finance. These areas are financial accounting, managerial accounting, and finance and investments.

Financial accounting is primarily concerned with recording the transactions of an organization. With oversight by the Financial Accounting Standards Board (FASB), accounting rules for recording such transactions (e.g., the inflow and outflow of assets, including cash) provide guidance on the proper methods for such documentation. A comptroller, who is often a certified public accountant (CPA), manages the financial accounting, which is primarily concerned with the comprehensive, consistent, and accurate recording of transactions that have already occurred or are occurring. The principles and tools that underlie financial accounting processes are described in Lecture #3.

In contrast, managerial accounting involves financial analyses that support management decision making concerning future activities such as investing in a new piece of equipment or program, or evaluating the performance of programs to determine future directions. Examples of managerial accounting tasks include capital project evaluation, budget variance analysis, and product costs. While these rely on data generated by financial accounting (i.e., recording transactions), the tasks require additional analysis and interpretation of financial data to effectively inform management decision making and strategic planning. Unlike financial accounting processes that are overseen by those with CPA degrees or equivalent preparation, managerial accounting analyses are often completed by master's-level prepared staff (in business, public health, and/or health management).

The third area of finance focuses on methods for financing new projects and strategies for investments. Fundamental areas for financial services and investment banks, these tasks are less important for most healthcare areas. Typically in the healthcare delivery setting, finance and investment responsibilities are held by the chief financial officer and treasurer.

Chapter Overview

This chapter, which focuses on the tools of managerial accounting in healthcare, is organized in three sections. The first establishes the relationship between management strategy and the tools of managerial accounting. The second provides primers for two applications of managerial accounting for strategic decision making in healthcare: (1) budgeting and budget variance analysis and (2) capital project evaluation. The final section summarizes the strengths and limitations of managerial accounting techniques and discusses approaches to promote ethical and effective financial decisions in healthcare management.

Tools of Managerial Accounting

The Budget

The budget has been referred to as the fourth financial statement, in addition to the traditional three: the balance sheet, the income statement, and the changes in financial position.[1] The budget can reveal important insights about the operation and performance of the organization, although the budget is not shared widely with external parties, as financial statements may be.

The budget is a detailed operating plan, derived from the strategic plan, expressed quantitatively in dollars. In essence, the budget describes how resources will be obtained and used during a specified period. Therefore, it is helpful to think of the budget as a managerial tool, rather than an accounting tool. The strongest budgeting processes integrate the budget development process with the strategic planning process, such that the vision of the organization is reflected accurately in its financial road map, or budget. Although most attention is paid to the operating budget, there are three types of budgets in most large healthcare organizations: the cash budget, the operating budget, and the capital budget.

Cash Budget   The cash budget is distinguished from the operating budget for those organizations that use accrual accounting, as described in Lecture 3. For organizations that use cash accounting, revenue is recorded when cash is received, and expenses are recorded when cash is paid out. However, most large organizations operate on an accrual accounting system. With accrual accounting, revenues are recorded at the time services are rendered, and expenses that reflect resources consumed in producing such services are matched to revenues. This ensures that related expenses are recorded as close as possible to the time that the revenue is recorded. A cash budget is particularly important for organizations in which revenues can be recorded without previously receiving the cash associated with that revenue. In such organizations, the cash budget ensures that adequate, liquid assets (i.e., cash and assets that can be converted to cash quickly and without penalty) are available to meet immediate needs, such as payroll.

In addition to ensuring adequate cash is available for immediate needs, the cash budget is used to assess the performance of investment strategies. The statement of changes in financial position (also termed the statement of cash flows) is relied upon for long-term cash and investments planning. The cash budget, however, is prepared on a monthly, weekly, or daily basis and used for short-term cash management.

Operating Budget   The operating budget is a combination of the revenue budget and the expense budget, and projects the surplus or loss for the organization. Unlike the income statement, which is prepared for the organization overall, the operating budget is prepared for individual business units to aid managers when monitoring the revenues and expenses over which they have some control. Because the operating budget is particularly important for health-care managers, the majority of this section focuses on the development and use of the operating budget.

Capital Budget   The capital budget describes the resources available for capital purchases as well as the planned capital investments. Capital items are defined as items that will not be used up within one year of purchase. Although the operational definition of capital may vary from organization to organization, it is typically valued above some dollar limit. For instance, anything costing more than $1,000 that will not be consumed within one year may be considered capital. Capital budgeting is typically completed annually and directed by the senior management team and the board, based on the strategic capital needs of the organization.

Developing an Operating Budget

In principle, the operating budget should reflect the organization's strategic plan. Ideally, the process of developing the operating budget begins with a statistical budget that provides the volume estimates for the next year's activities. Depending on the organization, volume may be patient days, lab tests, and/or members per month. These volume figures are considered targets, and outline what is known as the statistical budget. Once agreed upon, the statistical, or volume, targets are used to project associated expenses and revenues. The projected numbers are combined to create a draft operating budget, which is reviewed internally, revised as needed, and finalized.

It is important to recognize that this describes the ideal budgeting process. In reality, the budgeting process is much more iterative, with strategic volume targets defined interactively with expenses and revenues, ensuring the budget reflects desired financial outcomes. Therefore, depending on the result of the budget's first draft, the process may include a protracted period for revisions, in which assumptions about volume, reimbursement, and production costs are varied, until the final document reflects a realistic operational plan that also generates acceptable surplus. Thus, the budget in many ways reflects the political process in an organization. The volume and financial targets are set by politics as much as statistics.

A variety of methods are used for developing budgets in healthcare organizations, and multiple methods can be used within a single organization. Each method has its strength and weakness; the chosen method reflects the existing culture and goals of the organization and can significantly affect the future organizational culture and mission. For a graphic description of the advantages and limitations of each approach, see Table 4.1.

Incremental Budgeting In this method, the budget is developed based on last year's budget plus a uniform, incremental adjustment for all expenses and revenues. For instance, an incremental budget might take last year's budget and increase expenses and revenues by 3 percent across the board. The results are a similar distribution of resources across the organization and an equivalent surplus (or loss) as budgeted in the previous year. Needless to say, this approach has the advantages of ease, speed, and simplicity for managerial staff. In addition, incremental budgeting limits expense growth and pro-

Table 4.1 Evaluating Different Budgeting Methods

Budgeting Method	Ease	Promotes Strategic Planning	Limits Expense	Culture Expense
Incremental	+	–	+	Top-down
Request by exception	+	–/+	+	Bottom-up
Forecast budgeting	–	+	–	Top-down
Zero-based budgeting	–	+	+	Bottom-up
Flexible budgeting	–	–/+	–	Mixed

⁺Advantage
⁻Disadvantage

motes predictability in expense and revenue growth (assuming the budget is fulfilled).

However, this approach does not promote or reward strategic planning, and in fact, may conflict with assumptions in the strategic plan. This potential conflict is especially likely in current healthcare markets, in which the external environment and organizational goals change rapidly. Further, the incremental budget process signals a top-down approach to budgeting, as the incremental percent increase is typically set at the most senior levels, and variations in departmental activity are not recognized.

Request by Exception   In this method, the budget for next year is exactly the same as last year's (which may or may not include a specified increase across the board), except for departments or cost centers that request increases. Requested increases are assessed for their ability to pay for themselves (i.e., for their ability to generate revenue that exceeds the requested increase in expenses). Increased expenses are budgeted only if they can be financed through increased revenue.

The request by exception budgeting approach has some advantages to incremental budgeting. It is fairly easy, quick, and comprehensible to managers. Additionally, it generally limits expenses, and increases are predictable, again assuming the budget is fulfilled. Yet, request by exception budgeting can be more consistent with strategic planning goals than incremental budgeting. This is because profitable areas are budgeted to grow according to a strategic plan.

Although request by exception budgeting does demonstrate more sensitivity to the strategic plan, it is important to remember this approach rewards those managers or departments that develop and present credible financial analyses to demonstrate the revenue impact of their requested increases in expenses. Such financial analyses may be easier for some managers to conduct and present. As a result, there may be an inherent bias toward departments with adequate financial analytic support and may penalize departments with less. Finally, compared to incremental budgeting, request by exception demonstrates a more bottom-up approach to budget development, because programs and ideas from the department level may influence the final budget.

Forecast Budgeting   Forecast budgeting, like the ideal budget process described earlier, is driven by volume and productivity goals set by the strategic plan. Based on these goals, or statistics, the expense and revenue budgets are developed and combined. Although this budgeting approach is more complicated than the previous methods described, it promotes strategic planning in a way the other methods do not.

The forecast budgeting method does not explicitly limit spending, although strategic plans may be written with ambitious productivity goals and, therefore, may support limits on expenses. While there is some involvement in planning at the department level, forecast budgeting tends to reflect a top-down approach to budgeting, since most strategic plans are developed at high levels of the organization.

Zero-Based Budgeting   Zero-based budgeting requires each department to begin the development process with a budget of zero. Managers and department heads then specify their departmental objectives and the resources needed to fulfill these objectives. They then prioritize each objective based on specific rationale. At this point, senior management reviews these objectives, their associated expenses and revenues, and their relative priority as projected by the department heads. Based on this review, senior management decides which objectives will be budgeted. Objectives not budgeted are then deleted from the departments' yearly goals and budget.

Popularized in the 1970s by Jimmy Carter to manage the Georgia state government, zero-based budgeting has the advantage of involving all managers in an organization. In this way, it reflects a bottom-up budgeting method and can result in increased realism, understanding, and support for the budget throughout the organization. Furthermore, because the total expenses and total revenues are set by senior management, zero-based budgeting can be used to limit expenses in predictable ways consistent with an overall strategic plan, while still incorporating the interests and needs of the lower levels.

Zero-based budgeting, however, is extremely difficult to implement. The process is time-consuming and requires extensive expertise and access to data among department heads. In addition, interaction between departments, including spill-over effects when one department's activities facilitate others, can be overlooked because priority levels are set at the department, rather than organizational, level. For instance, medical records managers may not prioritize expenses for diagnosis coding as highly as they might prioritize expenses for retrieving records for new admissions. Timely diagnosis coding, however, may be highly valued by the billing department, which cannot submit claims until the coding is complete. Thus, individual manager's priorities may not be consistent with organization-wide priorities, and interaction between departments may be compromised.

Flexible Budgeting All the methods described so far result in a fixed budget. Once the budget is determined, it remains unchanged over the budget period, even if the actual volume varies significantly from the predicted, or budgeted, volume. In fact, flexible budgeting explicitly recognizes that the actual volume rarely matches the predicted volume. A flexible budget automatically adjusts budgeted expenses and revenues to reflect changes in volume over time.

For instance, if laboratory expenses were budgeted at $10 per test, and the budgeted volume was 100 tests, the fixed budget would be $1,000 ($10 × 100 tests). If instead, the actual test volume turned out to be 150, a fixed budget would remain at $1,000, the department would experience a $500 budget overage. However, a flexible budget would increase to $1,500 ($10 × 150 tests) automatically. The result is that any overage in the flexible budget is not due to changes in volume because the changes in volume are already accounted for in the budget. Overages are therefore due to increased expenses related to each test (i.e., increases in the $10 per test) rather than the increased number of tests performed.

The flexible budget has the advantage of clarifying the source of budget overages by accounting for changes in volume explicitly. In addition, flexible budgeting rewards busier units by increasing their budget rather than penalizing them for increased expenses associated with higher than expected volumes. Furthermore, flexible budgeting reflects a mixed approach between top-down and bottom-up budgeting. Productivity standards are set at high levels of the organization, yet volume changes (and associated budget changes) are derived from departmental activity.

Flexible budgeting, while extremely appealing, has significant limitations. First, the process of tracking appropriate volume and cost information frequently may be possible only in larger healthcare organizations. Second, the process is not easy for managers to understand, especially since the budget constantly changes as volume changes. Third, flexible budgeting does not limit increases in expenses, which may increase in unpredictable ways, given unanticipated changes in volume. Last, a flexible budget responds to the market, increasing budgeted resources based on the volume experienced. Since strategic plans are driven by market demands, flexible budgeting may be consistent with strategic planning. However, if the strategic plan involves promoting areas currently experiencing a volume decline, the flexible budget may penalize them by denying adequate budgeted resources for growth.

Accounting and Decision Making

Budget Variance Analysis

Budget variance analysis is an analytical tool used to assess organizational performance relative to its desired (i.e., budgeted) revenues and expenses.[2] A budget variance is a deviation from the budget. For instance, in the case of expenses, the budget variance is the actual expenses incurred minus the budgeted expenses for a specified time period. A budget variance can be calculated for every line item on the budget, and for the surplus or loss overall.

While an organization that is overbudget in its expenses (i.e., a positive variance in expenses) or underbudget in its revenues (i.e., a negative variance in revenues) may have a problem, this information alone does not explain why. Addressing the causes of poor performance based on total budget variance alone is often impossible. And although one may calculate budget variances specific to expense or revenue line items on the budget, the analysis of the causes often requires additional variance calculations.

Expense Variance There are two possible causes of a positive expense variance (i.e., actual expenses are above budgeted expenses). It is due either to increased volume or increased expense per unit of volume (or a combination of the two). Because each cause has different implications for the organization, it is helpful to break down the total variance into the *volume variance* (the portion of the variance due to changes in volume) and the *management variance* (the portion of the variance due to changes in the expense per unit of volume).

The management variance is also known as the *price variance*.[3] These variances are calculated as follows:

Volume variance =
(actual volume − budgeted volume)(budgeted expense/budgeted volume)

Management variance =
[(actual expense/actual volume) − (budgeted expense/budgeted volume)][actual volume]

Consider a laboratory in a hospital with the budgeted and actual expenses and volumes listed in Table 4.2. Note that in this case, the total budget variance indicates the laboratory's actual expenses exceeded its budgeted expenses by $1.5 million. Management wants to know how much of this overage is due to increasing volume and how much is due to reduced efficiency (i.e., increased expenses per unit of volume). The former is generally not under the control of the individual manager, while the latter is.

In this example, the volume variance accounts for a large portion of the total variance ($1.2 million of the $1.5 million in total variance). In contrast, the management variance accounts for substantially less of the total variance. The implication is that most of the budget overage is a result of increased volume, and little of it results from reduced efficiency, relative to the efficiency assumptions in the budget. Clearly, the management decisions will be different if the total variance is due to increases in expenses per unit volume (i.e., reductions in efficiency).

In this example, the volume and management variances both contribute to budget overages. But it is possible to have volume and

Table 4.2 Expense Variances in Example Laboratory

	Actual	Budget	Total Variance
Volume of tests	160,000	100,000	60,000
Total expenses	$3.5 million	$2 million	$1.5 million

Volume variance: [160,000−100,000][2,000,000/100,000] = $1,200,000
Management variance: [($3,500,000/160,000)−($2,000,000/100,000)][160,000] = $300,000
Total variance = volume variance + management variance = $1,500,000

management variances work in opposite directions. In fact, the total expense variance may be negative (indicating that actual expenses are less than budgeted expenses), yet the management variance may be positive, indicating worse than budgeted efficiency. This can occur, for instance, when a service experiences far less volume than budgeted.

In this case, total expenses may be below budgeted expenses, but this underage may be attributable to reduced volume. In fact, the management variance may indicate poor performance (i.e., a positive variance would indicate that actual expenses per unit of volume are above budgeted expenses per unit of volume). In such a case, the total variance shows that expenses are within budget, yet the underage at this level masks a problem in the operational efficiency. The problem is detected only if the portion of that total variance that is attributable to volume and the portion that is attributable to efficiency changes are distinguished.

Revenue Variance Revenue variances can be examined similarly. The total variance on the revenue lines is composed of the volume variance and the price variance, based on the following:

Volume variance =

(actual volume − budgeted volume)(budgeted revenue/budgeted volume)

Management variance =

[(actual revenue/actual volume) − (budgeted revenue/budgeted volume)][actual volume]

As in the analysis of expense variances, an analysis of revenue variances can determine the reason for observed deviations from the budgeted revenue. Increased volumes generally increase revenue. Understanding how much of the revenue increase is due to changes in the revenue per unit of volume, however, is important to isolate possible problems related to discounted charges, capitated arrangements, or revenue collections.

Often, revenue volume variances and price variances work in the same direction. As in the case of expense variances, however, changes in volume (in this case, increases in volume) may mask problems associated with decreases in revenue received per unit of volume. Given the different implications of these explanations for budget variances, a manager does well to identify the cause of the budget deviation prior to addressing the variance itself.

Quality of the Budget A central premise of budget variance analysis is that the budget is a valid yardstick against which to measure performance. If the budget is consistent with a realistic view of the market and the strategic plan of the organization, it should provide a sound yardstick against which to compare performance. Given the myriad and conflicting forces that might drive budget development, however, the final budget may have little to do with reality. In such cases, budget variances may be unavoidable and, in fact, necessary to meet the strategic plan. The analysis of budget variances is only useful if the budget itself reflects a consistent and realistic operational plan.

Capital Project Evaluation

Few managers are in their position long before they must evaluate whether to invest in a new program, a new technology, or other innovation. Typically, such projects require substantial commitment of resources or cash during their start-up and are expected to generate substantial benefits (pecuniary or nonpecuniary) in the future. How does one assess whether the expected future benefits are worth the required investment? This is the topic of the remainder of the chapter, and is a question common in both nonprofit and for-profit healthcare settings.

There are three common approaches to evaluating capital investment decisions: net present value, internal rate of return, and payback period. To apply any of these methods, one needs the following information. One must know (1) the initial cash outlay, (2) the expected life of the asset being purchased (i.e., the number of years the asset will be in use), and (3) the estimated future cash flows. Future cash flows include the timing and magnitude of cash expected to be generated (cash inflows) by the purchased assets and cash expected to be used (cash outflows) in activity related to the purchased assets.

A fundamental concept of net present value and internal rate of return is the *time value of money*. This refers to the added (or reduced) value money has if one receives it sooner (versus later). In other words, $1,000 received today is more valuable than $1,000 received in one year. This is primarily because the recipient of $1,000 today may invest the money and earn interest on it, so that in one year (assuming an interest rate of 8 percent), the recipient has not $1,000 but $1,080 ($1,000 × 1.08).

Note that the reason money received today is worth more than money received in the future has nothing to do with uncertainty of future receipt. Assume the individual is certain he will receive the $1,000 in one year. The person is still better off if he or she receives that money today, because of the investment opportunity the cash affords. This concept of the time value of money is essential to the accurate evaluation of capital investments in which cash inflows may be expected in the future, rather than immediately. Valuing those inflows properly is the crux of making good capital investment decisions.

Net Present Value This method of capital project evaluation requires the analyst to calculate the net present value (NPV) of the capital investment based on assumptions about future cash inflows and outflows. If the NPV is greater than zero, it will be profitable to undertake the capital investment under review. NPV is therefore calculated as follows:

$$NPV = \sum \frac{(inflows - outflows)}{(1 + i)^t}$$

The example in Table 4.3 demonstrates how projected revenues and expenses may be used to calculate NPV. If the organization uses accrual accounting, assumptions must be made concerning the timing of the cash inflows and outflows, relative to the timing of revenue and expense recordings. In this example, we assume that the cash inflows and revenue recording are close in timing. We also assume that the cash outflows are close in timing to the recording of expenses. Depreciation, an expense that is recorded on the income statement but does not represent an outflow of cash, is not included as a cash outflow in the calculation of NPV.

Assume the required cash outlay is $2,500 now (i.e., in year zero). To calculate the NPV, one first computes the estimated cash inflow minus cash outflow (Table 4.3) for each time period (here, a year) until the asset has no useful life left. In this example, we assume the technology will be outdated in 4 years, so the useful life of the asset is 4 years. Using the values in Table 4.3, the cash inflow minus cash outflow is –$2,500 for year 0 (because of the immediate

Table 4.3 Worksheet for Net Present Value Analysis

Line Item	YR1	YR2	YR3	YR4
Total revenue	$1,400	$1,500	$1,550	$1,800
Salary expense	$700	$600	$600	$400
Supply expense	$100	$100	$100	$100
Utilities expense	$150	$140	$150	$150
Depreciation expense	$350	$350	$350	$350
Total expense	$1,300	$1,190	$1,200	$1,000
Surplus/(loss)	$100	$310	$350	$800
Cash inflows	$1,400	$1,500	$1,550	$1,800
Cash outflows	$950[1]	$840	$850	$650
Cash inflow – outflow	$450	$660	$700	$1,150
Discounted cash flows	$416.67[2]	$565.84	$555.68	$845.28

NPV = −$2,500 + $416.67 + $565.84 + $555.68 + $845.28 = −$116.53

[1]950 = 700 + 100 + 150 (Do not count depreciation as a cash outflow because it is a non-cash expense.)
[2]Assumes discount rate of 8%.

required cash outlay), $450 for year 1, $660 for year 2, $700 for year 3, and $1,150 for year 4.

The next step is to discount each net cash inflow minus cash outflow values by the appropriate discount rate. That is, one divides by a factor related to the discount rate and the period in which the cash inflows and outflows are calculated, as described in the previous formula. Hence, $2,500 is discounted (i.e., divided) by the factor $(1 + i)^0$; $450 is discounted by the factor $(1 + i)^1$; $660 is discounted by $(1 + i)^2$; $700 is discounted by $(1 + i)^3$; $1,150 is discounted by $(1 + i)^4$. Once each of the net cash inflows minus outflows is discounted, one sums the discounted values to attain the NPV. The example in Table 4.3 assumes a discount rate of 8 percent.

As stated earlier, if this value is greater than zero, one should undertake the investment. In this example, the NPV is equal to −$2,500 + $416.67 + $565.84 + $555.68 + $845.28 = −$116.53. Because −$116.53 is less than zero, investing in this technology is not advisable based on financial considerations.

If two or more projects are compared, the NPV for each project should be calculated and compared. It is profitable to undertake both projects if both NPVs are greater than zero, with the higher NPV indicating the more profitable project. Further, one must always account for spillover effects of new investments. For instance, if investing in a new technology makes an old program obsolete, the lost revenue (and expenses) due to the diminishment of the old program must be included as cash outflows.

Internal Rate of Return   The internal rate of return (IRR) is a metric often used to assess whether a capital project should be undertaken, or which of several projects is most profitable. In essence, the formula for calculating the internal rate of return is identical to the formula for calculating NPV. However, one sets the NPV = 0 and solves for the interest rate (which is the IRR), rather than assuming an interest rate (or discount rate) and then solving for the NPV, as was done in the previous analysis. One should undertake the capital project if the IRR is greater than the interest that could be earned on the organization's next best foregone opportunity (i.e., the project they would forgo in favor of the chosen project).

Often organizations use a hurdle rate to judge capital project decisions. If the IRR is greater than the hurdle rate, the project is undertaken. Hurdle rates may reflect the organization's cost of capital or another rate deemed appropriate by senior management and the board. Again, multiple projects can be compared, and the one with the highest IRR is most profitable.

Note that if projects are indivisible and the organization has a fixed budget that will allow only one project to be undertaken, one should always calculate and compare the NPVs, rather than depending on comparisons of IRRs. An example will clarify this point. A smaller project may generate a high return (for instance, IRR = 20 percent) yet generate only $10,000 in surplus. A second project, much larger in scope, may generate a return of only 10 percent but a surplus of $100,000. If these projects were divisible, one should invest whatever funds one could in the first project and put the remaining funds in the second. However, if one must do the whole of each project (i.e., they are indivisible) and if investment in the first project prevents the organization from investing in the second project as well, the organization should invest fully in the second. The second project has the lower IRR but the higher NPV, which is based on the absolute surplus size, rather than the rate of return.

Payback Period   The payback period is not the recommended way to evaluate capital project investment decisions if profitability is the goal. However, the payback method is often used to provide a quick idea of when the cash outlay can be recouped. The payback period approach is less appropriate than the NPV and IRR approaches, since it is not a discounted cash flow approach and does not account for the time value of money. With the payback period approach, one calculates the net cash inflows minus cash outflows per period to assess when the initial cash outlay will be recouped.

In the example provided in Table 4.3, the payback period is between periods 3 and 4. This is based on the initial cash outlay of $2,500. At the end of year 1, $450 of that cash outlay is recouped; by the end of year 2, $1,110 (= $450 + $660) is recouped. By the end of year 3, $1,810 of the initial $2,500 outlay is recouped. By the end of year 4, $2,960 is recouped, more than the initial outlay of $2,500. Prorating the net cash inflow minus outflow in year 4, the payback period is approximately 3.6 years. All else being equal, projects with shorter payback periods are considered better.

Strengths and Weaknesses of Capital Project Evaluation

There are several pitfalls and complexities in capital project evaluation that deserve attention, although the issues cannot be fully resolved in this chapter. These issues include the role of uncertainty in future cash-flow analyses, the choice of discount rates, the issue of risk, and the valuation of nonpecuniary costs and benefits.

Role of Uncertainty   Estimating future cash inflows and outflows is fraught with uncertainty. This uncertainty pertains to both the cash flow amounts as well as when cash flows will occur. Uncertainty is magnified when the capital project involves a technological innovation (a new piece of equipment, for instance) for which the product life cycle and market robustness is unknown. Yet, formal analysis of capital investments remains important despite such uncertainty.

The best way to handle this uncertainty is to conduct *sensitivity analyses* in which assumptions about future volumes, future prices that can be charged, and the life of the asset are varied. The best sensitivity analyses are those that identify the level of the most uncertain variables (volume typically) that change the decision about proceeding with the purchase versus not purchasing the asset. Once such break points are known for each of the uncertain variables, the manager can assess how likely it is that the organization would face each break point. Such analyses can help inform the final decision, although there is no absolute way to eliminate the uncertainty inherent in making financial decisions based on estimates about future events.

Discount Rate The proper discount rate for NPV calculations should be the interest rate one would obtain in the next best foregone opportunity. However, estimating this rate is not easy. Often projects are assessed with a range of discount rates. This type of sensitivity analysis can be helpful to understand how sensitive the decision is to assumptions about the discount rate.

Risk Some projects carry more risk than others. Intuitively, organizations expect risky projects have higher returns to be equally valued. Yet how does one formally incorporate risk into capital project evaluations? Two methods are commonly used. The first is to increase the discount rate (if one is conducting NPV calculations) or to increase the required IRR (if one is conducting an IRR analysis). Alternatively, one may calculate the expected values for the numerator for the NPV calculation. The expected values are the estimated net cash inflows minus cash outflows multiplied by the probability that those estimates are accurate, for a variety of scenarios, each with its own probability of occurring. Although computationally more complex, this approach is also an acceptable method for accounting for risk in capital project evaluation analysis.

Nonpecuniary Costs and Benefits This chapter addresses only the financial analysis component of capital project evaluation. The best analyses make every effort to evaluate costs and benefits that can be stated in dollar values. However, nonpecuniary costs and benefits can be critical to management decision making. For instance, not investing in a new program may limit an organization's community influence, a benefit that is difficult to value in dollars. Similarly, investing in new technology may enhance the prestige and image of an organization.

Some of these prestige or image effects can be financially valued based on assumptions of increased volume or charges. Yet some of these effects may not be captured in dollar values but rather in greater stability of the organization in its professional market. In such cases, one must include these qualitative costs and benefits in decision making, although they are not explicitly valued in dollars. Typically, in the broader context of management decision making, financial analysis should be thought of as providing additional information, rather than determining the action to be taken.

Summary

This chapter introduces several commonly used tools in healthcare financial management. Performance evaluation can be promoted by appropriate budget development and variance analysis. Although variance analysis only evaluates the degree to which an organization meets its financial goals, such analysis can reflect broader strategic and operational performance as well if the budget is developed in an informed and realistic way. Budget variance analyses are especially important when volume is unpredictable, as is commonly the case for new services in the healthcare field. Assessing variances regularly provides a sense of the magnitude of problems that might exist. Disaggregating variances into their component parts can provide an important diagnostic tool for uncovering the causes of such problems.

Like budget variance analysis, capital project evaluation is a commonly used tool to enhance management decision making. Most frequently used to support strategic decisions, such financial analysis should be used as one aspect of future program and service design. As described previously, embedded in such financial analyses are substantial assumptions about future events. These assumptions often drive the results of the analysis. To ensure both intelligent and ethical behavior, managers using these analytical techniques should acknowledge their assumptions, disclose their methods, and report sensitivity analyses that demonstrate the sensitivity of their recommendations to the assumptions and methods used. Applied in such fashion, financial analysis can be an invaluable tool to aid effective managerial decision making.

Notes

1. Gapenski, L. *Healthcare Finance: An Introduction to Accounting and Financial Management*. Chicago: Health Administration Press, 1999.

2. Cleverly, W. O. *Essentials of Health Care Finance*. Gaithersburg, MD: Aspen Publishers, 1997.

3. Horngren, C. T., G. Foster, and S. M. Datar. *Cost Accounting: A Managerial Emphasis*. New Jersey: Prentice Hall, 1999; and Gapenski, L. *Healthcare Finance: An Introduction to Accounting and Financial Management*. Chicago: Health Administration Press, 1999.

How to Convince Someone an Idea Is Worth the Money

Stephen Rimar

The ability to persuade others to spend money is a precious skill. The reality of business is that if you can't pay for it, you probably can't do it. Managers often need to convince a boss or benefactor that an idea is worth spending money to make it a reality. Decision makers who receive the requests, therefore, often ask themselves the following question.

Why Should I Spend Money on This?

People spend money for three reasons: profit, preference, and necessity. Profit and preference motives are pertinent here. People spend money on lottery tickets or invest in the stock market because they believe they can profit. Preferring a new car to a two-year-old model impels others to part with their money. If an idea involves both profit and preference, such as purchasing a raffle ticket from a local charity—it's a winner. As with individuals, organizations seek activities to maximize profit (or minimize losses) that are consistent with their mission. For any proposal, convincing decision makers that money will be made or saved ends the financial argument. The only question is whether the idea is consistent with the decision makers' preferences.

Preference is extremely important in organizational decision making. If the head of an organization or other influential leaders support a plan, it is likely to be executed—sometimes regardless of cost. So knowledge of where a proposal might be numbered on an organization's list of preferences is extremely beneficial to someone looking for support. The required strength of the proposal's financial argument depends on its position. The further down the list, the more detailed and convincing the financial analyses and projections need to be. Sometimes a proposal's location is so far down that a powerful argument must be made just to get attention.

So how does one convince organizational leaders that an idea is worth financing? Persuading them that the idea solves a significant problem is often the first and most critical step. Dr. Sally Beecher was desperate to solve a problem observed in her intensive care unit (ICU). She developed an approach to convince the hospitals' administrators to address and resolve the problem.

The Problem of No ICU Beds

Intensive care units have a limited number of beds to serve critically ill patients. When ICUs are full, the options for patients requiring their services are limited (and undesirable): referral to another hospital or housing in a part of the hospital not specifically designed, equipped, or staffed to deliver ICU care. Having fewer ICU beds than ICU-type patients can significantly impact both physician and hospital revenues. In addition, it can considerably affect the image and reality of a hospital's quality. Unavailable beds contribute to frustration for patients, their families, and referring doctors because they delay care. Furthermore, they potentially compromise patient safety, spur deterioration of referral patterns (which take years to develop), and cause a tremendous expenditure of internal resources in shuffling beds to accommodate patients.

The simplest solution to the problem of too few ICU beds is to create more ICU beds. But beyond the need to secure permission to augment bed capacity, this requires a large amount of money for equipment, space, and staff. Convinced, though, that increasing the number of ICU beds was the best way to solve her ICU's problem and knowing that bed expansion is undertaken at the discretion of hospital leadership, not attending physicians, Dr. Beecher undertook the challenge to persuade the decision makers to finance her solution. Successfully completing the first step of that process—getting the issue on the organization's radar screen (it was not there)—was essential.

Dr. Beecher assumed that the initial cost of adding new beds would be high, both in terms of money and the politics of expanding the hospital. So rather than attempt from the outset to argue that the total cost of adding new beds would be financially worthwhile, she focused on the financial viability of the new beds as *if* they were already in existence. If her hypothesis that the revenue generated from additional beds would exceed their cost was correct, she believed she could jump-start a serious discussion about bed expansion. Her hope was to entice hospital administrators to perform a comprehensive analysis of the problem and engage her in that process and any subsequent decision making. Options for the hospital included using capital expansion funds to increase the unit size or adding ICU beds by decreasing adjacent non-ICU beds. Dr. Beecher hoped the financial data would argue strongly for additional ICU beds.

Spend Money to Make Money

Dr. Beecher's approach was financially based and began by identifying the three pertinent patient groups. The first group included those referred to the hospital but who were refused admission due to unavailable ICU beds. These patients were then referred to another hospital. The second set of patients included people who remained at home awaiting a postponed surgery date due to unavailable beds. In most cases, their surgery was rescheduled for another time, although occasionally it was booked at another hospital. The final group consisted of patients whose surgery was postponed because no ICU beds were available, but had been admitted to the hospital preoperatively and remained in-house awaiting a new surgical date and available ICU bed. From a financial perspective, the most noteworthy patients were the first group, those who were referred but refused. They represented lost revenue. (Inpatients for whom surgery was postponed also likely cost the hospital money because of increased length of stays during which few reimbursable services were provided.)

In order to show that revenue generated by additional ICU beds would more than compensate the cost of maintenance, Dr. Beecher chose to calculate their net present value (NPV) using existing costs and revenue. She reasoned that if the amount of revenue lost because of refusing referred patients was greater than that necessary to achieve a positive NPV, added beds would be profitable.

Dr. Beecher needed both cost and revenue data from the hospital to perform an accurate analysis. She received cost data, but was not given access to revenue information. Undaunted, she used a surrogate measure of hospital revenue. Dr. Beecher knew that in the combined hospital-physician case rates negotiated by her organization, the physicians received no more than 15 percent of the combined payment. Using this ratio, she calculated her lost professional revenue and multiplied it by 5.67 for an estimate of hospital revenues (assuming the hospital receives 85 percent of total physician-hospital revenues) (Hospital revenue = [85 × MD revenue] / 15 = 5.67 × MD revenue).

Fortunately, for the past year the ICU kept a log including information about every refused admission. (Had that not existed, as little as two months of prospective data could have been collected and extrapolated to derive annual figures.) Forty-five patients were referred to the hospital for ICU care but were refused admission in the last 12 months because beds were unavailable. Since the average physician revenue was $1,000 per patient, Dr. Beecher estimated that $45,000 of revenue was lost by her ICU physician group in the last year (45 patients × $1,000). Assuming a 15 percent to 85 percent physician-hospital split on revenue, the hospital forfeited approximately $255,150 (5.67 × $45,000) due to referred but refused patients.

Using actual cost data from the hospital, Dr. Beecher then calculated the revenue required to produce a positive NPV. At 6 percent and 8 percent, the amount of revenue needed to calculate a positive NPV was $114,000 and $115,000 respectively. Since both projected revenues are less than the estimated $255,150 lost, Dr. Beecher's calculations suggest that additional beds, once established, would be profitable. Her estimates were also substantial enough to persuade hospital administrators to redo her analysis using actual revenue. She reached her first goal of engaging administrators in serious discussions about the ICU bed situation.

How to Do It

1. *Estimate a preference rating.* How difficult will it be to sell your idea? If your proposal involves something that the organization's CEO is known to support, or is an add-on to a popular project, your strategy for presentation and likelihood of securing funds will be different than if it involves an unpopular or brand-new effort. Because leaders tend to earmark dollars for ideas they believe in, capitalize on links between your proposal and their plans or vision. In Dr. Beecher's case, there was some support for solving the problem because of its far-reaching effect, but the issue had not been viewed seriously enough to warrant discussing a solution. Her financial analysis provided the evidence needed to get the ICU bed shortage on the hospital's to-do list. Furthermore, it positioned her to suggest a solution.

2. *Develop an operational plan for the proposal.* In order to make your idea a reality, you need to describe it thoroughly. Dr. Beecher considered multiple questions regarding her proposal (some were related to its financial aspects, others were not). What will it mean to increase the number of ICU beds? Where might they be located? Must walls be torn down and rebuilt? What, exactly, will the additional staffing needs be, if any?

With the development of any proposal, begin by asking and answering (on paper) all the questions pertinent to each of its components. Also, envision other questions that your presentation might evoke given different audiences and try to address them. Next, ask, "If all issues I've already considered were taken care of, could my proposal be fully implemented tomorrow?" If the answer is yes, you have a well-articulated operational plan. If you answered, "Not tomorrow, because I haven't accounted for hiring two additional nurses needed," add the data associated with the hiring to your proposal. Repeat the question to yourself until the answer is a resounding yes.

3. *Cost it out.* Once you detail an operational plan, assign a cost to each item. The more detailed the plan, the better the cost estimate will be. A convincing financial model for costs includes an explicit list of assumptions and calculations. They are important because, if reasonable, they minimize the chances that the finance staff (or anyone) will find your model invalid or unrealistic. Dr. Beecher discussed her proposal's methodology and the validity of her NPV calculations with a finance person before presenting her plan to others.

4. *Estimate revenue.* The revenue estimate is just as important as the cost analysis, but people are usually better at projecting cost than revenue. This is because in most organizations (particularly large health-delivery organizations, like hospitals) many people work with expense budgets, but a much smaller group handles revenue. The process for developing a revenue model, however, mirrors that for a cost model. Clear assumptions and calculations are the key. Remember, assumptions and calculations must be realistic and practical to be convincing. Dr. Beecher's ICU project began with determining the number and types of patients affected by unavailable beds from the unit's log. This group was the source of data for her lost revenue figures. Accurately identifying them was critical to accurate revenue projections.

5. *Use nonfinancial measures of success.* Financial information is often weighed more heavily than nonfinancial information simply because it is quantitative. Everyone understands the concept of a dollar. But patient satisfaction, for example, is hard to measure, and survey results are sometimes suspect. Don't let this discourage you from obtaining as much data about nonfinancial costs and outcomes as possible. Patient satisfaction data can nicely supplement financial data. In the ICU's case, satisfaction scores and hospital admissions were declining at approximately the same rate. Postponed surgeries were mentioned as problematic by a number of respondents. A case could be made for some relationship between the two, suggesting that steps taken to improve satisfaction (e.g., ensuring availability of ICU beds) might also raise admission rates. Any data that supports your argument, whether clinical, operational, or financial, should be considered when making your case.

6. *Convince yourself.* You cannot possibly convince anyone to support your proposal if *you* are not convinced of its value. Before you seek support for an idea, carefully review it and ask yourself if you could honestly support your proposal. If you could not, hone it until you are convinced of its value. Then, run it by your allies. Do they find it feasible and desirable? Dr. Beecher presented her proposal to peers (her physician practice group) before taking it to hospital administrators.

7. *Present the right information to the right audience.* Many people find financial data uninteresting and refuse to understand it. Even some executives care little about examining financials, leaving it to their accountants. Others, though, scrutinize every detail. Regardless, a detailed financial analysis is an integral part of a good proposal. Sooner or later at least one financial person will scrutinize it—so develop your plan with that person in mind.

Find out what interests the individuals to whom you will present your proposal, and tailor presentations to suit them. Recognize too that proposals are rarely accepted without modification. Listen carefully to feedback from all sources, take the time to modify the proposal accordingly, and present it again.

Dr. Beecher's full ICU proposal consisted of two parts: (1) the patient data and associated equipment and personnel figures, along with an operational plan; and (2) the financials (cost and revenue projections). At the time of her presentation, Dr. Beecher sensed that hospital administrators were particularly concerned about the impact of unavailable beds on patients and referring physicians. This prompted her to put the detailed financial data in an appendix rather than the body of her written proposal and, when she spoke with the administrators, to focus on such things as satisfaction data, the frequency with which ICU beds were closed, and the consequences of closure. Dr. Beecher's adaptation of the written and oral proposals to the existing atmosphere made her argument more convincing.

8. *Frame a cost-benefit argument.* The decision to support or reject a proposal often hinges on perceived cost vs. perceived benefit. After completing your financial analysis, consider the potential of your idea to produce a profit or other benefit. Then find a cost-benefit argument that supports your case. Your idea should produce a profit in the short term, produce a profit in the long term, break even, or compare favorably to other investments. Projects that forecast a substantial profit in the short term are usually the easiest to sell. Long-term profit makers may or may not be acceptable depending on the number of years until profitability or the break-even point. Break-even propositions that will produce a nonfinancial benefit without costing a cent are usually supported if the benefit is consistent with, or at least does not impinge on, organizational goals. If you must provide an additional argument because the financial benefits are unclear, consider comparing it to other investments. You might even compare competing plans to yours. As a last resort, if the organization has reserves, consider comparing the cost of your proposal to keeping the money in the bank.

LECTURE 5

An Introduction to Economic Evaluation

A. David Paltiel

The healthcare market in the United States presents decision makers with increasingly constrained resources, rising costs, and intensified competition. In the absence of any viable plan for a universal health-insurance program, the onus has been placed upon the private sector to develop mechanisms regulating the delivery, financing, and consumption of services. Producers and consumers of medical care can no longer afford to base decisions solely on short-term considerations of safety and efficacy. More and more, buyers and sellers alike must also pay close attention to issues of long-run value. This chapter provides a clinician's introduction to the emerging field known variously as *health economics, decision analysis, pharmacoeconomics, cost-effectiveness analysis,* and *health program evaluation.*

Economics and Decision Making

Goal of Economic Evaluation

Economic evaluation aims to assist decision makers when choosing among competing medical alternatives, in situations of uncertainty and limited resources. This objective highlights a few critical features of economic evaluation worth noting:

1. *Economic evaluation is managerial in focus.* It is a pragmatic field, intended to provide practical assistance for decision makers.

2. *All economics is about choices.* There is no such thing as a cost-effective drug, for example, except in relation to some alternative use of resources.

3. *Real-world evaluations are performed and consumed in an environment of incomplete information.* Rigorous analysis helps decision makers understand and manage uncertainties.

4. *Trade-offs are inevitable.* Economic evaluation is premised on the assumption that we cannot afford all the healthcare we would like to consume and that it is useful to evaluate results if we allocate resources where they are likely to yield the greatest good.

Sadly, real-world economic evaluation in the health sector rarely lives up to these statements of principle. All too often, the method is used as a justification for downsizing, as a penny-wise and pound-foolish exercise in bean counting, as a means of second-guessing clinical judgment, and as a wedge to distance the clinician from the interests of the patient. It is not surprising, therefore, that clinicians view the field with some skepticism.

Chapter Overview

This chapter is intended to serve as an accessible introduction for clinicians who must either make use of health-related economic evaluations or are accountable for policies and procedures based on such methods. Contents include:

- An overview of key analytic methods
- Guidance for the design or critical reading of an analysis
- Brief discussions of emerging areas of consensus and controversy
- Information on additional readings

Theoretical Underpinnings

Nonsatiation

The goal of economic evaluation—to assist decision makers when choosing among competing alternatives, in situations of uncertainty and limited resources—is one that carries a number of implicit assumptions regarding the healthcare market. Among the most basic assumptions is that human wants are unlimited, while the resources available to satisfy these wants are scarce. The first part of this statement (sometimes referred to as the *principle of non-satiation*) might, at first blush, appear obvious; there are, however, some cases in which more is not necessarily better and human wants for a particular good can indeed be satisfied. While it is the exception to the rule in most economic situations, the existence of a saturation point may be fairly common in healthcare (i.e., there is a limit to how much therapy some patients can endure). Thus, maximizing an externally determined objective (such as survival) may not always be appropriate.

Inevitability of Choice

A second principle, following directly from the first, is the *inevitability of choice*. While demand for some goods may be finite, it is a general truth that not all wants can be satisfied. Resource limitations constrain consumers, forcing them to choose how scarce assets will be allocated among competing options. For any alternative selected, another alternative must be foregone. At the heart of economic analysis is the idea of *opportunity costs,* which is the value of activities precluded by a particular action or choice. From the standpoint of economic efficiency, the wisdom of investing in a particular program cannot be considered in isolation; rather, it should be measured in the context of alternate uses for those same resources.

The Market

The inevitability of choice does not in itself signal a need for formal economic evaluation and regulation. In what economists refer to as a perfectly competitive market, the invisible forces of supply and demand allocate resources efficiently with no need for external fine-tuning. In the healthcare market, however, economists have identified various sources of *market failure* that prevent this optimal outcome. One example is the presence of *moral hazard,* a situation where the individual making a decision about whether to consume a good (such as a medical treatment) does not pay the full price of that good. Privately insured patients receiving the benefits of a therapy, for example, generally pay only a fraction of the cost; the remainder is borne by their insurance company and fellow policy-holders. Because the individual's decision does not take into account the full societal cost of the treatment, moral hazard can lead to overuse of services.

A second source of market failure is the presence of *externalities,* situations where a person does not fully take into account the consequences of his or her actions on the well-being of others. Externalities are an important consideration in the context of infectious diseases like AIDS, where one person's decision to adopt preventive measures can affect the risks of infection population-wide.

In the presence of market failures, external intervention may be necessary to assure the efficient allocation of scarce resources. The methods of pharmacoeconomics, cost-effectiveness analysis, and cost-benefit analysis are rooted in the simple principle that decisions should be made from a careful comparison of marginal costs and benefits—the net benefits conferred for each additional unit of resources spent.

The preceding discussion provides only a cursory survey of the principles and assumptions that underpin the theory of economic evaluation. Decision makers should explore these issues further and draw their own conclusions as to the appropriateness of these arguments as an intellectual justification for the use of economic evaluation as an aid to decision making in medical care and public health. The remainder of this chapter is built on these foundations.

Analytic Frameworks

Economic evaluations provide information about the relative economic impact and consequences of alternative choices. Specific methods differ by the manner in which they measure costs and outcomes. This section describes the four most common analytic approaches.

Cost-Benefit Analysis

Cost-benefit analysis (CBA) is considered the gold standard for economic evaluation. It permits decision makers to compare drugs and medical interventions with widely different health outcomes. In a cost-benefit analysis, net resource costs and net health effectiveness are both measured in the same units, usually dollars. Results are then expressed in terms of an *expected net benefit*. The decision rule prescribed by CBA is that an intervention is deemed *cost-beneficial* if its expected net benefit is positive (i.e., if benefits outweigh costs).

Expected net benefit =
monetized value of net effectiveness − net resource cost

Practical and ethical considerations limit the use of CBA in the evaluation of many health-related activities and products. Although the conceptual framework for the approach is easy to understand, most people balk at the idea of assigning a dollar value to life, death, and the many intangibles that characterize the consequences of medical intervention. CBA is, therefore, usually applied only in instances where an accepted and credible method exists to quantify benefits in monetary terms.

Cost-Effectiveness Analysis

Cost-effectiveness analysis (CEA) is the most commonly used analytic framework for economic evaluation in healthcare. It is typically employed in situations where the economic input can readily be measured in dollars, but where it may be more appropriate to denominate benefits in natural units of value (e.g., in the case of healthcare, hospital days avoided). Such circumstances may arise when the alternatives under consideration aim to achieve the same objective.

In a CEA, no attempt is made to monetize the value of health benefits. The overall indicator of performance (known as the *cost-effectiveness ratio* or *C/E ratio*) reports the net cost per unit of effectiveness conferred.

Cost-effectiveness (C/E) ratio = net resource cost / net effectiveness

The C/E ratio represents the additional resources that must be consumed to produce an incremental unit of effectiveness relative to an alternative. If resources are allocated subject to a budget constraint, then all alternatives considered should first be ranked from lowest (best) to highest (worst) C/E ratio. Choices are then made from the top of the list downward until the budget is exhausted. The C/E ratio of the last project that receives funding represents a threshold (or hurdle) rate against which any subsequent opportunities should be evaluated.

Cost-Utility Analysis

Cost-utility analysis (CUA) is a special case of CEA in which effectiveness is measured in preference-based measures of well-being (such as the quality-adjusted life-year). CUA is considered, for instance, in situations where issues of individual preference or quality of life may be the driving criteria in the choice of one drug versus another. The CUA framework permits the analyst to capture patient (or clinician or organizational) preferences with regard to risk, quality of life, and other intangibles when framing decisions. At the same time, however, it adds a layer of complexity and ethical difficulty to the analytic process.

Cost-Minimization Analysis

Cost-minimization analysis (CMA) assumes that the competing interventions being analyzed are equivalent in terms of the outcome under consideration. The analysis, therefore, focuses on a cost comparison. A cost-minimization analysis may be appropriate, for example, in situations where two generically equivalent drugs have the same pharmacological effect. In such a circumstance, the question boils down to which drug is cheaper and more easily administered.

CMA differs from the other analytic methods previously listed in that no attempt is made to balance costs against the benefits conferred. As such, CMA violates the economic idea of *opportunity costs* (i.e., that choices should be based not only on the costs incurred but also with regard to the benefits foregone). Most experts agree that, while there is nothing wrong with identifying the economic consequences of decisions, care must be taken to ensure that CMA is not used merely to justify indiscriminate cost cutting.

USEFUL ECONOMIC TERMINOLOGY

Marginal analysis assesses the resources that must be consumed in order to produce an additional unit of health effect from a particular activity.

Incremental analysis compares the resources required to produce an additional unit of effect from a particular activity relative to the impact of devoting those resources to an alternative activity.

An activity's *opportunity cost* represents the value of the most productive, foregone alternative use of the resources.

Selecting an Analytic Framework

Choosing an appropriate analytic framework depends on the context of the analysis. Study design considerations, such as the nature of the decision at hand, the target audience, the planning horizon, and the relevant costs and consequences to be considered, all play a role in choosing the appropriate method. Each of these design issues is discussed in further detail in the next section.

Economic Evaluation Design

Health economic evaluations appear with increasing frequency, both in the medical literature and in industrial settings. They have even begun to figure prominently in national health policy debates. The growing importance of the field fuels refinement of analytical tools and creates a more sophisticated audience. This section considers those features of an economic evaluation that analysts generally agree are essential to a sound analysis. Every economic evaluation (e.g., cost-effectiveness analysis, cost-benefit analysis) should consider the following issues: (1) What is the decision? (2) Has the analytic perspective been specified? (3) What are the competing alternatives? (4) How are time horizons and preferences handled? (5) What are the relevant costs? (6) What is the outcome measure of interest? and (7) Have uncertainties been appropriately managed?

What Is the Decision?

The first step in any economic evaluation is an explicit statement of purpose and rationale of the analysis and a specification of the decision to be addressed. A well-constructed, clearly articulated description of the question is essential to the other design elements (such as the choice of an analytic perspective, the costs to be included, and the specification of relevant decision alternatives to be considered).

Achieving consensus on the question is often easier said than done. The key issues to be considered include

- *Definition of the target audience.* Who is the decision maker? Who are the likely consumers of the analysis? Are these people different? What are their respective information requirements? What reporting formats are most likely to serve those needs?

- *Selection of objectives.* What performance measures are likely to influence the choice faced by the decision maker? Can formal, analytic, yet understandable objectives and reporting formats be identified?

- *Exploration of competing interests.* In cases where there might be multiple questions and/or audiences, what are the various stakeholder concerns and incentives? Where are the likely areas of disagreement, and what kinds of answers can promote coalition building or resolution?

- *Examination of distributional issues.* It is often important to acknowledge and manage the fact that a decision will produce both winners and losers. Who pays under each alternative? Who receives more or less benefit under each plan? Do the answers to these questions create any legal, ethical, organizational, political, or economic implications that should be given weight in the analysis?

Has an Analytic Perspective Been Specified?

Healthcare decisions affect patients, providers, insurers, families, governments, taxpayers, and society. More often than not, the approval of a new drug, for example, or its inclusion in an HMO formulary, redistributes costs and benefits among these stakeholders. Depending on whose perspective is adopted, assessments of the drug's appropriateness and cost-effectiveness may differ dramatically. Any evaluation, therefore, should begin with a careful specification and justification of whose costs and benefits are considered relevant to the analysis.

Published academic evaluations typically focus on public health and global resource allocation decisions. For these evaluations, it makes sense to adopt a societal perspective in which all costs and benefits are included, regardless of whom they affect. It is generally a good practice, however, to consider a decision from multiple points of view. By considering the same decision from a variety of perspectives, it is sometimes possible to identify expected gainers, potential losers, and likely sources of conflict.

What Are the Competing Alternatives?

Economists define costs in terms of lost opportunities. The economic consequences of a decision only have meaning in light of the alternative activities foregone or precluded. To an economist, there is no such thing as a cost-effective decision until an answer to the question, "Compared to what?" is provided. That's why it is so important to specify the *comparator* against which the decision is to be assessed.

The choice of an appropriate basis of comparison is not always obvious. In general, a new drug or technology should be compared to the best available option or—if that choice has not yet been widely accepted—to the most commonly accepted alternative. If different options are available to decision makers in different settings, more than one comparator may be considered in the analysis.

One easy way to overstate the advantages of a new technology is to use an inappropriate, outdated, or expensive technology as a comparator. Many questionable evaluations of pharmaceutical interventions, for instance, fail to consider nonpharmaceutical alternatives as possible comparators.

Selection of relevant alternative(s) is of critical importance when interpreting the results of a study. Investigators should provide an explicit statement and justification of the choices considered. Consumers of economic evaluations should also question whether an appropriate comparator was chosen.

How Are Time Horizons and Preferences Handled?

The costs and benefits of a decision can continue to accrue long after the intervention itself. This is particularly true in the case of preventive activities, where many years may pass between the time of implementation and when benefits are finally observed. Choice of an appropriate planning horizon and an approach for handling the time value of money and health should reflect the expected flow of economic consequences.

Planning Horizon   A sound analysis should aim to capture all the relevant costs and consequences of an activity. It is generally advisable, therefore, to err on the side of inclusiveness and adopt a longer-run perspective. An appropriate analytic time perspective should be

- Relevant to both the decision under consideration and its expected effects
- Long enough to capture any seasonal variations in the accrual of costs and benefits
- Designed to account for both the fixed costs of start-up and the ongoing costs of program maintenance
- Sensitive to the downstream consequences of interventions that have either long payback periods or that involve intergenerational transfers

At the same time, however, the time horizon should not broaden the limits of credibility. An analysis that extends too far into the future may fail to capture critical technological innovations and environmental changes.

Time Preferences   Discounting is employed in economic analysis to account for the time value of costs and benefits. In general, people prefer to receive benefits as soon as possible and delay costs indefinitely. Discounting quantitatively incorporates these preferences into economic analyses by weighing costs and benefits less heavily the further into the future they occur. Thus, a future benefit does not look as attractive as an immediate benefit, and a future cost does not weigh as heavily as an immediate cost.

The discounting of monetary costs and savings has met with general acceptance. Objections are often raised, however, to the discounting of nonmonetary effects, such as lives saved (for a medical therapeutic decision). The notion of valuing immediate changes in health more highly than future changes strikes some people as distasteful and possibly unethical; these objections are often based on concerns that discounting nonmonetary effects, such as lives saved, biases our decisions against prevention programs, against the elderly, and against future generations.

In recent years, academics reached a general (although not unanimous) agreement that all costs and benefits should be discounted at the same discount rate. Rates in the 3 to 5 percent range are commonly recommended. So long as the issue remains a thorny one, however, most analysts recommend that sensitivity analyses be performed to assess the robustness of the results with respect to an even wider range of values. Sensitivity analyses should include an analysis in which effects are not discounted at all.

What Are the Relevant Costs?

Economics is about resources consumed and opportunities fore-gone. To an economist, the cost of an activity is understood as the net change in resource consumption resulting from that activity compared to a competing alternative. Direct costs (those attributed to the activity itself) indirect costs (those which result from the activity), and intangible costs (such as psychological stress or anxiety) should all be considered in any evaluation.

What Is the Outcome Measure of Interest?

Devoting resources to a particular intervention means foregoing the benefits that might be conferred by a competing, alternative activity. Outcome measures are the currency in which such benefits are denominated. Ideally, an outcome measure should capture the value of all relevant changes.

Have Uncertainties Been Appropriately Managed?

The results of an economic evaluation often vary considerably depending on the estimates of a few highly influential variables. Given the imperfect information that underpins so many evaluations, sound practice requires that the uncertainties be clearly identified and explored. A number of techniques are available:

- *Sensitivity analysis* varies the estimates of one or more variables at a time and analyzes the effects of this variation on the results. Greater confidence grows from a result that is robust across broad variation in critical variables. While sensitivity analysis is simple to perform and its results are easily interpreted, the method has significant problems: the analyst might not choose the right variables to test; the analyst might not choose the right range of values to examine; and the method may fail to detect interactions between variables.

- *Scenario analysis* explores the effects of changing more than one variable at a time. Analysts can consider best-case and worst-case scenarios by setting parameter values to their most and least favorable levels.

- *Monte Carlo simulation* techniques take advantage of fast computers to perform simultaneous sensitivity analyses on many uncertain variable estimates. A multitude of different parameter values are mixed and matched at random in order to produce a more complete picture of the influence of uncertainty in shaping the results of an evaluation. This method requires that some assumptions be made about the distributions of the parameters to be varied, but offers advantages over traditional sensitivity analysis.

- *Threshold analysis* searches for values that underlying variables would have to assume to change the recommended decision. This can be a useful form of sensitivity analysis in situations where it is impossible to pinpoint the value of an important variable. In such instances, it is sometimes helpful to identify the value of that parameter at which the decision maker would be indifferent between two courses of action.

Bibliography

Brett, A. S. "Hidden Ethical Issues in Clinical Decision Analysis." *New England Journal of Medicine* 305 (1981): 1150–1152.

Detsky, A. S. and G. Nagalie. "A Clinician's Guide to Cost-effectiveness Analysis." *Annals of Internal Medicine* 113 (1990): 147–154.

Drummond, M. E., G. L. Stoddart, and G. W. Torrance. *Methods for the Economic Evaluation of Health Care Programmes.* 2nd ed. Oxford: Oxford University Press, 1997.

Eisenberg, J. M. "Clinical Economics: A Guide to the Economic Analysis of Clinical Practices." *JAMA* 262 (1989): 2879–2886.

Gold, M. R., J. E. Siegel, L. B. Russel, and M. C. Weinstein. "Cost-effectiveness in Health and Medicine." *Report of the Panel on Cost-effectiveness in Health and Medicine.* New York: Oxford University Press, 1996.

Haddix, A. C., S. M. Teutsch, P. A. Shaffer, and D. O. Dunet. *Prevention Effectiveness: A Guide to Decision Analysis and Economic Evaluation.* New York: Oxford University Press, 1996.

Hadorn, D. C., "Setting Health Care Priorities in Oregon: Cost-effectiveness Meets the Rule of Rescue." *JAMA* 265 (1991): 2218–2225.

Sloan, F. A., ed. *Valuing Health Care: Costs, Benefits, and the Effectiveness of Pharmaceuticals and Other Medical Technologies.* New York: Cambridge University Press, 1995.

Journals about economic evaluation. *Medical Decision Making. Value in Health. International Journal of Technology Assessment in Health Care. PharmacoEconomics. Health Economics. Journal of Health Economics*

How to Evaluate a Proposal

Stephen Rimar

Case 4 is about selling a proposal. But what if you are the person being sold to? Individuals and groups continuously bring proposals to managers, committees, boards and the like for action. Some proposals are thoroughly prepared and in writing, while others are no more than vague ideas shared during conversation. Depending on the decision-making authority of a proposal's recipient and the state of development of the proposal, the action will vary. Sometimes recipients assume the role of supporter, coach, or reviewer because they lack authority to determine a proposal's fate. Other times, however, it is their job to decide the value of a proposal and recommend action.

Seems Like a Good Idea

Dr. Vincent Gulisano, chief medical officer of a large hospital, was a member of a committee to whom the CEO sent a proposal for the establishment of a new dental clinic. The committee represented a wide variety of disciplines and served as the CEO's primary advisor on matters of this type.

The hospital offered no outpatient dental services and influential physicians strongly supported the clinic's establishment. The reasons proposed for its development were convincing: The local population was underserved; the addition of a dental residency would enhance the prestige and educational mission of the hospital; and more importantly, the clinic would serve as a vehicle through which patients could flow to other hospital clinics. Despite compelling arguments in support of the proposal, the committee needed more information before responding to the CEO's question, "Should we establish a dental clinic?"

The proposal presented to the committee was poorly developed. It offered no analysis or implementation plan. Rarely would a proposal in this state make it to the committee, but the CEO was interested in the prospect of helping the underserved in the community while attracting new patients. At this point, the committee could have asked those who created the proposal to supply the missing information and analysis. That is a reasonable step under normal circumstances and an acceptable response for a proposal recipient. A combination of factors, however, prompted the committee itself to investigate the value of the proposal. The first factor was the interest the CEO displayed in the project and his accompanying (though unspoken) demand for quick action. The second reason stemmed from the first: Committee members commanded resources and held expertise well beyond the proposal's originators. They could accurately assess the proposal's merits. The originators would be consulted if necessary, but because of time constraints and their inadequate proposal preparation, they essentially relinquished control of their proposal. These circumstances, though not particularly unusual, can have unpleasant consequences, including blurring the identity of the idea's source. Not a problem if it's a bad idea, but. . . .

Reworking the Proposal

Dr. Gulisano volunteered to head the ad hoc group to evaluate the proposal before the committee made a recommendation to the CEO. They began by conducting a financial review. To estimate expenses, they used a model of a typical dentist office and practice, and applied hospital costs and services to it. They estimated the salaries of a receptionist, dental assistant, hygienist, residents, and attending staff (including fringe benefits and malpractice), as well as rent, communication services, billing/collections fees at the same rate as other hospital clinics. They also approximated start-up costs associated with the purchase of new dental office equipment, including x-ray machines.

Hospital costs could be estimated by comparing projected space and service requirements with those of existing clinics, but since the hospital had no experience with dental outpatient services, revenue projections were difficult to determine. Assuming the same patient/payer mix as other hospital clinics, the ad hoc group obtained a representative billing profile (i.e., the frequency and mix of billing codes) from a local community dental practice. Estimations of patient volume in the first two years of the practice were based on patient volume in the other hospital clinics relative to similar community practices.

After reviewing cost and revenue projections, it was clear that, at best, the dental clinic would break even in two years, excluding the start-up costs. A sensitivity analysis using the most conservative cost estimate and the most liberal revenue projection supported this assessment. For many proposals, particularly those with popular support, a break-even projection would be acceptable. But Dr. Gulisano's group knew that considerable expenses would be incurred long before revenues appeared for this clinic. Given the worsening state of hospital services funding, they thought it unwise to initiate an effort that lacked the prospect of immediate profitability. Even in the most favorable economic scenario, the clinic would operate at a loss for the first two years. They knew the hospital could not afford to support such a proposal at that time.

A Way Out

Dr. Gulisano, however, pressed his group to look beyond the financials in estimating the value of the dental clinic proposal. Specifically, they needed to address supporters' claims that the clinic would provide access to dental care for the underserved and attract patients to other clinics (thereby providing additional revenue). They found little evidence to suggest that either would occur. Two city-based dental clinics, eight school-based dental clinics, and 10 dentists in private practice were found in close proximity to the hospital. An informal poll of current clinic patients found them happy with their existing dental services, including access to care, and unlikely to switch to a hospital dental clinic. Finally, Dr. Gulisano's group noted that creating a new clinic would require displacing existing services, which might jeopardize existing business. It was clear to the group that the hospital should not invest in this effort.

The group summarized its findings. The final report, while it contained a detailed financial analysis, devoted a significant amount of space to the reasons suggested for the clinic's establishment. This was included in hopes of mitigating the inevitable response of the influential physician supporters. Dr. Gulisano's group also left the door open for a clinic in the future. They stipulated conditions under which the decision should be reexamined: if reimbursement for services increased, if the number of dental care providers in the community decreased significantly, if there was evidence of a growing number of clinic patient visits, or if funding to cover start-up costs could be obtained by a grant or donation. Providing this list conveyed two messages to the proposal's supporters. The first implied that the idea was a good one, but simply not feasible given the existing conditions. The second message conveyed ways to change some of these conditions.

The conclusion of Dr. Gulisano's group, that the hospital should not establish a dental clinic, was supported by the full committee and eventually the CEO. Had they been a less diligent group, the committee could have supported the proposal without appropriate investigation, or denied it simply because they didn't think it would work. Instead, they supplemented an inadequate proposal using their own resources.

How to Do It

1. *Determine your role.* Sometimes it is clear why a proposal comes your way. Perhaps you are the boss, or chair of a committee, or president of a foundation with the power and resources to turn an idea into action. Sometimes though, it is because the proposal's creator thinks you can offer help in another way. He may view you as a knowledgeable source of the proposal's subject or the process for getting one funded or approved. Or you may simply represent a willing listener or supportive colleague. In addition, you may be sought as a collaborator. Discussing your role with the author and establishing what is wanted of you, and what you can and will do, is the first step when someone approaches you with a proposal. Clarifying expectations simplifies personal as well as business relationships.

2. *Assess the completeness of the proposal.* If you are asked to accept or reject a formal proposal (which could range from a plan to switch thermometer vendors to an application for a large foundation grant), the first step is to determine whether the proposal is complete. If there is a format for presentation, does the proposal conform to it? This can be reviewed by support staff, or in the case of a committee, by a subgroup of the committee so that time is not wasted. If the format was not established beforehand, take a few minutes to write down what you expect to find in the body of the proposal after reading the introduction. Compare the proposal's content with your list. Is everything essential included? If so, it's time to move to assessment of quality and comparative value.

3. *Decide what to do with incomplete proposals.* If the proposal is incomplete and you're not going to reject it outright, at least three options are available: Return it to the originators with explicit directions as to what to do before resubmitting; dedicate your own resources to fill in the blanks, without involving the originators; and work with the originators to produce a complete document. Factors such as the nature and importance of the proposal, the decision deadline, and the availability of resources will inform the choice.

4. *Consider the pros and cons.* Once you have a completed proposal, list the advantages and disadvantages of implementing it. Consider the strength of data associated with both. As needed, consult knowledgeable sources (e.g., people, print media, the Internet), and remember that a different perspective, even regarding aspects of the proposal in which you consider yourself expert, can be illuminating.

If you need to choose among competing proposals, consider developing a scoring system for evaluation. This can decrease evaluator bias and simplify the logistics of reviewing multiple proposals. The items on a scoring sheet along with their weights should reflect the importance of the characteristics of both the proposal and those responsible for implementation. The quality of a proposal—how comprehensive or well written, for example—may not reflect its likelihood of success.

5. *Communicate decisions and provide feedback.* People who submit a proposal deserve, at the least, prompt notification of a decision. This gesture of respect, however, is more valuable if accompanied by information that might inform resubmissions or new proposals. And winning as well as losing proposals merit feedback. Dr. Gulisano's group, for example, clearly articulated the conditions under which the proposal could be reexamined. In sharing such specific feedback, you can potentially avoid some postdecision work and Monday-morning quarterbacking and remain in good standing with both supporters and detractors. It is also an opportunity to learn how to develop a better proposal the next time around.

Organizational Management

LECTURE 6

Leadership Style: Managing the Decision-Making Process

Victor H. Vroom

Introduction

For the last quarter century, I have researched leadership based on what is called a situational or contingency approach. Put succinctly, this approach posits there is not just one right answer when it comes to leadership (i.e., no set of leadership characteristics or behaviors is effective in all situations). Effective leadership requires matching appropriate leader traits or behaviors to the situation.

In our research, we have not been concerned with all aspects of leadership but rather with one very important dimension—the extent to which the leader involves members of the work team in decision making. This is often referred to as leadership style or, more specifically, the degree to which a style provides opportunities for participation by direct reports. The scale of participation and the terms applied to different degrees of participation are in Figure 6.1.

Leadership Styles

At the left-hand side of the scale (Figure 6.1), we have a style frequently referred to as autocratic in which the decision is made by the leader without influence by team members. The next two styles, consult (individually) and consult (group), include team members'

Figure 6.1 Taxonomy of leadership styles.

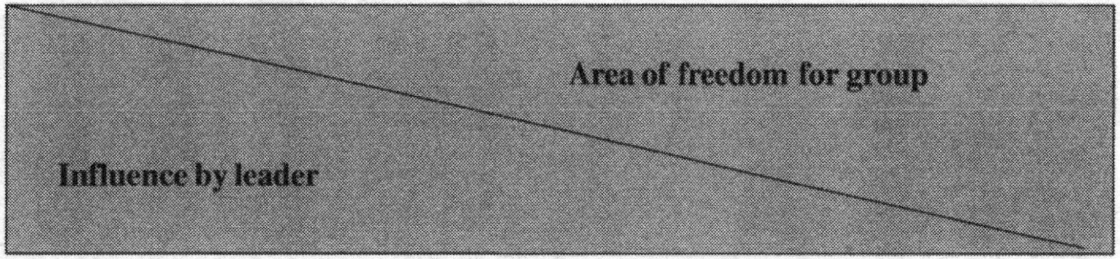

Area of freedom for group

Influence by leader

| 0 | 3 | 5 | 7 | 10 |

Decide

You make the decision alone and either announce or sell it to the group. You may use your expertise in collecting information that you deem relevant to the problem from the group or others.

Consult (individually)

You present the problem to the group members individually, get their suggestions, and then make the decision.

Consult (group)

You present the problem to the group members in a meeting, get their suggestions, and then make the decision.

Facilitate

You present the problem to the group in a meeting. You act as facilitator, defining the problem to be solved and the boundaries within which the decision must be made. Your objective is to get concurrence on a decision. Above all, you take care to ensure that your ideas are not given any greater weight than those of others simply because of your position.

Delegate

You permit the group to make the decision within prescribed limits. The group undertakes the identification and diagnosis of the problem, developing alternative procedures for solving it, and deciding on one or more alternative solutions. While you play no direct role in the group's deliberations unless explicitly asked, your role is an important one behind the scenes, providing needed resources and encouragement.

involvement as consultants. Their advice and counsel is solicited by the leader either individually or in a group meeting. Moving further right we have a style designated as facilitate in which the leader serves as chairperson, moderator, or facilitator in a meeting aimed at gaining consensus. Finally, in the style termed delegate, solving the problem or decision making is given to a team who then has total responsibility for making the decision. The numbers corresponding to each alternative (0, 3, 5, 7, 10) depict the relative amounts of influence or opportunities for participation afforded the team members during the decision making process.

Antecedents and Consequences of Leadership Style

We use this scale both normatively and descriptively. In our normative work, we seek to develop a prescriptive model to guide leaders and managers toward the styles that are consistent with the particular problems and challenges they face. In this normative work, thousands of decisions were studied in which both the style used and the effectiveness of the resulting decision are known. The normative model has received numerous revisions in the past 25 years with changes being informed by evaluation studies carried out by us and by other researchers in the field.

In our descriptive work, our principal data collection method has consisted of a set of standardized situations or cases, usually 30 in number, each depicting a leader with a problem to solve. Managers are asked to put themselves in each situation and to specify which style they would use. Well over 100,000 managers have been studied in this fashion. Descriptively, we are concerned with understanding the factors that influence the styles people use.

I use the term *we* advisedly and in two senses. First, there is the proximal *we*—my colleagues Philip Yetton and Arthur Jago who at different stages in evolution of these ideas worked closely with me in developing earlier versions. Then there is the distal *we*—the hundreds of social scientists worldwide who have spontaneously joined us in testing and elaborating these ideas. At last count, there were almost 50 doctoral dissertations and 150 scientific articles dealing with this work.

More complete summaries may be found elsewhere. It is not my intent to summarize this work in this lecture. Instead, I focus on its major import for the practicing physician/manager. I first examine the normative model and then turn to some of our descriptive work.

Toward a Normative Model

Decision Quality

Let us examine what is at stake in the choice of how much and in what way to involve others when solving problems and making decisions. The first outcome, and undoubtedly most important, is the quality of the decision. Above all we want wise, well-reasoned, and analytically sound decisions that are consistent with the end goals and that consider available information about the consequences of alternative means of achieving them.

What happens to decision quality as one moves from an autocratic process to the more participative processes? Undoubtedly, the nature of the decision and its quality change as we move across the scale. But does decision quality increase or decrease? A conservative answer, and one which we believe is consistent with the available research evidence, is that the effects of participation on decision quality depend on certain observable features of the decision-making situation. These effects depend on where the relevant knowledge or expertise resides—in the leader, in the group, or both. They also depend on the goals of the potential participants, particularly on the extent to which group or team members support the organizational objectives embedded in the problem. Finally, the amount of synergy exhibited in team-based processes depends on the interpersonal skills of team members including their ability to collaborate to solve problems.

Decision Implementation

While the quality of the decision may be the most important component of its effectiveness, it is not the only component. Many high-quality decisions are ineffective because they are not effectively implemented. The effectiveness with which a group or team implements a decision depends on the extent of their commitment to its success. Here the evidence is clear and less equivocal. People support what they help build. Under a wide range of conditions, increasing participation leads to greater buy-in, commitment to decisions, and motivation for effective implementation.

To be sure, there are some situations in which the motivational benefits of greater commitment are nonexistent or irrelevant to the implementation of the decision. Sometimes the team may not be involved in the implementation; in other situations, the team views the leader as the expert or as the person with the legitimacy to make the decision and, as a result, fully supports whatever decision the leader makes.

Costs of Decision Making

Apart from considerations of decision quality and implementation (which determine the ultimate effectiveness of the decision), there are considerations of efficiency relevant to the decision process. Use of any decision-making process consumes resources, and at the same time can add to resources, albeit of a different kind. The resources consumed are called costs which are expressed in the amount of time spent in the decision-making process. Increasing the amount of participation increases the elapsed time to make the decision and, to an even greater degree, the number of hours consumed by the process.

Both values of time constitute liabilities of participative leadership styles. Seeking consensus slows down the process and consumes substantially more hours than the directive or even consultative methods of decision making. The first of these costs, increasing the time interval between the occurrence of a problem and obtaining a solution, is most relevant in emergencies where a quick or immediate response is necessary. The second consideration, the hours consumed, is more generally relevant.

Development

Developmental benefits from increased participation potentially offset these costs. Moving from the autocratic to highly participative styles increases the potential value of the team to the organization in three ways: (1) It develops the knowledge and competence of individuals by providing them with opportunities to solve problems typically handled by higher organizational levels, (2) it increases teamwork by providing opportunities to collaborate as part of a team, and (3) it increases identification with organizational goals by giving people a voice in making significant decisions in *their* organization. These developmental benefits may be negligible when the decision lacks significance, such as when the issue is trivial and lacks consequences to the organization. Furthermore, the development benefits may be nominal if the group or team members have a nonexistent or tenuous future within the broader organization.

An inefficient style wastes time without a commensurate return in development. Conversely, it is efficient when used judiciously in precisely those situations in which sufficient developmental benefits are realized. It is interesting to note that costs (time) and development, the two components of efficiency, are realized at different points in time. The time costs are immediately realized. The slowness of response and the number of hours consumed in a meeting have immediate effects. However, the growth and development of individuals and teams may not pay off for a substantial period of time.

From Analysis to Synthesis

Models of Leadership

So far our discussion identified four participation outcomes, each contingent on one or more situational factors. To be useful to leaders, we must supplement our analysis with a suitable tool for synthesizing the effects postulated. Figures 6.2 and 6.3 depict decision matrices exemplifying such a tool. Figure 6.2 shows the time-driven model. Its orientation is short term, since it is concerned with making effective decisions with minimum investment of time. No attention is placed on employee development.

In contrast, Figure 6.3 shows the development-driven model. It may be thought of as a long-term model since it is concerned with making effective decisions with maximum developmental consequences. No attention is placed on time.

Use of these two models requires a decision problem that has two properties. First, it must fall within your area of freedom or discretion (i.e., it must be up to you to decide). Second, there must be an identifiable group of potential participants in the decision.

Figure 6.2 Time-driven model.

Source: Reprinted from *A Model of Leadership Style* by Victor Vroom.
© Vroom 1998.

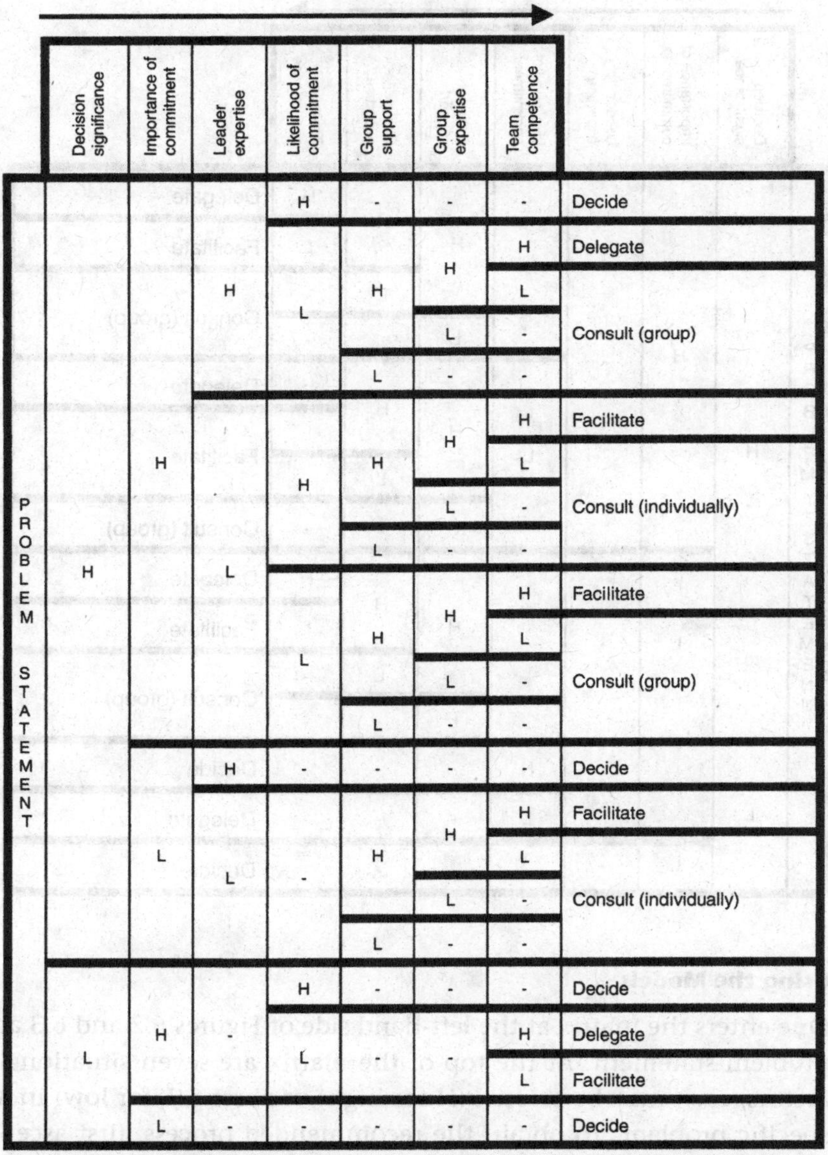

Decision significance	Importance of commitment	Leader expertise	Likelihood of commitment	Group support	Group expertise	Team competence	
H	H	H	H	-	-	-	Decide
			L	H	H	H	Delegate
						L	Consult (group)
					L	-	
				L	-	-	
		L	H	H	H	H	Facilitate
						L	Consult (individually)
					L	-	
				L	-	-	
			L	H	H	H	Facilitate
						L	Consult (group)
					L	-	
				L	-	-	
	L	H	-	-	-	-	Decide
		L	-	H	H	H	Facilitate
						L	Consult (individually)
					L	-	
				L	-	-	
L	H	-	H	-	-	-	Decide
			L	-	-	H	Delegate
						L	Facilitate
	L	-	-	-	-	-	Decide

(Left margin spanning label: **PROBLEM STATEMENT**)

Instructions: The matrix operates like a funnel. You start at the left with a specific decision problem in mind. The column headings denote situational factors which may or may not be present in that problem. You progress by selecting High or Low (H or L) for each relevant situational factor. Proceed down from the funnel, judging only those situational factors that a judgment is called for, until you reach the recommended process.

Figure 6.3 Development-driven model.

Source: Reprinted from *A Model of Leadership Style* by Victor Vroom.
© Vroom 1998.

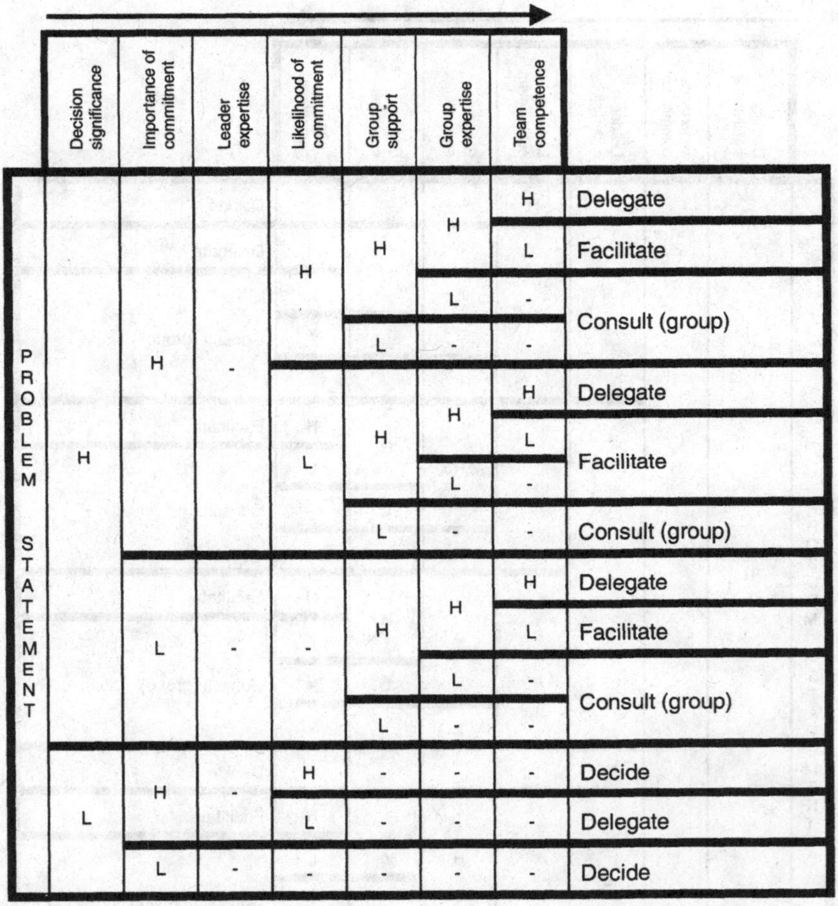

Decision significance	Importance of commitment	Leader expertise	Likelihood of commitment	Group support	Group expertise	Team competence	
H	H	-	H	H	H	H	Delegate
						L	Facilitate
					L	-	Consult (group)
				L	-	-	Consult (group)
			L	H	H	H	Delegate
						L	Facilitate
					L	-	Facilitate
				L	-	-	Consult (group)
	L	-	-	H	H	H	Delegate
						L	Facilitate
					L	-	Consult (group)
				L	-	-	Consult (group)
L	H	-	H	-	-	-	Decide
			L	-	-	-	Delegate
	L	-	-	-	-	-	Decide

(Left margin label: PROBLEM STATEMENT)

Using the Models

One enters the matrix at the left-hand side of Figures 6.2 and 6.3 at
problem statement. At the top of the matrix are seven situational
factors, each may be present (H for high) or absent (L for low) in a
specific problem. To obtain the recommended process, first ascer-
tain whether the decision to be made is significant. If so, select H
and answer the second question concerning the importance of

gaining commitment from the group. Continuing this process (while avoiding crossing any horizontal line) provides a recommended process. Sometimes a conclusive determination is made based on as few as two factors (e.g., L, L); others require three (e.g., L, H, H), four (e.g., H, H, H, H,), or as many as seven questions (e.g., H, H, L, L, H, H, H).

Submitting the same problem to both the time-driven and development-driven models can be instructive. Sometimes the two models yield identical recommendations. Where they differ, the development-driven model recommends a higher level of participation. Occasionally, the difference may be greater than one position on the participation scale, in which case intermediate alternatives are acceptable, but they are neither the fastest nor the most developmental.

While the situational factors that identify the columns in Figures 6.2 and 6.3 are sufficient for the experienced user of these matrices, a less experienced user may wish to refer to explanations of the situational factors in Figure 6.4. Figure 6.5 contains three cases and the results obtained by applying each of the decision matrices.

A Computer-Based Model

These decision matrices are simple—perhaps too simple. For example, they require high or low answers to continuous variables. They also require a choice between time-driven and development-driven models, when in fact both time and development might be important. Furthermore, they ignore potentially important situational factors.

To overcome these limitations, our research moved from a pencil and paper model to a computer program. The computer model has a number of features not found in the paper decision matrix. These include (1) use of 11 situational factors rather than the seven shown in the matrices, (2) permitting five possible responses corresponding to the degree to which situational factors are present, (3) incorporating the value of time and value of development as situational factors, rather than portraying them as separate matrices, and (4) guiding managers through the process of analyzing situations with definitions, examples, and other sources of help.

Figure 6.4 Situational factors in the normative model.

Decision significance	How significant is the decision to the success of the project or organization?
Importance of commitment	How important is it that the group members be committed to the decision?
Leader's expertise	To what extent do you have the knowledge or expertise necessary to solve the problem?
Likelihood of commitment	How likely is the group to commit themselves to a decision that you might make on your own?
Group support for objectives	How much do group members support the organizational objectives to be obtained in this problem?
Group expertise	To what extent do group members have the knowledge or expertise required to solve this problem?
Team competence	To what extent do group members have the social and interpersonal skills needed to work together in solving this problem?

Figure 6.6 shows the basic screen of a Java-based version of the computer program. Figure 6.6 shows the program as it might have been applied to the manufacturing problem described earlier. The case is analyzed by addressing the 11 situational factors. Note that each factor is rated on multiple levels (typically five). Once the evaluation is completed, a calculate tab is selected and the bar graph display at the top of the figure is produced. This particular bar graph is based on all four outcome variables and is labeled overall. To illustrate the trade-off and different effects, each outcome may be selected by clicking on the appropriate tab and observing its effects on the bar graphs.

Figure 6.5 Applying the matrices to the sample cases.

Setting: Manufacturing plant
Your position: Plant manager

You have recently been appointed manager of a new plant, which is presently under construction. Your group of five department heads has been selected, and they are now working with you in selecting their own staff, purchasing their equipment and generally anticipating the problems that are likely to arise when you move into the plant in three months.

Yesterday you received from the architect a final set of plans for the building, and for the first time you examined the parking facilities that are available. There is a large lot across the road from the plant intended primarily for hourly workers and lower-level supervisory personnel. In addition, there are seven spaces immediately adjacent to the administrative offices, intended for visitor and reserved parking. Company policy requires that a minimum of three spaces be made available for handicapped parking, leaving you only four spaces to allocate among yourself and your five department heads. There is no way of increasing the total number of such spaces without changing the structure of the building.

Up to now there have been no obvious status differences within the group. To be sure, there are salary differences, with your administrative, manufacturing, and engineering managers receiving slightly more than the quality control and industrial relations managers. Each has recently been promoted to the new position and expects reserved parking privileges as a consequence of his/her new status. From past experience, you know that people feel strongly about things that are indicative of their status. You are reluctant to do anything to get their relationships off to a bad start.

ANALYSIS
      TIME DRIVEN: LHLL: Facilitate
      DVPT DRIVEN: LHL: Delegate

(continued)

153

Figure 6.5 (*Continued*)

Setting: Electronics plant
Your position: Manufacturing manager

You are manufacturing manager in a large electronics plant. The company's management has always been searching for ways of increasing efficiency. They have recently installed new machines and put in a new simplified work system, but to the surprise of everyone, including you, the expected increase in productivity was not realized. In fact, production has begun to drop, quality has fallen off, and the number of employee separations has risen.

You do not believe that there is anything wrong with the machines. You have had reports from other companies who are using them and they confirm this opinion. You have also had representatives from the firm that built the machines go over them, and they report that they are operating at peak efficiency.

You suspect that some parts of the new work system may be responsible for the change, but this view is not widely shared by your supply manager or your immediate subordinates who are four first-line supervisors, each in charge of a section. The drop in production has been variously attributed to poor training of the operators, lack of an adequate system of financial incentives, and poor morale. Clearly, this is an issue about which there is considerable depth of feeling within individuals and potential disagreement between your subordinates. You seriously doubt that any of your group knows for sure the real cause of your productivity drop.

This morning you received a phone call from your division manager. He had just received your production figures for the last six months and was calling to express his concern. He indicated that the problem was yours to solve in a way that you think best but that he would like to know within a week what steps you plan to take.

You share your division manager's concern with the falling productivity and know that your people are also concerned. The problem is to decide what steps to take to rectify the situation.

ANALYSIS
> TIME DRIVEN: HHLLHL: Consult (Group)
> DVPT DRIVEN: HH_LHL: Facilitate

Figure 6.5 (Continued)

Setting: Coast Guard
Your position: Captain

You are the captain of a 210-foot, medium-endurance coast guard cutter, with a crew of nine officers and 65 enlisted personnel. Your mission is general at-sea law enforcement and search and rescue. At 2:00 A.M. this morning, while en route to your home port after a routine two-week patrol, you received word from the New York Rescue Coordination Center that a small plane had ditched 70 miles offshore. You obtained all the available information concerning the location of the crash, informed your crew of the mission, and set a new course at maximum speed for the scene to commence a search for survivors and wreckage.

It is now 10:00 P.M., 20 hours later, and you are currently on duty on the bridge along with three junior officers sharing the watch with you. This is your first voyage with these officers and, indeed, the first time that they have worked with one another. For each it is a first experience as an officer on an extended mission aboard a large vessel. You were summoned from your berth by your executive officer who was concerned about the 50-knot winds and 20-foot seas, which are making it difficult to control the vessel. Your last communication from the New York Rescue Center, before atmospherics and deteriorating weather made further communications impossible, advised you that a severe storm was building to the southwest.

A decision must be made whether to abandon the search and place the vessel on a northeasterly course to ride out the storm (thereby protecting the vessel and your crew but relegating any possible survivors to almost certain death from exposure) or continuing a potentially futile search and the risks it might entail.

ANALYSIS
        TIME DRIVEN: HHHH: Decide
        DVPT DRIVEN: HH_HHL: Consult (group)

Figure 6.6 Java version of the normative model.

Source: Used with permission. © Vroom 2000.

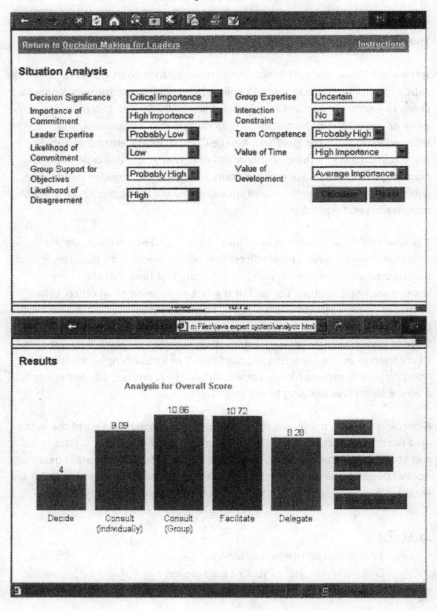

Other screens available in the computer program contain menus of help screens explicating various features of the model. For example, Bibliography contains a complete bibliography of the research underlying the model. Technical Issues explicates in general terms the theory underlying the model. Framing the Problem describes guidelines for stating the problem in a manner most likely to prove helpful in generating a solution. Forming the Team presents guidelines for team creation of a team or taskforce where none readily exists.

Studies of Participation

Our research on leadership styles has not been restricted to the development and refinement of normative models. We have been interested not only in what managers should do but also in what they do, in fact. In the latter, our principal data-collection method has been a set of cases, typically 30 in number. Each case involves three elements: a leader, a group or team, and the problem to be solved or decision to be made. These cases vary markedly in institutional context. The leader may be an army captain, a corporation president, a city mayor, or a dean of a business school. All problems are based on real-life events. For each case, managers are asked which decision process (shown in Figure 6.1) they would use in that situation.

The most important feature of a problem set resides in its design. The situational factors shown in Figures 6.2–6.4 are systematically varied across the set in accordance with a multifactorial design. This feature enables us to determine which situational factors influence the managers' choices, to what degree, and in what manner. It also shows what factors they apparently ignore.

Early in our research program, we developed computer programs for evaluating the correspondence between a manager's choices and the normative model showing his or her effectiveness in achieving both quality decisions and the commitment needed to ensure their effective implementation.

Currently, our individualized computer analysis is five pages long and includes recommendations aimed at increasing each person's leadership effectiveness. Not surprisingly, these analyses proved useful not only informing our research but also for the managers themselves.

Managers and Decision Making

Here we focus not on what *managers learned* from having a mirror held up to them, but rather what *we learned from managers* about how they choose when and where to share their decision-making power. In a world in which it is common to label managers with terms like autocratic, or participative, or Theory X, or Theory Y, it was instructive to observe managers make different choices in different situations. In fact, it makes somewhat more sense to label autocratic and participative situations rather than autocratic or participative managers. The differences in behavior among managers are about one-third the size of differences among situations.

Situational Behavior

Managers behave situationally. They adapt their behaviors to the situations at hand. Furthermore, the kinds of situations that evoke autocratic and participative styles are very similar to those in which the normative model would recommend such styles. Each of the seven situational factors at the top of Figures 6.2 and 6.3 affects the average manager in roughly the same way as it affects the behavior of the model. Managers make more participative choices on highly significant decisions, when they need the commitment of the group, when they lack expertise, when the likelihood of commitment to an autocratic decision is low, when the group's expertise is high, and when the group has a history of effective teamwork.

But not all managers behave that way! Some are influenced by only one or two of these factors and appear to ignore the rest. Still others are affected by one factor but (in what we believe to be) the wrong way. For example, one-fifth of the U.S. managers we studied (and three-quarters of the managers from Poland) are more likely to involve others in insignificant, trivial decisions.

Configural Behavior

One important function of feedback is to draw each individual's attention to those aspects of the situation they are overlooking. We should make it clear that the model not only responds to the seven situational factors but does so configurally—that is, the effects of one factor depend on the level of certain other factors. For example, where the knowledge resides (in the leader, in the group, with both, or neither) has more effect on leadership style in highly significant decisions.

Of great interest to us is that managers also behave configurally; that is, they attend to combinations of factors rather than being influenced by each factor separately. However, these effects are weaker among managers than in the model, suggesting that only a small number of managers behave that way or, for the typical manager, the configural effects are small in relation to those that are linear.

Differences among Managers

We stated earlier that the situational effects dwarfed the differences among individual managers. While that is true, it does not imply that differences among managers in their typical or overall behavior are insignificant or inconsequential. If one averages the choices of a manager on the 30 cases, the mean score reflects the average of where he or she stands on the scale in Figure 6.1. We turn now to consider some of the correlates in mean scores on our 10-point scale of participation.

Timing and Culture Early in our 27-year period of data collection, we noticed that managers were becoming more participative. Something seemed to be moving managers toward higher involvement, more participation, greater empowerment, and more frequent use of teams over time. We do not know precisely what produces this, but we suspect it reflects changes in (1) the external environment of organizations (greater rates of change, greater complexity), (2) the flattening of the pyramid (greater spans of control resulting in difficulties in hierarchical control), (3) the growth of information technology makes it easier to get information closer to the occurrence of problems, and (4) the changing nature of the labor force (higher education, higher independence needs, etc.).

Of the demographic factors, the culture in which the organization functions accounts for the greatest variance. High-involvement managers are more likely in countries with high per capita GNP, with a strong democratic tradition, and a highly educated workforce.

Gender We also investigated gender differences and found women managers to be significantly more participative than their male counterparts. Supporting this conclusion, we found sizeable differences in the reactions to autocratic men and women managers. In general, being participative is valued by direct reports, but this is truer for women than for men. Participative men and women are equally valued but autocratic males are strongly preferred to autocratic women.

Organizational Level   Use of participative leadership styles is also associated with level in the organization. In most of the organizations we studied in depth, the higher the level in the organizational ladder, the more participative the manager. To be sure, we never carried our investigation up to the level of CEO because we cannot rely on sample size and the law of large numbers to cancel out chance factors due to personality or to measurement.

Bias in Self-reports   Our findings, while generally consistent with those reported by others using different research methods, are restricted to what managers say they would do on a standardized set of cases. While managers have no incentive to lie (since it will only decrease the accuracy of the computer feedback that they alone receive), we have no guard against self-deception. As a possible check on such tendencies, we give the same problem sets to both the manager and his or her direct reports. The latter are asked to describe how their manager would respond to each case. The result is striking. Virtually all managers are perceived by their direct reports as closer to the left side of the scale than they see themselves. We refer to this difference as the autocratic shift. We do not know whether the biases are in managers' self-conceptions, the perceptions held by their direct reports, or both.

Conclusion

The search for the one best leadership style has not been productive. Nor has the vacuous truism that one must vary one's style with the situation. In this lecture, I argue that many of the situational factors on which choice of an appropriate style must depend are known. Furthermore, it is possible to offer a framework that can guide leaders, whether they are physicians, mayors, or CEOs to decision-making styles, which have a higher likelihood of being effective and efficient.

I will be the first to admit that the models presented here are far from perfect. The decision matrices and computer programs are not tools to be slavishly embraced. They are support systems designed to help leaders of tomorrow through the important task of wading through the challenges presented by today's complex and rapidly changing environment.

Selected Bibliography

The original inspiration for this body of work may be found in an article written in the *Harvard Business Review* by Bob Tannenbaum and Warren Schmidt. "How to Choose a Leadership Pattern." *Harvard Business Review* 36 (1958): 95–101.

My initial work on leadership was done with Philip Yetton (*Leadership and Decision Making*. Pittsburgh: University of Pittsburgh Press, 1973). Subsequently, I collaborated with Arthur G. Jago in writing *The New Leadership* (Upper Saddle River: Prentice-Hall, 1988).

Those who wish to learn more about the specific findings cited, or the computer programs that are referred to in this article, may contact me at victor.vroom@yale.edu or at The Yale School of Management, 135 Prospect Street, P.O. Box 208200, New Haven, CT 06520-8200.

CASE 6

How to Be a Leader

Stephen Rimar

Everyone knew the lab was a disaster. Absenteeism, turnover, and infighting were rampant. The number of complaints about lost specimens and slow turnaround time rose to an all-time high. As Dr. Jack Treadwell assumed the position of lab director, he knew something must be done. However, the challenge of handling a dysfunctional organizational group was new to him. His career was spent as a clinical pathologist, and while he oversaw the introduction of new technologies, and even served as director of quality control for the labs, this was different. This was a new problem—not of technology or process, but of people.

A Problem of People

The lab suffered a long history of disharmony, much of it traceable to an administrative separation enforced several years before into a hospital section and a medical school section. Despite sharing physical space, half the staff was employed by the hospital and half by the medical school. Each group had its own supervisor and policies and procedures for sick time, overtime, vacation, and so on. In addition, the school's employees were union members, whereas the hospital employees were not.

The hospital and the medical school jointly funded Dr. Treadwell's position and gave him the task of solving the problems in the lab. Knowing the problems were people-related, he appropriately dedicated much of his time to communicating with staff. Soon after becoming director, Dr. Treadwell scheduled a meeting with each employee. The sessions began with Dr. Treadwell relaying the concerns of the hospital and the school about the lab's performance, including timeliness of reports and efficiency of specimen handling. He took the time to ask a number of open-ended questions and spent a lot of time listening. He was particularly interested in employees' impressions of the problems' causes and their suggestions for improvement. Staff consistently identified poor interpersonal communication, blurred roles, and unclear reporting lines as problematic. They acknowledged their inability to work effectively as a team, and claimed things were so bad, even staff with the same employer had trouble working together.

Dr. Treadwell developed a recovery plan. It included (1) clarifying, with the help of human resources from both organizations, all staff roles and reporting structures; (2) establishing work groups along product lines (e.g., the staff that perform blood chemistries); (3) developing a performance measurement system, based on user satisfaction and productivity measures; (4) convening weekly meetings with the two lab supervisors to discuss operations and human resource issues; (5) holding weekly staff meetings to discuss all lab issues; (6) holding monthly staff meetings with a consultant from human resources to address common communication problems; and (7) sponsoring lunch on Fridays in the staff area near the lab (this was to be a social gathering only).

The Best-Laid Plans

At the first large staff meeting, Dr. Treadwell discussed the components of his plan and announced its goals: to make the lab a better place to work and, in doing so, to improve performance. The initial response was silence. Only one person spoke and her comment was that they had tried this before but it didn't work. This was not what Dr. Treadwell hoped would happen. He was looking forward to a lively discussion of the plan.

So he held individual meetings, this time with the two supervisors, the one technician whom he recognized as particularly influential, and the person who had spoken at the meeting. Their remarks indicated that staff did not talk together and were afraid of the retribution their comments might evoke from supervisors and peers. Dr. Treadwell surmised that before staff would freely express their views, they needed to spend some time together, in his presence, without being expected to say much of anything. He allowed the format of the lab meetings to be more informational than interactive. He communicated information and reviewed progress— hoping to create an environment in which people could discuss their opinions.

Two months passed, and Dr. Treadwell saw little progress. His regular meetings produced no discussion and many changes he wanted to implement were stalled by the lack of staff involvement. In desperation, he installed a suggestion box in the lab—for staff to anonymously comment to him alone. He needed a spark to get the group moving.

Three days later he found a single comment in the box: No one in the lab had voice mail; if staff were away from the phone running a test, the call was lost. Dr. Treadwell saw this as an easy problem to correct, and perhaps the thing that would get the group moving. Within a week, he had voice mail up and running. One week later, two more suggestions and one more complaint appeared in the box. Dr. Treadwell had the spark he needed.

How to Do It

1. *Take charge personally.* Leadership cannot be delegated. It is neither an academic exercise nor something that can be addressed from a corporate office. Dr. Treadwell knew he could not deal exclusively with the supervisors and expect them to implement his plan. The only way to solve the lab's problems—both his and theirs—was to personally engage each employee. For Jack Welch, the legendary CEO of General Electric, that means, make a religion out of being accessible. For Jack Treadwell, it meant meeting with many people and working with them to accomplish their common goals.

2. *Fix something quick to gain momentum.* In any organization, large or small, there is always something that can be fixed quickly and easily. Look for it. Even if you solve only a simple problem (e.g., the lack of voice mail), you will show your ability to get things done. The suggestion box provided Dr. Treadwell with a means of identifying one quick fix. It also gave him an opportunity to examine and discuss communication in general. As the staff member pointed out, they had been through this before, and it didn't work. Dr. Treadwell needed to prove that this time would be different, and a quick fix helped.

3. *Be prepared for a marathon.* Quick fixes only serve to feed momentum. They may treat a symptom but not the disease. Leadership requires patience, and Dr. Treadwell's served him well. It enabled him to act only when the group was ready. For physicians accustomed to a fast-paced world in which immediate results are the norm, waiting is not easy. Leading an organization, however, is like treating a chronic disorder. Evaluation and treatment may take years, and acute exacerbations should be expected.

4. *Have a plan and communicate it.* Developing a plan is not enough. You must communicate it, which means more than simply sharing it. The plan must be understood by all those it affects, and everyone needs to be clear about his or her role in its implementation. Physicians spend years learning to communicate patients' signs and symptoms as precisely and as efficiently as possible. Unfortunately, for many doctors, describing disease and response to treatment is the only topic they're comfortable communicating.

Dr. Treadwell had little experience communicating a message to a group, particularly a dysfunctional one. By meeting with each employee and holding regular staff meetings, he was able to state the plan repeatedly. And once the group became engaged, specific issues about implementation could be addressed.

5. *Choose the right leadership style.* Victor Vroom's research demonstrates a spectrum of decision-making styles, ranging from dictatorial to democratic (see Lecture 6). He further distinguishes between a decision in which time is critical and one in which the development of the group is crucial. It follows that each decision should be handled in a manner appropriate to the needs of the organization. For instance, an organization in which the leader traditionally makes all the decisions may find it quite difficult to decide things in his absence. A group whose leader prefers that consensus be reached before announcing a decision may flounder considerably when required to make controversial decisions alone.

Medical practice also necessitates use of a variety of decision-making styles. In handling acute emergencies (Vroom's time-driven model), physicians make decisions alone, but in chronic conditions (Vroom's development-driven model), they seek advice and consensus, knowing that these situations are very different, and require different paths to success. The same is true for organizational leadership. For Dr. Treadwell, whose situation was more chronic than acute in nature, the need was to develop the group in order to solve problems, rather than mandate new policies and dictate behavior. Good leaders use the right approach at the right time.

6. *Support rather than command professionals.* Leading a group of professionals, such as physicians, requires a special understanding of a leader's role. In business schools, an orchestra conductor is a popular example of one who must lead a group of professionals with different skills, all of whom are necessary to meet a goal. A conductor can place music in front of musicians, but he can neither force them to play nor make them play together. He must find a way to support and direct each musician while synchronizing the performance of the entire group.

This leadership style is in contrast to that used by the military, whereby a leader gives orders that are obeyed without question. The military model serves the armed forces well because failure to obey can result in serious consequences. In the past decade, many healthcare organizations have tried unsuccessfully to lead physician groups using a military model. Physicians, however, are much more like musicians than soldiers. They must be supported and convinced, and they bristle (or much worse) if ordered. The same is true with other healthcare professionals—nurses, lab technicians, and so on. After all, healthcare professionals believe the patient is ultimately their boss. Dr. Treadwell knew that simply ordering change in the lab wouldn't make it happen.

7. *Address major detractors strongly, directly, and early.* Here is your opportunity to lead in the way most people understand leadership. The image of a leader—strong, confident, no-nonsense—matches the reality of the leader needed for one thing: dealing with detractors. Give them clear notice of your plan, whether it involves closer observation of their work or initiation of a formal disciplinary procedure, or termination, and then follow through. It may be necessary to warn several times what is going to happen, but it's essential to establish your resolve. Remember that others in the group will likely hear about these interactions, even if you keep them confidential. Strong action against detractors can serve to boost your supporters. Call on your boss (or the equivalent) for help if you feel the need. Sometimes just invoking his or her name can be effective (provided the boss knows about it).

8. *Avoid unnecessary confrontation.* Leadership involves confrontation. But think carefully before being drawn into it. Your involvement in a confrontation should only follow careful reflection on the need for your involvement (rather than someone else) and the likelihood of you improving the situation (rather than aggravating it). The job of a leader is to build, not destroy. Be sure that it is business, not personal issues that drive the interaction.

Bibliography

Tichy, N. and R. Charan. "Speed, Simplicity, Self-confidence: An Interview with Jack Welch." *Harvard Business Review* (Sept./Oct. 1989).

7
LECTURE

Leading and Managing a Negotiation Process

Christopher McCusker

This chapter offers a perspective on managerial negotiation that draws on the field of negotiation research. It reviews some core negotiation concepts, describes two fundamental processes of negotiation, and concludes with a discussion of leadership in negotiation. Readers may find it helpful to read Case 7 first (which follows this chapter), because frequent references are made to the case.

The Doctor as Negotiator

Most of us are familiar with negotiation because we do it every day. Some common examples include buying a car or a house, making vacation plans, deciding on a work schedule with coworkers, or merging into rush hour traffic. Negotiation, which derives from *neg* (not) + *otium* (leisure), is also common for physicians. Examples of doctor as negotiator include heart-to-heart talks with patients about treatment options, meetings with colleagues about policies and procedures, memos to and from a hospital's president about budget allocations, or pep talks with new members of a medical team about their roles and responsibilities.

While physicians negotiate in a wide variety of settings, it can be said that no two negotiations are exactly alike. Like human beings, each one is different even though all are constituted in somewhat similar ways. In this chapter, we focus on those similar aspects of any negotiation. The aim of this chapter is to present an overview of negotiation dynamics, and, in doing so, draw on academic research. This is not a comprehensive literature review of the field, but a summary of the most important ideas. A more comprehensive review of negotiation research can be found elsewhere.[1]

The Nature of Negotiation

Each of us enters a negotiation process with assumptions about the nature of the process. This can best be assessed by choosing a personal metaphor for negotiating. Personal metaphors are an excellent means of discovering one's assumptions about a person or process. For example, a common metaphor is time as money. We often think of time as money when we save, spend, budget, or waste it. It is similarly possible to develop a metaphor for negotiation. To do so, simply complete the following sentence: "To me, negotiating is most like ____."

To understand your own assumptions about negotiation, consider the metaphor you've chosen. Is your metaphor an individual activity, like running a marathon? Or, is it a group activity, like playing poker? Does it involve competitive strategies, like playing chess, or cooperative ones, like sailing a boat? Does it involve fear and desire, like dating or marrying? Or is it rational and calm, like doing a crossword puzzle?

Professional negotiators believe there is no single metaphor to describe negotiating. Each negotiation process involves a different set of assumptions and circumstances. And each negotiator enters the process with his or her own approach. But the successful negotiator begins by understanding his or her own assumptions. Choosing a metaphor sharpens this understanding. As you read this chapter, evoke your own metaphor and compare it to the ideas discussed. This will enable you to manage the negotiation process better, by understanding your own biases. And as discussed, understanding one's own assumptions is the first step to leading the negotiation process.

Core Concepts

Like human beings, no two negotiations are exactly alike. Several concepts, however, are helpful in identifying and making sense of negotiation situations. They are context, conflict, and interdependence.

Context

Negotiation always occurs within a situational context, or defining environment. The situational context can be thought of as a set of forces that are external to negotiators, but impact the structure and process of negotiation. Negotiation research places an emphasis on the situational context.[2] This is noteworthy because situational factors are powerful determinants of behavior, yet negotiators can easily underestimate their impact. Instead, a common tendency is to focus on personal characteristics. Underestimating the importance of the situational context is known as the "fundamental error of attribution."[3] It means that causes of negotiation behavior are commonly assumed to be characteristics of others (e.g., size of ego, presence or absence of classical virtues, level of intelligence) rather than circumstances (e.g., time pressure, budget constraints, busy schedule). Managing a negotiation process requires overcoming this tendency and focus on the circumstances within which a negotiation process is embedded.

Generally, a negotiation context includes more circumstances than we can analyze productively. For example, a negotiation context can include structural factors, such as whether negotiation is embedded in a market or an organization, how many issues there are, whether there is time pressure, whether parties are face-to-face or on opposite sides of the planet, and so on. In addition, there are social factors that can make up the context, such as the degree of intimacy between parties (e.g., strangers or romantic partners), norms about proper conduct (e.g., who should lead the discussion), or whether the parties expect to work together again in the future.

Negotiators must actively interpret and shape their context because negotiator strategy should match the particular context at hand. This matching of situational factors to group processes is consistent with the logic of Vroom and Jago's models of leadership and decision making (Lecture 6). This matching idea is addressed again when we discuss the contingency approach for determining a strategy in negotiation.

For now, consider your metaphor for negotiating. What kind of context does it suggest? How well does that metaphoric context correspond to your organizational context? Several factors are worth mentioning because they will relate to our analysis of the contingency approach. The negotiation context for doctors includes many memberships. Physicians may belong to a hospital or medical school or both; within an organization, they may belong to several practices or moonlight on an emergency medical team. In addition, physicians are members of one or more professional societies and may even do research, teach, or take courses. In addition to membership considerations, physicians also maintain many working relationships over time. Therefore, it is likely that colleagues will work together again in the future. In addition, a reputation is important. The complexity of their professional interests and the significance of long-term relationships are two important situational factors that surround negotiation problems.

Conflict

Conflict is "the appearance of difference."[4] Often conflict is associated with negative emotions and destructive actions between parties. Strikes, boycotts, protests, sabotage, avoidance, and the like are all destructive responses to conflict. For example, some students of negotiation perceive a negotiation as war metaphor. An academic perspective on conflict is neutral about whether conflict is inherently good or bad. The critical issue is how conflict is managed. The response to conflict is what can create positive or negative consequences. An effective negotiation process is a constructive response to conflict.

Two kinds of conflict are a part of negotiation. *Conflict of understanding* occurs when there is a difference in what appears to be *true*. This kind of conflict occurs when there are different interpretations to the question, "What is going on here?" For example, two physicians may observe a set of symptoms and then disagree about diagnosis. *Conflict of interest* is a difference in what appears to be *good*. For example, physicians may agree about a diagnosis but disagree about treatment. Any negotiation will include conflict of interest as well as areas of compatible interest. In a medical practice, for example, quality patient care is a common interest. At the same time, different interests emerge from a variety of sources.

A single doctor will have many professional interests, and negotiation situations can be analyzed from multiple points of view. Two or more doctors will have even more interests at stake and between the two some will be common and others different. The example in Case 7, which follows this lecture, illustrates conflicts of understanding and interest. Dr. Davids needs to staff his emergency department, but unlike his colleagues, he does not want to hire just any warm body. The decision to hire appeared to be a conflict of interest. His colleagues felt a warm body would be good, and he disagreed. This difference led to strong emotions and open conflict. Dr. Davids reconciled this conflict of interest by finding areas of compatibility. At the same time he removed the conflict of understanding about the nature of their disagreement by sharing information. By talking about the underlying reasons for their different positions, Dr. Davids diffused the emotional conflict and restored attention to the situational context. The discussions led to a deeper understanding of the problem, and he discovered a way to resolve the conflicts.

Interdependence

Ben Franklin, upon signing the Declaration of Independence, said, "Surely, if we do not all hang together, we will all hang separately." Franklin recognized that, in declaring their independence, the patriots became highly interdependent. Interdependence occurs when outcomes are the confluence of one's own decisions and those made by others.

Negotiation requires parties who perceive their mutual dependence. Both sides recognize that they need each other in order to realize their interests. For example, Dr. Davids (Case 7) eventually realizes he needs the cooperation of his team of physicians in order to realize his goal. Negotiation, however, can create a complex form of interdependence. On the one hand, opposing negotiators must cooperate in order to reach an agreement. On the other hand, they are bound to compete over which agreement is accepted. Each side prefers the best possible terms for itself. As discussed in the following, the choice between a cooperative or competitive approach to negotiation depends on how the parties think about their interdependence.

This mixture of motivation causes the basic strategic choice in negotiation. Should one adopt a cooperative or competitive strategy? Think back to your metaphor for negotiation. What kind of relationship exists between participants? What kind of strategy do you tend to follow in negotiation? Why?

Summary of Core Concepts

In sum, situations are powerful determinants of behavior, and understanding a negotiation context is vital for making strategic choices. For example, since Dr. Davids kept his mind on the long-term vision for this group, he was able to see the value in apologizing and reopening the negotiation. A negotiation opportunity arises when interdependent parties perceive some form of conflict. Sometimes this is one party hanging up the phone on the other. Negotiation is a response to conflict. It is an attempt by two or more parties to reach agreement about how to advance their interests and includes cooperation and competition.

Models of Negotiating

Two models of negotiation receive attention in negotiation research, *distributive negotiation* and *integrative negotiation.* They correspond to competitive or cooperative strategies, respectively. An example of the difference between the two approaches comes from Mary Parker Follett, a pioneer in negotiation research.[5] She described the difference between distributive and integrative negotiation with a story of two sisters bickering over possession of a single orange.

Both sisters want the orange. One sister wants the orange to make some juice. The other sister wants it to make jelly. On the one hand, the sisters can approach their problem with distributive negotiation. A fair *distributive* solution would be to divide the orange in half. This would provide each sister with half an orange. On the other hand, an *integrative* approach recognizes that they want the orange for different purposes. Since one sister wants only the peels and the other only the pulp, it is possible to divide the orange accordingly. All the peels should go to one sister and all the pulp to the other. This integrative solution provides each sister with twice as much as they would have received from the distributive solution.

Distributive negotiation can be summarized as an attempt to capture value, or divide the negotiation pie. Integrative negotiation can be summarized as an attempt to create value, or grow the negotiation pie. Most negotiations contain elements of both, and negotiation can move back and forth between the two. However, it is useful to distinguish between the two for analysis.

Distributive Negotiation: Competition for Its Own Sake

One approach is to give consideration to one's own interests and approach negotiation as an opportunity to advance them as much as possible. The idea is that negotiation puts a certain amount of happiness at stake and one's task is to reach an agreement that captures as much happiness for one's side as possible. Capturing value is another term for the distributive negotiation process, which assumes negotiators enter the situation with opposing interests— what is good for one side is bad for the other.

Games of strategy, such as poker or chess, are useful metaphors for distributive negotiation. Those who play the game of distributive negotiation well do so by recognizing that it involves a competitive exchange of information. In many ways, the process of capturing value amounts to an intentional conflict of understanding. Negotiators want to create a favorable impression while withholding, or at best selectively revealing, information. Playing poker well, for example, involves bluffing, not revealing one's cards. Yet, negotiators should actively seek as much information about the other side as possible.

However, the competitive nature of distributive negotiation can lead to emotional conflict, and too much emotion might lead negotiators to make irrational decisions.[6] For example, one of the physicians in Case 7 is ready to quit after the conflict becomes emotional. So the first issue to address is limits, which can function to prevent distributive negotiation from spiraling out of control.

Limits and BATNAs   There are two mistakes that negotiators can make when it comes to capturing value. The first is to accept an agreement that should have been rejected. The second is to reject an agreement that should have been accepted. Both mistakes hinge on a negotiator's ability to create a reasonable standard from which possible agreements can be evaluated.

A limit is a standard for judging whether an agreement is acceptable. For example, consider a simple negotiation over a used car between a buyer and a seller. Steve, the seller, wants a high price. He will set a limit that is the lowest price he will take. Sally, the buyer, prefers a low price and will set a limit that represents the most she will give.

A limit can come from a variety of sources. For example, Sally may set a limit of $8,000 for the car because that is all the money she has available. Or Steve may set a limit of $7,000 for the car because that is how much he needs for a down payment on a new condo. The best way to form a limit is to develop a BATNA, or Best Alternative To Negotiated Agreement.[7] A BATNA refers to those outcomes that will occur if no agreement is reached. For example, suppose that before negotiating with Sally, Steve received an offer of $7,000 from another buyer. That would make $7,000 his best alternative to reaching an agreement with Sally, and he would enter his negotiation with Sally with a limit of $7,000.

Negotiators should be careful about sharing their limit with the other side. This is a case where telling the truth can be costly. For example, Raiffa describes experiments in which one side in a negotiation was given the other side's limit.[8] Negotiation agreements strongly favored the party who was informed about the other's limit. At the same time, negotiators should actively attempt to find out the other side's limit. Once the other side's limit is known, it is possible to insist on a solution that will leave the agreement slightly above their limit.

Making the Opening Offer The most important offer is always the first one, or the opening offer. In many cases, such as buying a car or house, the opening offer is made when sellers list an asking price. In organizational situations, an opening offer might be a position that one hopes gets adopted. For example, Dr. Davids' decision not to hire the unacceptable applicant was his opening offer.

Research has shown that negotiators who overbid, or make extreme opening offers, end up with more value from an agreement than those who make low opening offers.[9] Extreme offers can anchor the negotiation around favorable agreement points. For example, Dr. Davids could have started out his negotiation by stating that the applicant would not be hired and that the current team will have to provide full coverage. This more extreme offer might have anchored the negotiation on the best possible terms for Dr. Davids and any movement would be seen as his concession.

However, there is a risk in making offers that are too extreme. It is possible that the other side might dismiss the possibility of reaching an agreement because it seems impossible. For example, Dr. Davids' team might collapse as its members found another place to moonlight. Or extreme offers may be insulting to the other side. By making an extreme offer, Dr. Davids might reopen the wounds from the emotional episode and end up in a worse position than before. But if the situation is sufficiently ambiguous, or the other side is poorly prepared, an extreme opening offer can lead to better results.

Understanding Concession Patterns Negotiation situations are characterized by partial information. Each side knows for sure only its own preferences and circumstances. Concession patterns can be a useful source of information in distributive negotiation.

Concessions often follow the *norm of reciprocity*. This means that negotiators are expected to make similar concessions in terms of size and frequency. For example, when Dr. Davids apologizes to his colleagues, he makes a concession by admitting his mistake. The other doctors reciprocate and concede to work with Dr. Davids in finding a solution without hiring the unacceptable applicant. The reciprocity norm is very powerful, and negotiators should be prepared to make concessions. In addition, negotiators should insist on reciprocity. If the other side is not following this pattern for one issue, perhaps there is something else that can be done on another. For example, since Dr. Davids agreed to request a small raise for his team, he might ask his physicians for their help in finding more applicants.

A second issue involving concession patterns concerns *resistance*. Research has shown that concessions tend to decrease in size and frequency when a negotiator is approaching a limit. As limits are approached, fewer concessions are possible, so concessions get smaller. One tactic for negotiating would be to make smaller and smaller concessions. This gives an impression that you are nearing your limit.

Time Pressure   Time pressure is an important factor in negotiation. Usually, the negotiator with less time pressure will capture more value than one under pressure. Finding out the other side's deadline is a tactic for capturing value. At the same time, hiding your own time pressure might be necessary. For example, if Dr. Davids had only one month to find a new person for this team, a different result might have occurred. Maybe he would have agreed to hire the unacceptable person just to save the team.

Summary   Distributive negotiation involves attempts to capture as much for one's own side as possible. The process of capturing value usually entails a competitive exchange of information and creating conflict of understanding. Negotiators may overbid, or start by asking for more than what they really want. In addition, they can ask questions to infer the other side's limit and keep their own secret. Negotiators should rely on the norm of reciprocity. Distributive negotiators believe that what is good for one side is bad for the other. But true success in distributive negotiation should be based on how well one did with respect to a reasonable standard, such as a limit. The best limit to have is a BATNA.

Integrative Negotiation—Cooperation for Its Own Sake

Students of negotiation often express concern about the nature of distributive negotiation and tactics of capturing value. Images of smoke-filled rooms, politics as usual, and late-night compromises are easily evoked. However, it is an approach worth learning about because research has shown that most people enter negotiations with a distributive mind-set.[10] The capacity to recognize which strategy another person is following is important for defense and persuading them to negotiate differently. Finally, there are times when negotiation situations are purely distributive.

In integrative negotiation, the overriding goal is to create value. A metaphor is that a negotiation problem is a puzzle. A set of interests is put on the table. Perhaps those interests appear completely irreconcilable. To create value, one must solve the puzzle. An integrative agreement is one that advances the interests of all parties. Integrative negotiation involves sharing information freely about interests, working together to brainstorm options and create agreements of mutual advantage. In the following, we describe several tactics that have been shown to underlie effective integrative negotiating.

Establish Rapport   Integrative negotiation requires that parties work together cooperatively. But there is a risk in integrative negotiation. It is possible only through valid information exchange. A major lesson of distributive negotiation is that sharing information is risky business. It is possible that the other side might be playing a trick—pretending to do integrative negotiation but secretly trying to get information in order to capture value. For this reason, it is important to establish mutual cooperation early in the negotiation process. Morris et al. showed that negotiators are more likely to reach integrative agreements if they first establish rapport.[11] There is no magic bullet when it comes to establishing rapport. In general, the function of rapport is to make negotiators more comfortable working together. In Case 7, Dr. Davids' apology functions to establish rapport. Good will is restored and all sides coordinate with mutual cooperation.

Focus on Interests, Not Positions   Each participant in negotiation enters the situation with an interest or set of interests. Interests are the stuff of negotiation, and negotiators will bring different interests to the table. However, as Fisher, Ury & Patton argue, most parties will begin negotiations with a discussion of their respective positions.[12] A position is a preferred solution for satisfying an interest. Positional bargaining, as described by Fisher et al. is akin to distributive negotiation.[13] Parties state their own position and then dig in their heels in order to get that position adopted. A better approach is to move toward an analysis of underlying interests. Once interests are understood, then negotiators can work together to explore options, and, ultimately, adopt a position that satisfies all interests.

Also, the relations between interests are often different from what is assumed. Negotiators tend to begin negotiation with a distributive mind-set and assume that they have opposing interests. Sometimes interests are compatible. Fisher et al. suggest that negotiators start with areas of compatible interest and build momentum.[14] For example, Dr. Davids is able to get all sides to recognize their common interests in building a specialty team and not working nights.

Consider Multiple Interests and Priorities   Integrative negotiation is especially important when there are many interests at stake. This is because some interests will be valued differently and those of less value can be conceded. For Dr. Davids, it is extremely important to avoid hiring a poor performer. There were already complaints about nonspecialty physicians in the ED and he cannot risk poor performance. For the other physicians, it is extremely important to avoid working nights. The hiring of the applicant was their position for that interest. So, Dr. Davids is able to take advantage of this difference in priority. He realizes his most important interest and is able to work out a schedule that keeps most nights free for his physicians and compensates them a little more for their willingness to work some nights. By finding multiple interests, and understanding the different priorities, Dr. Davids is able to create value for all sides.

This example illustrates that power in integrative negotiation comes from how well parties can exchange information. This means that the challenge of creating value in negotiation comes down to how well parties listen to each other and eliminate any conflict of understanding. Power listening consists of two basic activities—asking generous questions and listening for understanding.

Asking Generous Questions   Questions are the sparks that ignite the process of information exchange. Generous questions are those that pertain to circumstances, not personalities. This idea is related to the earlier discussion of the fundamental attribution error. In addition to the tendency for social actors to underestimate situations and focus instead on personal characteristics of parties, research shows that there is also a tendency to make self-serving attributions. This is the tendency to attribute success to personal characteristics and failure to situations.[15] For example, students who do well on a test will attribute that success to their intelligence, but those who do poorly will assign cause to some external condition, like a busy schedule. The self-serving bias implies that a person is willing to give himself the benefit of the doubt when he fails. That is, he is willing to look to the situational context for an explanation. Applied to negotiation, this means that focusing questions on situations rather than personalities is a generous thing to do (this is how we tend to treat ourselves). Generous questions in negotiation are those that focus attention away from the personalities involved and toward the circumstances that surround the negotiation problem. This facilitates creating value because it helps negotiators become situated in the same subjective reality and maintain a positive working relationship.

Generous questions can also avoid the tendency for naive realism. This is a tendency for disputants to believe that they see the world as it really is and that others who see it differently are irrational in some way. For example, in a speech about the plans for defense spending, a well-respected politician stated, "Anyone who dismisses our serious readiness problem . . . is either willfully uninformed or untruthful (*New Haven Register,* September 3, 2000). Many agree that the problem of military readiness is a real concern, but the statement reflects naive realism. Those who disagree are either stupid (willfully uninformed) or immoral (untruthful). It is generally more effective to focus on a situational context (e.g., threats to security, an insufficient level of resource allocation for defense) rather than intellectual or moral defects in those who see a problem differently.

The other part of power listening concerns the mind-set that negotiators adopt while listening. Carl Rogers and Fritz Roethlisberger, in a classic *Harvard Business Review* article, distinguish between listening for understanding versus listening for evaluation.[16] Listening for understanding is an attempt to understand what the other person is saying without judging the content of the message. The focus is on learning what the other person believes to be true. A more natural tendency is listening for evaluation. This tendency is to immediately judge what another person is saying according to whether it seems good or bad. In negotiation, this is especially challenging since what the other party has to say tends to be an unacceptable position.

Brainstorming In integrative negotiation, parties should work together to generate as many possible solutions to a negotiation problem as possible. In Case 7, for example, Dr. Davids meets individually with each of the moonlighting physicians and then devises a solution. A brainstorming approach would include an additional meeting to work together to compile multiple solutions.

Research has shown that brainstorming processes should be done without evaluation. Rather, the focus should simply be on generating as many options as possible, even though some are obviously unacceptable. It is possible that a bad idea from one person can trigger a good one for someone else. This can be done in many ways. One method is to have separate meetings for brainstorming and evaluation.

Use Objective Standards Evaluation of possible agreements in integrative negotiation should be done after parties have generated options. Fisher et al. argue that standards should be agreed upon and objective.[17] For example, the number of nights each emergency physician should work is objective and concrete. In addition, agreements should be evaluated based on the extent to which they produce a mutual advantage. That is, all sides should be better off from the agreement. This might mean that there are many standards to consider when evaluating options.

Summary Integrative negotiation involves attempts by negotiators to reach mutually satisfying agreements through the process of creating value. Such a process is generally aimed at removing conflict of understanding between parties. It entails establishing rapport, focusing on interests not positions, handling more than one issue at a time, asking generous questions, listening for understanding not evaluation, generating options through brainstorming, and evaluating agreements based on objective standards and mutual advantage.

The Contingency Approach—Choosing Strategy A or B

The contingency approach to negotiation addresses the issue of whether it is better to pursue a distributive or integrative strategy. The approach assumes that under some conditions one strategy is preferred to the other. Negotiation research suggests that there are three situational factors that can impact the strategic choice between a distributive or integrative approach.

A distributive approach seems to make sense when there is a fixed resource to be divided, such as a pot of money or governance of a city. Negotiation over a single issue often has a distributive flavor. For example, a buyer and seller in a market need to decide one issue—price. In addition, distributive negotiation matches a context in which there are limited relationships between parties, like anonymous participants in a market of buyers and sellers. Because the approach is highly competitive, there is no guarantee that an agreement will be favorable to all sides. Research suggests that getting a raw deal in one negotiation can make negotiators tougher in subsequent negotiations.

Physicians operate in health organizations, which contain multiple interests and ongoing relationships, and so place participants in an integrative context. When there are many issues at stake, negotiation problems are too difficult to handle with distributive negotiation. Also, if each side attempts only to capture value, they will miss out on opportunities to take advantage of different priorities between interests. Also, long-term relationships match an integrative approach. Integrative agreements lead to mutual advantage and are more stable and more likely to be implemented than distributive ones.[18] In addition, when parties expect to interact again in the future, hardball tactics of distributive negotiation can harm the relationship.

Leadership in Negotiation— Negotiating the Negotiation

The function of leadership in negotiation is to determine which strategy should be followed and to guide others along that path. This leadership role itself can be thought of as a negotiation about the way in which the negotiation will proceed.

Leading an Integrative Negotiation Process

While integrative negotiation is often the preferred approach, most negotiation processes begin with distributive attitudes and positional bargaining. How can physicians in a medical practice shift negotiation processes away from distributive strategies and tactics and toward integrative ones? One possibility is through effective leadership. Leadership can be defined as going first to a new place and being followed. This definition of leadership can be applied to the challenge of creating an integrative negotiation environment.

Persuading others to adopt an integrative approach can be difficult. It is not always as easy as in Case 7. Dr. Davids gathers infor-

mation about interests and priorities from his colleagues and virtually solves the negotiation problem alone. At times, others will be
reluctant to forgive an emotional outburst or share information
about their true concerns. In addition, several brains are needed for
some problems, and this is possible only if negotiators have bought
in to an integrative process.

Given the reluctance of some to adopt an integrative approach,
negotiating the negotiation might require that leaders provide a
vision for the negotiation process itself. That is, a discussion of the
negotiation procedure might become necessary. The chapter concludes with four principles that can guide such a discussion. Each is
a virtue that can be used in articulating a vision for an integrative
process of negotiating.

The idea of virtue corresponds to the strategy of integrative
negotiation. Henry Sidgwick distinguishes between duty and
virtue.[19] Duty is something we expect of one another. It is one's
duty to pay taxes, care for elderly parents, and obey the law. Virtue
is doing more than one's duty. Some examples of virtuous conduct
are volunteering one's time to do community service, paying a little extra in income tax, recycling more than the law requires, or car-
ing for someone else's parents. The difference between virtue and
duty is helpful when applied to negotiation processes. Integrative
negotiation consists of activities that are inherently virtuous.
Specifically, four virtues can be applied to integrative negotiation.

The Virtues of Integrative Negotiation

Wisdom Wisdom refers to the degree to which an act or event
seems good from more than one point of view. For example, when
adopting a new policy an administrator can think about its effects
for a specific work function, for the practice as a whole, or even for
broader communities. Wisdom is the extent to which the policy
seems good from those different vantage points. In negotiation,
wisdom is consistent with the idea of an integrative, or win-win
agreement. Leading an integrative negotiation means that one
holds and will cultivate the belief that it is possible to find a solution that benefits all sides.

Prudence Prudence is a self-regarding virtue that concerns the
degree to which a wide time horizon is allowed for solving prob-

lems. Taking a longer view of negotiation problems is likely to underline the importance of relationships and promote cooperative strategies. For example, Dr. Davids gets the other physicians to consider the long-term vision for the team. This helps them see how hiring the unacceptable applicant is a poor idea. Leadership in negotiation can entail taking a longer view of problems.

Benevolence Benevolence comes in many forms but generally refers to the consideration given to others. In negotiation, finding common interests, sharing information, working together to generate options, and striving for mutual advantage are all examples of benevolence. In addition, benevolence can mean that the right people are included in the negotiation. Dr. Davids could have worked out a solution with his superiors and then passed it down to his team. Instead, he includes them in the process. Leading an integrative negotiation might also mean that one has to go first in sharing information and making concessions.

Veracity This concerns telling the truth. Veracity is critical for integrative negotiation. Truthful exchanges of information are required in order for parties to create value. Each side must accurately understand the interests that are brought to the table, respectively. Moreover, priorities must be shared as well as standards for evaluation. Veracity is also important when it comes to recognizing mistakes. Since Dr. Davids is honest about his mistakes, it is more likely he is honest about other things.

Summary

In sum, leading an integrative negotiation process is a difficult challenge. The shift from a distributive to integrative strategy will require that leaders negotiate the negotiation. This might include articulating a vision for how the process might unfold. Integrative negotiation is a function of wisdom, prudence, benevolence, and veracity. Those virtues can be thought of as guiding principles that underlie integrative negotiation.

Notes

1. Lewicki, R. J., D. M. Saunders, and J. W. Minton. *Essentials of Negotiating*. Chicago: Irwin, 1997; Pruitt, D. G., and P. J. Carnevale.

Negotiation in Social Conflict. Pacific Grove, CA: Brooks-Cole, 1993; Pruitt, D. G., and J. Z. Rubin. *Social Conflict: Escalation, Stalemate, and Settlement.* New York: Random House, 1986; Thompson, L. "Negotiation Behavior and Outcomes: Empirical Evidence and Theoretical Issues." *Psychological Bulletin* 108 (1990): 515–532; Walton, R. E., and R. B. Mckersie. *A Behavioral Theory of Labor Negotiations: An Analysis of a Social Interaction System.* New York: McGraw-Hill, 1965.

2. Pruitt, D. G., and P. J. Carenvale. *Negotiation in Social Conflict.* Pacific Grove, CA: Brooks-Cole, 1993.

3. Ross, L., and R. E. Nisbett. *The Person and the Situation.* New York: McGraw-Hill, 1991.

4. Follett, M. P. "Constructive Conflict." In *Dynamic Administration: The Collected Papers of Mary Parker Follett,* edited by H. C. Metcalt and L. Urwick. New York: Harper, 1940.

5. Ibid.

6. Bazerman, M., and M. A. Neale. *Negotiating Rationally.* New York: The Free Press, 1992.

7. Fisher, R., W. Ury, and B. Patton. *Getting to Yes: Negotiating Agreements without Giving In,* 2nd ed. New York: Penguin Books, 1991.

8. Raiffa, H. *The Art and Science of Negotiation.* Cambridge, MA: Belknap Press of Harvard University Press, 1982.

9. Chertkoff, J. M., and M. Conley. "Opening Offer and Frequency of Concessions as Bargaining Strategies." *Journal of Personality and Social Psychology* 7 (1967): 181–185; Weingart, L. R., L. L. Thompson, M. H. Bazerman, and J. S. Carroll. "Tactical Behaviors and Negotiation Outcomes." *International Journal of Conflict Management* 1 (1990): 7–31.

10. Thomspon, L. "Negotiation Behavior and Outcomes: Empirical Evidence and Theoretical Issues." *Psychological Bulletin* 108 (1990): 515–532.

11. Drolet, A. L., and M. W. Morris. "Rapport in Conflict Resolution: Accounting for How Face-to-Face Contact Fosters Mutual Cooperation in Mixed-Motive Conflicts." *Journal of Experimental Social Psychology* 36 (2000): 26–50.

12. See note 7 above.

13. Ibid.

14. Ibid.

15. See note 3 above.

16. Rogers, C., and F. J. Roethlisberger. "Barriers and Gateways to Communication." *Harvard Business Review* (1952).

17. See note 7 above.

18. Pruitt, D. G., and J. Z. Rubin. *Social Conflict: Escalation, Stalemate, and Settlement.* New York: Random House, 1986.

19. Sidgwick, H. *The Methods of Ethics.* Indianapolis, IN: Hackett Publishing, 1907.

How to Negotiate

Stephen Rimar

Dr. Barry Davids was recruited to the academic medical center two years ago to develop an emergency medicine program. Although the hospital had an emergency room for nearly 30 years, Dr. Davids was the first board-certified emergency physician to work there. A handful of internists, pediatricians, and even surgeons worked in shifts in the emergency room to earn extra money, but no group of physicians considered the ER their home or emergency medicine their specialty. Mindful of the growing emphasis on specialty physicians in this area and the potential liabilities of an amateur medical staff, both the hospital's president and the dean of the medical school supported Dr. Davids and his plan to build a program.

24/7

At the heart of Dr. Davids' program was a plan to staff the emergency department 24 hours a day, 7 days a week with specialty-trained emergency physicians within two years. During the first year of his tenure, Dr. Davids successfully recruited two emergency physicians. The three physicians provided 16 hours of coverage a day. This decreased the number of moonlighting physicians needed as well as the time they spent in the emergency department. Overall, the hospital was pleased with the change, particularly following an excellent review by a certifying agency that commented on the improved caliber of physician leadership in the emergency department. The next step for the group was to provide round-the-clock coverage. To make this possible, Dr. Davids developed an elaborate call schedule to which the other two physicians agreed. The proposed schedule necessitated hiring one more emergency physician.

For several months, Dr. Davids interviewed candidates for the position. None, however, was acceptable. Only one was even tolerable. So the group decided not to offer the position to anyone, but to recruit again in six months. When that time came, however, there were no qualified applicants. No matter how many phone calls he made or how many ads he placed, Dr. Davids found no one suitable. He was prepared to wait another year. The hospital president and the dean, however, were not. They were concerned about the program's schedule. Total emergency department coverage by specialty-trained physicians was supposed to occur that year. Furthermore, complaints about nonspecialty physicians were escalating and moonlighting coverage cost both organizations more than they wanted to pay. The message was clear: Dr. Davids' group had six months to hire another emergency physician or take up the coverage slack itself.

An intensive recruitment campaign was undertaken during the following six months but, once again, no first-rate candidate appeared. One physician, however, was very interested in joining the staff. Dr. Davids found him professionally and personally unacceptable and the other physicians agreed. Yet Dr. Davids' colleagues made a plea to hire the doctor. They did not want to cover the eight hours each day that would be unassigned with the elimination of moonlighting. Discussions among the trio turned to arguments as Dr. Davids' vision of an emergency program clashed with the group's unwillingness to work more, particularly the overnight hours. They felt working the additional hours would compromise their performance and certainly make their jobs less enjoyable. "Let's face it," they said, "a warm body is better than nobody at all."

Dr. Davids, however, was determined not to hire this applicant. As far as he was concerned, rounding out his section with a warm body was a big mistake. Furthermore, he was offended that his colleagues didn't trust his judgment. In a fit of anger, he stormed out of a group meeting, shouting, "I'm the chief, and what I say goes." One physician responded, "Then do it by yourself, I quit." Later that night, Dr. Davids worried he had destroyed everything he built. So he picked up the telephone, called his colleagues, apologized for his behavior, and set up another meeting for the next day. His goal was to find a solution acceptable to everyone.

Compromise

Dr. Davids met with the two members of his group individually. He reiterated his vision of a separate section and program, the vision they all shared when they joined the group. He found that each of them was committed to developing the program. They were concerned about working more hours, but primarily because it would detract from their educational efforts and outreach work with EMTs. They were also concerned about working the night shift; if they were awake all night, they would not be productive the next day. Finally, neither really wanted the proposed candidate to join their group.

Dr. Davids understood how they felt. He did not want to work more nights and weekends either, but he was not about to jeopardize the future of the emergency program by hiring an unacceptable physician. He needed a temporary solution while the search for the right person continued. So he talked to his colleagues again, asking them what, specifically, they liked least about providing 24-hour coverage. It was working after 1 A.M. This was truly a graveyard shift in their emergency department. They also wanted two complete weekends off each month. Using this information, Dr. Davids constructed a compromise schedule that decreased the department's moonlighting needs by 75 percent and still satisfied the group's primary demands. In addition, he proposed a slight salary increase for each person to compensate for the additional time worked. The group agreed to his schedule.

Dr. Davids prepared to offer the hospital and medical school administration his temporary solution and to commence an aggressive recruitment campaign. The plan, with its near elimination of moonlighters (only four doctors, who rotated, remained) and slight increase in salaries, would actually save money and allow the group to remain relatively content until a new physician was hired. Dr. Davids now had to convince the president and dean to support the proposal.

How to Do It

1. *Recognize a negotiation.* Most of us think of a negotiation as a formal process that results in a written contract. The most common examples people cite are of a financial nature—purchasing a house or a car, or even arguing with a managed-care organization about a fee schedule. But negotiation is the process of compromise and agreement between parties. It occurs nearly every day, and touches everyone. In order to negotiate wisely, however, one must first recognize a negotiation process as such. Initially, Dr. Davids didn't realize he was in the middle of a negotiation. He was focused on his need to carry out an order from his superiors, in exactly the way he interpreted it. Most orders in business, however, leave room for negotiation, if approached properly. By the end of his story, Dr. Davids actually negotiated an acceptable alternative with his group and was about to approach the dean and president.

2. *Control emotion.* Failure to recognize a negotiation left Dr. Davids stranded between his need to execute his superiors' orders and his colleagues' refusal to submit to his. This led to frustration, anger, and an emotional outburst. When doctors encounter a situation in which their orders are refused or ignored, too many react as Dr. Davids did. They are unaccustomed to having orders disobeyed. But physicians and nonphysicians alike cannot hope to influence others if they cannot control themselves in the workplace.

The key to staying in control in such situations is to place them in the proper context. Dr. Davids would have done well to remember the line from *The Godfather*—it's business, not personal. The issue for his colleagues was not related to him or his leadership, but was about their own needs.

But what if the group's reaction is directed personally at the leader? Sometimes individuals resort to this tactic, usually when they are angry and frustrated. The best advice for a negotiator leader in this circumstance is to avoid engaging them on the same level in public, and to address the issue with the individual in private. Personal battles, unfortunately, interfere with management in many organizations. Your role as leader is to prevent this from happening in yours.

3. *Recognize mistakes and correct them quickly.* Because opposing parties usually begin negotiating with the goal of getting what they want, and no less, negotiating mistakes are common. The form they take varies. In Dr. Davids' case, his mistake was allowing his emotions to obscure his thinking and affect his actions. Fortunately, he was smart enough to recognize this and immediately corrected the situation. First, he acknowledged he was out of line. Next, he considered his colleagues' perspective rather than his own. This enabled him to begin a productive dialogue. Be vigilant in your assessment of what you're doing and how you're doing it throughout a negotiation and quickly attend to mistakes and miscommunications.

4. *Focus on a common goal.* Negotiation occurs within groups that share a common goal as well as between groups with conflicting objectives. Dr. Davids' group had a common concern—they wanted to minimize the amount of overnight duty—but they were at odds over how to achieve it. Each member of the group, however, was also committed to building an emergency medicine group in Dr. Davids' vision. He used this common goal to negotiate an acceptable solution. In the process, his group was forced to declare themselves a team. In a sense, team building is a continuous negotiation between all members of the group including its leader.

5. *Find out what the other side wants.* While Dr. Davids eventually reached a negotiated agreement with his group, he was unprepared to negotiate adequately with his bosses. The dean and the president told him they wanted the emergency department staffed by full-time specialists and the cost associated with moonlighting reduced. But had they really delivered an ultimatum that left no room for negotiation, or were they amenable to alternatives? When the case presentation ended, Dr. Davids needed to return with a counterproposal, yet was unsure of how they would respond.

One key to successful negotiation is finding out what the other side wants—all the other sides. In his case, Dr. Davids had two negotiations to conduct: one between the dean and president and himself, and the other between him and his ED group. As the leader of his group, he found it easy and convenient to speak with the other physicians and explore their thoughts. But he knew little about his bosses' wishes for the emergency department or his program except what they communicated about coverage and moonlighting costs.

How does one find out what others want and what their priorities are? The most direct way is, of course, to ask them. Take advantage of this opportunity if it occurs. Usually, however, such information is gathered from a variety of sources (e.g., past experience, business plans, colleagues, social contacts) and pieced together. It is also helpful to imagine yourself in their place and ask what you would want. Sometimes knowing other issues on the table can be helpful. For example, if Dr. Davids knows that the nurse administrator is negotiating with the hospital for more staff in the emergency department, they could both share information and strategy. Finally, get a sense of the importance of the issue to the organization. If Dr. Davids knows, for example, that decreasing costs is more important to his bosses than providing coverage by emergency specialists, or vice versa, it is easier to create an acceptable solution.

6. *Be creative with a solution.* Anything that restricts opportunities for creative solutions threatens the negotiating process. For example, many negotiations begin with an aggressively worded demand put forth by the party who initiated the proceedings. Such a presentation can stifle imaginative thinking because harsh words command the attention and time of both sides and leave little energy for addressing underlying issues. Negotiation experts recommend focusing on issues rather than demands. Focusing on an issue tends to promote creative thinking and position refinement, whereas focusing on a demand may precipitate a stalemate. And remember that there may be more than one creative, acceptable solution for any problem. Dr. Davids, unfortunately, approached the dean and president with a single acceptable alternative to their charge. If he is not successful in selling it, his effort has failed. He would be in a better position if he identifies at least one more acceptable alternative. Which brings us to the BATNA.

7. *Determine your BATNA.* No one should enter a negotiation of any kind without knowing (and being able to clearly articulate) a Best Alternative To a Negotiated Agreement (BATNA). Unlike a bottom line, which is a threshold for an acceptable offer, the BATNA is what will be done if no agreement is reached. In the case presented, Dr. Davids invested considerable time and effort developing his group's position, but made no provisions for dealing with rejection of his proposal. He never determined the BATNA with either his group or his bosses.

Individuals who, like Dr. Davids, assume the role of negotiator as part of their job must consider the impact of the negotiations on their own lives and careers. That means developing a BATNA. What was Dr. Davids'? Would he leave his position if the group or the medical center leadership, or both, failed to reach an agreement acceptable to him? Failing to consider this put him in a disadvantage in the negotiations. If he couldn't persuade the other side to agree to his terms he *had* to concede to theirs. He had no alternative.

Determining your own BATNA is difficult enough, but how do you find out someone else's? A bottom line (threshold for action) and a BATNA are merely extremes of a person's wants and interests. Dr. Davids determined it was after 1 A.M. that was the most difficult time for his colleagues to work. But he should have asked more questions to determine the extent of their willingness to extend themselves. For example, if they did not want to work many more nights, exactly how many more did they mean? He might also have determined their plans if the medical center leadership rejected their proposal. Knowing their BATNA, particularly if it is their resignations, might provide Dr. Davids with some leverage during his negotiations with his bosses. As it stands, he has no idea how the other doctors would respond to his bosses' potential rejection of his proposal.

LECTURE

Contemporary Marketing in Healthcare

Jeffery T. Wack and William Gombeski Jr.

Marketing with a Capital M

Overview

The telemarketer who interrupts one's dinner is to many the very personification of marketing. To others, it is the cultural stereotype of the used car salesman: Leading the prospect around the car lot, he'll say anything to make a sale—right now. And then there is one of healthcare's original marketers, famous from portrayals in black-and-white Westerns: the mustachioed character who sells bottles of snake oil from the back of his covered wagon. He assures everyone his elixir will cure whatever ails ye—and guarantees the money back if it does not. Of course, he skips town under cover of darkness before anyone can make a claim.

These popular images convinced many that marketing is synonymous with sales and advertising, and that effective marketing is a matter of cunning, guile, and deceit. These are powerful images to overcome as one strives to educate healthcare managers and physicians as to what contemporary marketing is actually about. On the one hand, marketing's application is to support sales of products, even ones injurious to health: Cigarettes, alcohol, and handguns are a few that come readily to mind. On the other hand, most are unaware that marketing concepts also support many public health campaigns ranging from population control, to seat belt usage, to organ donation.[1]

The purpose of this chapter is to reeducate physicians and managers as to what contemporary marketing—that is, marketing with a capital M—is about. The reader should start by memorizing the mantra, "Marketing is *not* merely advertising and selling."

Definitions

Webster's offers two definitions of marketing that only begin to convey what it is about: (1) a buying or selling in the market and (2) the total of activities involved in the moving of goods from the producer to the consumer, including selling, advertising, and so on. This definition presents the conventional view of marketing as a largely one-directional, producer-to-buyer process that was captured in an early popular definition of marketing as getting the right goods to the right people at the right time and at the right price with the right communication and promotion.

Recent definitions capture marketing as the two-way street between buyer and seller that it has truly become. One example is a definition in one of the most popular business school textbooks: "Marketing is a social process by which individuals and groups obtain what they need and want through creating and exchanging products and value with others."[2]

Marketing management, then, is the analysis, planning, implementation, and evaluation of the organization's (or firm, business, practice, etc.) programs designed to create and maintain mutually beneficial relationships and exchanges with targeted markets for the purpose of achieving the organization's objectives. For long-term viability, any organization must therefore monitor the market to ensure that they continue to offer products or services that customers value, and value at least as much as those offered by the seller's competitors. This is the essence of contemporary marketing.

Essential Concepts

Customer

There are no organizations without customers, although they have different labels. Passengers, fares, students, users, guests, taxpayers, and tourists are all customers; in healthcare they may be called clients, patients, referrers, payers, even employers. Employees of organizations view their customers more narrowly than does the marketer. Most would describe the customer as the person who is receiving services. In contrast, contemporary marketers' view of the customer also includes prospective customers who've never used the providers' services, as well as *former* customers.

Exchanges and Transactions

All customers seek something from the organization, and what is common to these organizations (be they called firms, governments, hospitals, or providers) is that they, in turn, want something of equal value in return. This is usually money, but it may also be recommendations, referrals, or even votes. A fair exchange of equal value is central to an effective market, and an unfair exchange—in either direction—can result in the loss of a customer.

In healthcare, this exchange is often not as direct, or simple, as in a retail transaction where cash is exchanged directly for goods. Historically, the insurer has been an intermediary between the provider and healthcare's customer: Physicians and hospitals provide the service to the patient, but payment comes indirectly through reimbursement by the insurer. This mechanism requires exchange relationships among all three parties, which many would contend complicates the efficient exchange of value between the buyer (the patient) and the seller (the healthcare provider).

Many healthcare transactions have become more direct and marketlike, and it's likely that the trend will continue. For example, the office copayments mimic the transactions to which those in a market economy are accustomed. Medical savings accounts permit patients to effectively fund their own healthcare accounts and directly pay providers. In addition, defined contribution plans by employers may signal the start of a new era in healthcare payment.

Products, Services, Ideas

Healthcare also differs by the nature and complexity of its product. When we think of customers and transactions, we imagine physical, tangible products. However, a marketer refers to the product as anything offered to satisfy a need or want. This could be a product (e.g., crutches, drugs), a service (e.g., diagnostics, surgeries), or even less tangible items of value like information or ideas (e.g., health promotion and attitudes). In healthcare, patients' needs are generally more complex than can be met by the products. For example, most customers easily determine the quality of a television picture. They are far less capable, however, of determining the quality of their physical exam or appendectomy. Because of this, other benefits are sought by the customer as part of the exchange. Many of these benefits are highly intangible and, from the perspective of the provider, seemingly irrelevant. Speed, convenience, and interpersonal skills, for example, are central to the customers' perception of quality in healthcare.

Satisfaction and Value

Continued success of an organization depends on delivering value to the marketplace, which is the sum of the mutually satisfactory exchanges between customer and provider. Mutually satisfactory means service was provided to the customer, while the provider received something from the customer (or his agent) in return, and each was of fair value to the respective parties. Emergency departments are notoriously unsatisfying settings. Hospitals feel unfairly compensated by the market for medical care provided in their EDs. Customers in turn feel abused because of the perceived inattention to many of their considerations. Given the choice, few patients would suffer the waits required in most emergency rooms. In the patients' mind, satisfaction begins with the first phone call and continues through the visit to the postvisit follow-up. Medical competence is usually taken for granted.

Managing Customer Relationships

The contemporary practice of marketing is perhaps most distinctive in its definition of the customer. Organizations tend to focus their energies and resources narrowly on the customer at hand, whereas the customer's experiences with the provider are much more extensive. Marketing reminds the provider that the nature of customer relationships with the provider transitions through several phases.

Marketing's roles and goals, as well as those of the provider, evolve accordingly, and are generally long-term (Figure 8.1).

Customer as Prospect

The first phase of the customer's relationship with the provider is that of prospect. This is the arena with which marketing has been most closely associated: recruiting new customers. Marketing in this phase involves a cascade of objectives intended to move the customer from a lack of awareness of the provider to using the provider's services. A sequence of measurable and manageable objectives define this process of customer cultivation beginning with creating awareness of the provider. This awareness is followed by conveying an appealing image, then enhancing preference and disposition to use, and ultimately trying the service.

Customer as User

The next phase of the relationship is that of user, buyer, or patient. This is the period of engagement during which most would identify the person as a customer. The delivery of health services has traditionally been viewed as the sole responsibility of operations and caregivers, central among them doctors. However, marketing's insistence on achieving customer satisfaction, not limited to medical quality, has focused attention on the broader customer experience. Service delivery objectives like speed, efficiency, com-

Figure 8.1 Customer relationship management process objectives.

Customer phase	Marketing's objectives
Prospect	Awareness
	↓
	Preference
	↓
User	Choice
	↓
	Satisfaction
	↓
After use	Loyalty
	↓
	Commitment

munications, and customer handling, even the experience of a patient's family members, are marketing concerns because performance on the nonmedical tasks also contributes to market success. And the delivery of these satisfiers depends on a much wider cast of employees.

Customer after the Sale

Marketing's interest in the customer does not end with the sale or use of services. To marketing, even after they've fully recovered from surgery, the patient remains a customer. Marketing strives to build on the relationship of the former user for important business purposes: to ensure repeated use by patients or their families; to encourage word-of-mouth (the most cost-effective and credible form of advertising); and to discover opportunities to cross-sell new services.

Marketing's influence in this area—growth through retention— is becoming common through a variety of relationship management programs. Examples include telephone calls made to patients postvisit, cards sent to remind patients to schedule checkups, provider-sponsored support or interest groups, disease-specific Web sites, and other tactics intended to support the strategy of building loyalty to the provider by supporting the patient.

The model is simple and obvious. For many years, marketing has been delegated the limited role of recruiting new customers when in fact marketing has as much to contribute to the handling of current and former customers. Indeed, retention is arguably more important to volume and revenue growth than customer attraction.

Strategic Marketing Planning

The notion of developing and continuously strengthening customer-provider relationships (from customer as prospect to customer as user, to customer as loyalist) is fundamental to contemporary marketing. A second integrative model that frames thinking and management is the strategic marketing planning model (see Figure 8.2).

In addition to pinpointing the benefits customers seek, marketing must help the organization meet these needs. Strategic market-

Figure 8.2 Basic strategic marketing planning model.

Market information, research, analyses	Marketing planning and strategy	Execution of marketing tactics
-*Internal*	-*Goals*	-*Tactics*
-*External*	-*Objectives*	-*Actions*
-*Trends*	-*Strategies*	-*Programs*

ing planning imposes discipline on the business by causing management to consider which objectives are priorities, by fostering development of integrated efforts to achieve the objectives, and by prompting continuous assessment of the effectiveness of these efforts.

Marketing Information and Analysis

The first phase involves collecting the information required for a solid analysis of the shape and dimensions of market demand and patterns of purchase or utilization. Most organizations have computer-resident financial information—volume, gross, and net revenues—readily available. Because of the ubiquity of financial information and budget, rather than market-driven planning methods, many organizations neglect to collect the market-relevant information needed for a thorough market analysis. A comprehensive marketing information system should also include: measures of product/service quality and trends, product/service or customer segment profitability (payer mix), competitive intelligence, demographic trends and patterns of demand, market share and volumes relative to capacities, referral channel dynamics, and consumer research such as image, decision making, and satisfaction.

Market Planning

Marketing information informs the planning phase. Firms may differ in how they label plans, including financial plans, business plans, strategic plans, and long-range plans, but the one test common to all plans is that they should actually work when applied to the market. Too often they neglect customer and market dynamics.

Planning is typically focused on achieving a profit, preferably by increasing revenue as opposed to reducing costs.* Achieving revenue objectives depends in turn on pricing, which in healthcare means volume. Market analysis and marketing planning are the methods required to gauge what objectives are reasonable and how to achieve them.

Execution

The last step in the strategic marketing model is the action phase of the plan, the execution of tactical elements. These activities are not limited to the production of brochures, events, public relations, ads,—in marketing parlance, promotional strategies—though that is often what even senior managers in healthcare seem to believe. Rather a host of tools, categories of actions referred to as the marketing mix, may be used depending on the situation and objectives. The elements of the marketing mix are outlined in the following, but suffice it to say that, in addition to promotional strategies, the mix includes changes in the nature of the product or service to enhance its desirability, adopting different methods of distribution of the product/service, and pricing considerations.

Evolution to Contemporary Marketing

Experience suggests that healthcare organizations are growing into strategic marketing. Initially, they focus on promotional activities, apparently believing that the louder one *shouts* at the market about existing products and services, the more customers will appear. The result is often the antithesis of strategic marketing: How many hospitals have, for example, promoted money-losing services to shrinking markets that competitors better serve?

---

* Most firms' goals include attracting larger volumes of users, patients, members, or whatever customers are termed. However, marketing is equally applicable to the management of other forms of demand management. For example, in healthcare, there is often too much demand—for unnecessary medical procedures, for access to certain healthcare settings, for unhealthy products, as examples—and the objective may be to reduce, or at least better manage, demand. In other situations—pediatric practices, emergency services, flu inoculations—the problem is often uneven demand, high during some hours, low during others. These are marketing, not merely operations, problems, and marketing (in this context sometimes referred to as demarketing) can be effectively applied to mitigate them.

Later, budgets increase, internal expertise develops, and experience grows. These organizations begin to allocate marketing resources based on objectives and likely return. For most organizations, however, planning remains at the mercy of budgeting requirements, and objectives are driven by political considerations as much as by market analyses. At least planning fosters a more integrated and coordinated approach, though the objectives and priorities may be misdirected.

Sophisticated organizations eventually enter the first analytic phase to guide planning. At this point, instincts and gut feelings for setting market goals and general marketing tactics are trumped by the reality of customer behavior, preferences, and trends. From a marketing model of fire-fire-fire, the organization matures to Marketing as ready-aim-fire.

The Marketing Mix

Perhaps the most powerful heuristic in the marketer's repertoire is the marketing mix, the set of tools considered in the planning phase to alter levels of demand according to objectives. The marketing mix has four components, known as the 4 P's: Products, Price, Places, and Promotion. Demand can be modulated by producing better or worse *products;* by increasing or decreasing *price;* by making the product more or less accessible by changing the *places* of distribution (or changing their hours of operation); and/or by altering the market's awareness of offers via *promotion.*

The general framework of the marketing mix—a set of categories of tactical tools that can be adopted or modified to adjust demand—remains fundamental to how the marketer thinks about markets. The remainder of the chapter describes an expanded marketing mix model, which the authors have found useful in guiding the marketing strategy and tactics of healthcare organizations.[3]

The Marketing Mix and Healthcare

The marketing model described here has been adapted for healthcare organizations. Although it lacks the simplicity (and mnemonic) of the 4 P's, it offers several distinct advantages. First, it is better suited to market complex programs and services, unlike classic marketing of manufactured goods. Second, it is extremely practical and designed specifically for the healthcare market. Finally, it was developed from the actual practice of healthcare marketing, rather than from a conceptual model.

Eight major marketing principles, or elements, comprise the mix and guide planning. They are internal marketing, benefits development, program/product development, targeting, relationships, differentiation, selling, and positioning. The three phases of strategic marketing planning—analysis, planning, and execution—pertain to each principle, and together they describe strategic marketing management.

Internal Marketing

Marketers must manage internal processes to assure that the organization and its employees understand the commitment required and steps to follow to successfully compete for customers. The development of internal marketing strategy begins with an organizational market assessment, or audit, that assesses employees' understanding of the organization's market strategy and their willingness to support it. The audit also might examine employee skills, systems, department structures, and resources to gauge the extent to which the organization is ready to support marketing. Many brilliant marketing strategies fail because of an inadequate marketing management infrastructure.

The organizational assessment identifies strengths and weaknesses, and aids the development of internal marketing objectives. These objectives, in turn, determine the work plan, the tactics necessary to reach the goal. Key internal marketing tactics include allocating marketing staff and dollars; developing systems; educating employees about the organization's products and services; and creating a market- and service-driven culture.

Most internal marketing tactics that healthcare marketers use fall into the education/training/motivation category. They include meeting with employees company-wide in small groups, providing marketing orientation sessions for new employees, developing marketing task forces to involve employees, generating an internal marketing newsletter, sharing the marketing plan and activities with employees, and creating visibility by walking the floor each day. The desired long-term outcome is a change in employee behavior that optimizes market effectiveness.

Benefits Development

Providing benefits to customers is key to the viability of any business. Understanding customers' needs, desires, expectations, satisfactions, and decision-making processes and determining the benefits they seek, and the products and services features they value is essential to successful marketing. This information strengthens customer and employee communication. Many marketers, however, continue to myopically promote product and service features, such as great medical training or the latest equipment, without realizing that customers are also looking for personal attention, assurance, and availability. The challenge for marketers is to uncover why a feature is important.

A variety of techniques help marketers listen to their customers, such as focus groups, surveys, complaints, and feedback from the sales force. Patient satisfaction surveys are common in healthcare. Some providers even use mystery shopping programs to identify successful tactics employed by competitors. These analyses are critical to the development of a marketing plan.

Program/Service Development

Because organizations and marketers have limited time and resources, it is impossible to support every product or service equally. Too often, decisions about marketing resource allocation are dictated by tradition or fiat rather than capacity, profitability, mission, and strategic need. Choosing which products to support is part of planning and strategy. The planning of new and better features, determining which to emphasize, and to which customers, is a key aspect of this approach.

Targeting

A market segment is a set of potential buyers with common needs who are similar in how they perceive, value, buy, and use a product or service. Marketers have long recognized that segmentation usually generates a higher return on market investment than a mass-market approach because efforts can focus on those segments most likely to use or buy. Markets can be segmented in many ways: demographically, geographically, psychographically, culturally, or by insurance coverage or utilization. By segmenting markets and customers, marketers choose to focus on a subset of the market that can be influenced more effectively.

Most healthcare marketers must replenish lost patients with potential customers who can generate a high net income for the organization. This usually entails aggressive prospecting. For example, instead of trying to bring in more men with urology problems, marketers try to bring in a richer mix of patients by focusing on men with more profitable diseases, such as prostate cancer. Increasingly, healthcare marketers use techniques to qualify potential patients so that marketing resources, such as newsletters and brochures, are sent only to the most desirable customers. Tactics include clinical trial recruitment, support groups, health talks, and asking current, desirable patients to identify others with similar problems.

Channels

Distribution channels are people and institutions that perform the functions necessary to move a product/service from a producer/ provider to an end user, the customer. In healthcare, this concept is broadened to include understanding and managing referrals, the steps by which patients come to use particular providers. A channel analysis is the first step toward developing strategy. Generally, a study of customers and their decision-making processes when choosing a service or product is needed to identify the factors that affect distribution.

Healthcare marketers have long recognized the role of physicians as a channel for hospital admissions and medications, and women as a channel for pediatric care. Increasingly, however, healthcare decisions are made by patients with input from multiple sources, including social workers, case managers, and even HMOs. Recognition of these influential roles is fueling more sophisticated channeling efforts. For example, the growth of parish nurse programs shows that appropriate customers can be influenced and guided to specific doctors and hospitals. Some examples of new ways to steer customers include orthopedic surgeons' focus on athletic trainers for sports medicine patients and emergency room physicians' focus on EMS personnel.

Differentiation

Differentiation is used to maximize an organization's competitive advantage by distinguishing the organization and its products from competitors. Providers may strive to maintain positions of better technical quality, innovation, accessibility, service, low cost, or value. The role of marketing is to develop and communicate those attributes that positively set their products and organizations apart.

Regulatory agencies, benchmarking, and outcome reporting can reduce healthcare to a commodity through the standardization of products and outcomes. However, one gains competitive advantage in a market by offering something different—by giving reasons for the consumer to choose you. By using competitive analysis, an organization can learn about competitors' positions, customers' market perceptions, and future competitors' products and services. This information can form the basis of a differentiation strategy.

Selling

The ultimate goal of a marketer is a sale, whether it involves the acceptance of a product, service, behavior, or idea. Although healthcare marketers use established sales tactics like television, radio, and print advertising, new techniques like Internet forums, point-of-sale marketing, and message cosponsoring with other organizations, are growing in popularity. Other techniques include health education/promotion, health fairs, public relations, direct mail advertising, packaging, and sales calls.

Positioning

Positioning, or branding, is designing a company's image so that the target market understands and appreciates what the firm stands for compared to its competitors. It is how an organization wants to be perceived, and the message that customers associate with an organization and its products. Positioning, which is embodied in the mission, corporate values, and vision of the organization, is the cumulative result of small, consistent activities that create positive or negative perceptions about a person, organization, or product. Effective positioning does more than differentiate the organization or service from its competitors. It also reflects an attribute valued by the marketplace and originates from a fundamental strength of the organization or service.

One way to establish a position is to highlight a relative uniqueness of one element in the marketing mix. In most organizations, positioning is reflected in all the marketing plan's elements, including the products and services, distribution channels, and communications. In industries with intense marketplace competition, organizations must consciously position themselves, or their competition will do it for them.

Frequently a variety of positioning strategies are evident in any market. For example, a university-based teaching and research organization has a high-tech, innovative position; the county/public hospital is the center for the poor; and community hospitals are positioned as good-neighbor, customer-friendly organizations.

Price

Nonhealthcare marketers are surprised to see pricing excluded from the marketing mix. However, pricing has traditionally been a weak tool for altering demand in healthcare because of the third party role position between a patient and a provider. However, there are some segments of the healthcare marketplace, such as cosmetic surgery, that are responsive to price and trends in healthcare payment, which suggests that price may play a greater role in the future.

Another dimension of price is the nonmonetary, or emotional, costs associated with the use (or not) of healthcare services. Why do patients sometimes refuse free healthcare? What motivates the use of alternative medicines and providers? Why do people avoid dentists or delay mammograms? Often the answer is fear, anxiety, or embarrassment, all very real emotional costs. Healthcare organizations are increasingly interested in this aspect of price and are taking steps to use it to gain market advantage.

Using the Mix to Create a Plan

Figure 8.3 illustrates how the marketing principles collectively contribute to developing the marketing objectives and strategies that

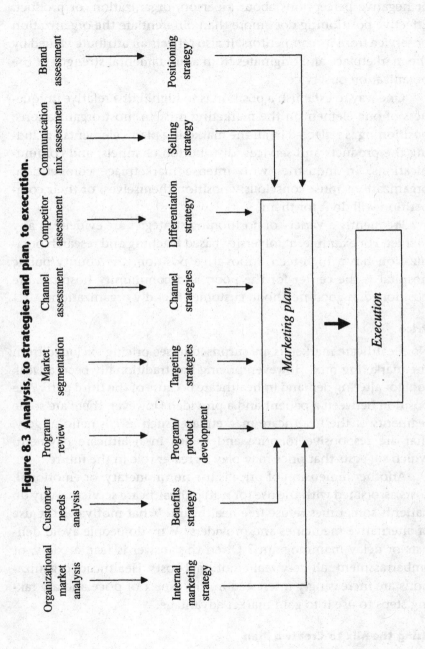

Figure 8.3 Analysis, to strategies and plan, to execution.

comprise a marketing plan. Research drives the strategies for each element of the mix. Using the model involves a rigorous analytic process for each element of the mix, resulting in plans, strategies, and priorities based on market information and analysis.

Figures 8.4 and 8.5 provide an expanded, more detailed version of the model, showing the many factors that comprise each mix element. While not all factors are relevant to every marketing situation, the model ensures a comprehensive review of marketing factors that can be used for planning. To complete the strategic marketing planning model, the execution and implementation phase addresses specific tactics and actions that flow from the plan.

The marketing strategy development model simplifies marketing planning and strategy development, makes marketing easier to understand, plan, and manage, explains marketing behavior, and helps to organize, prioritize, and communicate the marketing direction in a logical fashion. It also serves as a framework for a comprehensive marketing research program providing the focus for proactive research, tracking, and program evaluation.

From a practical point of view, healthcare providers can use the model to

- Assess a marketing situation and develop a plan to address it.

- Focus on the most important opportunities and problems.

- Ensure that all the key marketing principles or elements are addressed and incorporated into the plan.

- Show the relationship of one element to the others and how change in one element affects the rest.

- Allow the marketing process to be initiated at any of the strategy columns.

- Focus on building the business vs. communicating the business.

Summary

Contemporary marketing offers a framework for ensuring that businesses continue to have customers—because without customers, there is no business. Marketing encourages understanding cus-

Figure 8.4 Developing a marketing strategy.

Organizational market analysis	Customer needs analysis	Program review	Market segmentation	Channel assessment	Competitor assessment	Communication mix assessment	Brand assessment
Skills	Knowledge	Disease	Demographic	Consumer	Technical quality	Word-of-mouth	Product
Resources	Attitudes	Capacity	Geographic	Professional	Access	Public relations	Organization
Shared values	Behaviors	Strategic importance	Psychographic	Payer	Service	Promotion	Personality
Systems	Unmet needs	Technology	Utilization	Employees	Cost	Advertising	Symbols
Structure	Expectations, satisfaction	Profitability situation	Purchase	Organizational	Value	Sales	Royalty
Other	Other	Other	Other	Other	Other	Other	Other
Internal marketing strategy	Determination of desired benefits	Program product development	Targeting strategies	Relationship strategies	Differentiation strategies	Selling strategy	Positioning strategy

Marketing plan

Figure 8.5 Additional elements for each marketing principle.

Internal marketing	Selling	Differentiation
Employee motivation	Direct mail	Sponsorship
Employee behavior	Internet, intranet	Seal of approval
Marketing orientation	Place based	Reliability
of organization	Community relations	Speed
Staffing	Telemarketing	Technology
Organizational culture	Price	

Program/product development	Benefit identification	Positioning
Market potential	Motivations	User imagery
Product life cycle	Relationships	Customer
Range of choices	Culture of customer	relationships
Consumer intimacy		Credibility
Supply-side management		

Channel strategy	Targeting
Government	Degree of relationship
Media gatekeepers	Continuum of care
Community influentials	Behavioral
Parish nurses	Values
Comanagement	Culturally

tomers and analyzing markets, and focusing and prioritizing the organization's resources so that the market can be addressed in an integrated and coordinated fashion. Marketing, then, is not to be a job assigned to just anyone, nor is it limited to attracting new customers. It certainly is more than advertising and sales. Rather, marketing concerns exist at every point where the organization makes contact with the customer. From advertising and the handling of telephone inquiries, to bedside manners and the quality of the care, to sustaining and reinforcing the postcare relationship, properly practiced marketing (that is, Marketing with a capital M) is comprehensive and essential to successful management.

Notes

1. Manoff, R. *Social Marketing: New Imperatives for Public Health.* Westport: Praeger, 1985.

2. Kotler, P. *Marketing Management.* Englewood Cliffs, NJ: Prentice-Hall, 1997.

3. Gombeski, W. "Better Marketing through a Principles-based Model." *Marketing Health Services* (Fall 1998): 43–48.

CASE

How to Position a Practice to Get More Business

Stephen Rimar

The common perception was that Dr. Keith Lustig's group controlled the local market for his subspecialty service. Indeed, it had grown considerably, and he began to think about hiring yet another partner. But if he already had more business than everyone else, were there enough additional patients to support another physician, and could his practice attract them? Dr. Lustig decided to do his own market research to find out.

What Is Your Market?

First, Dr. Lustig needed to know his actual market share. Fortunately, his subspecialty kept a national databank that included data on all patients treated for the conditions of interest to him. He obtained data from three years earlier that showed his practice had 24 percent of the cases in his area, which he defined as an hour's drive or less from his location. This volume seemed surprising low to him, given his reputation as the market leader and the extremely limited number of specialists. Second, he compared the area's case numbers with that of per capita national averages using the same databank. To his surprise, he found that in his area, 30 percent fewer cases than the national average were being treated. Since the demographics of the population in his market were similar to those of nearby markets with higher case volumes, he concluded that patients in his area were going out of the market (more than an hour's drive) for treatment. He verified this by polling his current patients. Many of them said they had looked at practices outside the market for treatment.

In order to grow his practice, Dr. Lustig needed to know why patients traveled a considerable distance for care that he could provide more conveniently. Patients who traveled for treatment were also likely motivated enough to explore multiple treatment and practitioner options, and perhaps had researched his practice. He found that anyone could get a significant amount of information about his practice (e.g., number of cases, success rate, adverse outcomes) by consulting this databank via the Internet. And as he studied this databank he found (as would have prospective patients) that his practice had a much lower treatment success rate than others in neighboring markets. He recalled that questions about his treatment success rate were among the most common asked by new patients. It occurred to him the group might be losing prospective patients because of this data, which was readily available to anyone.

Understanding this, he sought to uncover the reasons for his poor success rate. By consulting both the national databank and his own patient records, Dr. Lustig determined that his patient population was primarily comprised of individuals in a high-risk category—one in which the likelihood of a successful treatment was poor. His patients' outcomes simply reflected their case mix. In addition, inquiries by his partners and staff, as well as patients, led him to believe that practices in his neighboring markets were more aggressive in their treatment initially. His group tended to begin with more conservative therapy. Perhaps this affected the overall success of therapy and patient satisfaction. If the group's initial treatment plan did not seem aggressive enough to patients, they could readily find a physician whose therapy was consonant with their desires.

Market Strategy

Armed with these facts, Dr. Lustig developed a three-part strategy to increase the volume of his practice. The first involved verifying that his success rate as reported in the specialty database was accurate. The number of cases was correct, but a problem became evident when he looked closely at the definitions of the database's terms. The definition of success was less stringent than the one he used in preparing his data for entry into the system. Therefore, he recalculated his success rate and found it to be slightly better than before (although still lower than his competitors' rates). After several discussions with the administrators of the database, he was allowed to resubmit his data.

Dr. Lustig's second approach involved an effort to understand his patients better. He added questions to the practice's intake form about the source of patients' referrals and the reason for their choice of his practice. Most patients had been referred by other physicians, but quite a few had found the group through the Internet.

Finally, he decided to advertise to referring physicians and directly to patients. Since patients were interested in success rates, and his practice's success rate was lower than others because of his patient base, Dr. Lustig decided to advertise his results to them, but with an appropriate qualifier. His message emphasized his vast experience with high-risk patients and those that other doctors deem hopeless. The campaign that he launched with all the referring physicians in the area started with the production of a one-page monthly newsletter addressing issues in his subspecialty.

How to Do It

1. *Look at your practice from the outside.* Most physicians believe they know their practice. But as Dr. Lustig found, one can know everything about a practice but have no understanding of how others perceive it. In order to understand patients' perceptions, he needed to put himself in their place. For Dr. Lustig, consulting a regional databank proved enlightening. Other physicians have asked patients and referring physicians for their opinion. Some even approach patients and referring physicians who decline their services, the so-called dissatisfied shoppers. If you can find out why people do *not* use your practice, you have valuable information with which to increase your patient volume.

2. *Define your market.* Dr. Lustig initially defined his market as the geographic area within an hour's drive. After completing his research, however, he concluded that he must broaden his definition because people were willing to drive more than an hour for the type of care he provided. His pool of potential patients was then significantly larger. He had opportunities for growth he hadn't considered before.

3. *Measure carefully against your gut.* Market data can be useful for your practice, but so is carefully reflecting on what years of experience have demonstrated to you. Market research, no matter how sophisticated or impressive, is based on sampling. Its results only accurately reflect the opinions and actions of a portion of the population of interest. As with medical research, how it is conducted drives how narrowly or broadly its findings can be applied. Critique its methods, consider its source, and use it accordingly. If what market research tells you conflicts with gut feelings, dig deeper, as Dr. Lustig did. He knew he was at least as competent as his peers although the data suggested otherwise. The discovery that his definition of success and his patients' case mix differed from that of his colleagues provided an explanation for varying success rates and proved his gut right.

4. *Learn what's out there.* If any organization tracks data that reflects the performance of your practice and makes it available to the public, either directly or indirectly, you'd better pay attention. They are shaping your practice's image. While physicians and hospitals have been reluctant to report outcomes for a variety of reasons, patients are finding information about performance and quality with increasing frequency. The growth of the Internet has greatly simplified access to such data. Regularly examine databases, Web sites, and so on that contain information on your practice. Think about how new or surprising information might be used to your advantage. Also scan the landscape for information about your competitors and do the same with it. Dr. Lustig used data he discovered about his own and competing practices to position his practice as the best choice for treatment of difficult cases.

5. *Use market data to develop a strategy.* The purpose of Dr. Lustig's strategy was to attract more patients, both from his own and neighboring markets. What he discovered through his market research suggested the right method. Investigating the databank entries led him to correct his record so that information seekers would get accurate statistics about his practice. It also indicated that the image of his practice needed attention (his success rate was poorer than that of his peers) and prompted him to promote his difficult case niche to potential patients and referring physicians. His questions to patients on the intake form suggested that he should broaden the area he considered his market and seek to attract patients who lived more than an hour's drive from his office. Each step was prompted by market data. It was therefore easier not only to justify any costs, but also to track his plan's results.

6. *Consider advertising—carefully.* To most doctors, marketing means advertising. Although once controversial, advertising by medical practices is now commonly used by practitioners in search of patients. But the role of advertising to increase a practice's business depends on many things including the nature of the practice, the patients, and the referral patterns. Dr. Lustig, for example, focused his promotional (advertising) campaign on referring physicians because they were the source of the majority of his patients—they received his monthly newsletter. Considering how your patients first come to you is a good step when deciding if you want to embark on an advertising campaign.

7. *Listen to patients who chose not to see you.* Many physicians survey their regular patients to gain their perspective on the practice's strengths and weaknesses. What these surveys fail to capture, however, is information from patients who chose *not* to use their practice. If you want to find out what you're *not* doing right, or how to attract patients who *do not* use your services, pay attention to other doctors' patients.

But how can you access these lost customers? One way is to review your office's scheduling logs to find new patients who scheduled visits but did not keep their appointments, or who came for an initial visit but never returned for follow-up care. Contact the patients by telephone or mail and ask why they never showed up or didn't return to your office. (And remember to give them a small token of appreciation for their time—perhaps a small, useful item with your contact information on it!)

8. *Become a benchmark.* Consumers and their advocates who demand information about patient outcomes are increasingly important in healthcare. Much of the data they currently access is found in voluntary registries, such as the one Dr. Lustig investigated. Find out which organizations are collecting data related to your practice and contribute your data—if it's favorable. Some registries have so few participants that your data may serve to highlight you as an outstanding performer. This kind of information, whether patient satisfaction data, outcome results, or patient profiles, can be enormously helpful in promoting your practice.

9. *Hire yourself as your marketing consultant.* Dr. Lustig found out a significant amount about his practice without hiring a consultant. You too can become a marketing consultant for your practice if you're willing to spend the time and keep an open mind. And while you may require the assistance of an expert for some aspects of a marketing campaign or for an extensive undertaking, conducting limited surveys and some promotional activities are easily within your capabilities.

Essential Management Skills

The Business Plan

Stephen Rimar

"Let me see your business plan." Why do these words intimidate physicians? Many say it's because they don't really know what a business plan is. Few have ever read one, and it is a rare physician who has written one. But composing a business plan is well within the ability of practically all doctors, as is mastering most business tasks.

Overview

Previous chapters refer to the presentation of a new idea as a proposal. *Proposal* is a general term used to describe any plan offered to others in an effort to gain their support. The type of support requested may be essential to a proposal's success, for example, money for needed supplies. It may also be optional, nonfinancial, or both. A physician in solo practice may share a proposal with his office staff to hire a nurse practitioner simply to increase the likelihood that they will welcome the individual. In either case, the support is desired and viewed as important to the venture's success.

A business plan is a specific kind of proposal most often associated with the development of a new business (or a significant extension of an existing one). It describes the essential aspects, assumptions, and financial projections for the new business and is almost always designed to convince a person or group to provide supporting funds.

A good business plan is like a good note from a consulting

221

physician. It provides the reader with a complete and detailed summary of a problem and its solution in a format that is simple and widely accepted. The best ones are comprehensive, succinct, and easy to read. Physicians can learn to write a successful business plan by using many of the skills learned in their medical training.

The Purpose of a Business Plan

Business plans vary in content and slightly in format, but their purpose is the same: to provide a clear and comprehensive snapshot of a proposed business to an audience whose response will largely determine its fate. Whether venture capitalists, loan officers, or hospital executives, the audience looks for evidence that the proposal will succeed, and that, in some way, its success will benefit them. That audience will relentlessly question all aspects of the plan in an effort to expose potential flaws. As a result, despite the amount of thought and effort put into developing business plans, many are rejected.

The Key to Success

So what makes a successful business plan? That question is most easily addressed by discussing why plans fail. Experts suggest that business plans fail for two reasons: poor packaging and inadequately addressing the investors or the market.[1] *Packaging* refers to the physical appearance and organization of the plan. Poor packaging is easily remedied and is, in fact, inexcusable. Business plans should always be neat; using only high quality paper and graphics, for example, helps. Most business plans presented to venture capitalists are less than 40 pages, but the appropriate length for any given plan depends on the nature of the proposal and its reviewers. Sometimes a review group expects a proposal of a certain length; knowing and adhering to their expectations provides an advantage to presenters. The cover, title page, and executive summary are other critical pieces of the business plan package. Most reviewers read these before looking at the rest of the business plan. If the title and executive summary don't attract their attention, it's unlikely the rest of the plan will. Finally, reviewers find a table of contents quite helpful, particularly as they study the plan in detail.

Adequately addressing the investors and the market is more difficult than creating an attractive package. Understandably, most business plans are written from the perspective of the entrepreneur seeking support. The reviewers, however, are concerned with investors' needs (the people or organization that fund the business), which involve satisfying the market (prospective clients of the new business). If the business plan fails to demonstrate a benefit to the investors, usually by its projected or de facto appeal to the market, it stands little chance of securing funding. That is why successful business plans usually highlight an organization's solution to an important problem in the market—for example, the convenience and speed of buying airline tickets over the Internet rather than over the telephone or through a travel agent. Reviewers by nature have little concern for the entrepreneur's needs beyond how well the organization satisfies their investment.

Developing and Writing the Business Plan—Medical Analogy

The Assessment

Developing a business plan is very much like performing a medical consultation. Both begin with a description of the problem, perhaps unclear at first (i.e., the chief complaint), proceed to better define and articulate the problem (workup and diagnosis), and conclude with a plan to solve it (recommendations). To the consulting physician, the problem comes in the form of a patient's chief complaint (CC). The *chief complaint* is a simple statement of the patient's problem in the patient's words. It indicates why the patient sought the physician's help. To the business plan writer, the problem is often a need identified through personal experience or observation, or by a third party.

Both the medical consultation and the business planning process require a significant amount of background work before the final product (the written note or plan) can be prepared. Each begins by exploring the history of their problem, in depth. In medicine, the history of present illness (HPI) and the review of systems

(ROS) serve as the basis for the construction of a narrative that starts with the chief complaint. The HPI and ROS also help determine the complaint's relationship to the real problem underlying a patient's distress. The more serious the HPI and ROS, the greater the need to understand the chief complaint. The patient's past medical, family, social, and occupational history can also contribute to establishing a correct diagnosis and a successful treatment plan.

For the business plan writer, a systematic and sequential elaboration of the business problem serves the same function as the CC, HPI, ROS, and past history. Detailing how long a problem has existed, its influence on the market, and the manifestations of its effect helps to demonstrate its significance, and consequently the importance of finding a solution. Examples of the issues or circumstances created by the problem reinforce this importance. An accurate story of the problem's development along with accounts of previous unsuccessful or semisuccessful solutions can provide further justification for the new plan.

Although the medical history goes a long way in establishing a diagnosis and suggesting a treatment, it is the physical examination and diagnostic testing that confirm both. Similarly, a business plan is most convincing when supported by a market analysis that includes the current state of the market and opportunities for new business. If neither the problem nor the solution is unique, there must be something unique about the market to support a new business. Many good ideas fail to take root because the market, in its existing condition, does not support them.

The Diagnosis and Treatment Plan— a.k.a. the Business Plan

Once the assessment is complete, the consulting physician is ready to produce a diagnosis and treatment plan, and the business plan writer can draft a business plan. Each begins by articulating the problem in simple, clear terms. Sometimes, for the sake of clarity, it also makes sense to describe what the problem is *not* before moving to a solution.

The business plan for a new Internet shopping enterprise may address the problem of busy consumers who prefer the convenience of shopping during off-hours or who want to avoid traveling from store to store to make purchases. A full problem statement for this business might read like this:

> The desire of consumers to shop from their homes has been well demonstrated in the past few years. The success of catalogue shopping has proven that consumers will take advantage of opportunities to shop from home. They enjoy the convenience of shopping whenever they like and avoiding the hassle and expense of traveling between stores to buy merchandise. But consumers are becoming increasingly dissatisfied with the limited variety of products offered by catalogues as compared to stores. Our Internet sales business will provide all that they want: the variety of style and pricing that is found in conventional stores and the convenience of home-catalogue shopping. We will use the power of the Internet to bring that variety into their homes.

Compelling problem statements alone, however, rarely convince business plan reviewers to support them.

The plan to resolve the problem follows its identification. Whereas the consultant's note describes all elements of the recommended therapy after the diagnosis is presented, the business plan delineates the constituents of the business process designed to solve the problem. It includes a detailed description of the proposed product or service, a financial analysis of its cost and projected revenues, and a description of the structure and management of the people who will comprise the new business.

Who's Caring for the Patient?

Once investors know *how* a business plan will solve a real problem in a supportive market, they want to know *who* will make it happen. Who are the people that will serve in the leadership roles in the business? What is their background and education? What type of experience do they bring with them? Have they been involved in similar businesses before? It is also important to include people and experience that are not necessary in the development of the business but are essential as the business grows. The description of this start-up team may be more critical to a business plan's acceptance than anything else described in the document.

The Business Plan—Format

Business plans, like many medical communications, have a standardized format. Funding groups and analysts expect a business plan to contain certain information and to be assembled in a particular way, just as physicians expect of medical information. Both consist of an organized, systematic structure for the development and presentation of a plan. As with the medical consultant's note, it is acceptable to vary the exact format of a business plan, provided the essential elements are included. There are a variety of books and publications that provide advice about format, and the Internet provides a potentially unlimited source of sample business plans. Regardless of the format used, however, the following essentials should be included.

Executive Summary

The executive summary is the single most important part of the business plan. Its purpose is to grab the reviewer's attention. The executive summary should include the problem that the business will solve as well as a brief description of how it will do so. This defines the purpose or mission of the business. Many experts suggest writing the executive summary last, after the entire plan has been articulated.

Market Analysis

This section provides information to suggest the relevance and significance of the problem to be solved. It should also explain the context in which the proposed solution will occur and establish the need and demand for the product or service proposed. Market analyses usually include information about potential customers, size of the market, recent trends, and an overview of the competition. If the reviewers are unfamiliar with the specific area of the market a business plan addresses, consider including an overview of the industry itself.

Organizational Description

The organizational description delineates those responsible for the plan's execution. Specifically, it recounts the leaders' education and previous experience and who will be responsible for what. It also describes how their roles interact.

Product or Service

The executive summary introduces the reader to the product or service that will solve the problem. The body of the business plan contains its detailed description. A common reason for rejection of business plans is the absence of sufficient detail in this section to describe the business adequately.

Structure and Management

Even the best solutions fail if they are not managed correctly. This section should present the management structure in detail—who will be responsible for what functions and what personnel, and how they will oversee the delivery of the service or product. It should address as many potential operational problems as possible (e.g., not enough staff, errors in production or delivery) and include management solutions to each.

Financial Analysis

Included in the financial analysis should be a projection of the costs and revenues of the proposed business, as well as a thorough and honest analysis of the financial risks. The format of this section is very important since financial experts will review it. All financial assumptions should be clearly stated to allow for appropriate review. Depending on the nature of the proposed business, a cash flow statement, balance sheet, and/or income statement might be included. Also a cost-effectiveness or break-even analysis may be appropriate. Remember that the purpose of a business plan is to obtain financial support. It is, therefore, essential that it include a detailed funding request and description of expected return for investors.

Refine and Revise

Remember, successful business plans, like other successful written works (including a good consultant's note), are the result of continuous refinement and revision. It is not enough to commit words to paper once and present what is a clearly a draft, in terms of its quality, as a final business plan. As the details of the idea become clearer, so should the business plan.

Note

1. Rich, S., and D. Gumpert. "How to Write a Winning Business Plan." *Harvard Business Review* (May/June 1985); Sahlman, W. "How to Write a Business Plan." *Harvard Business Review* (July/August 1997).

CASE 9

How to Develop a Plan for a Practice

Stephen Rimar

The purpose of a formal business plan is to win support, financial or otherwise, for a new business venture. But an established business also needs support from its customers, employees, and financial backers. Successful businesses, in fact, are continuously evaluating their existing support systems, creating ways to increase them, and looking for new sources. This process is similar in many ways to the formal business planning required for a new enterprise. The difference, however, is that it involves planning within and for a real organization, rather than one that exists only on paper.

Formalized planning for an existing business is often called strategic planning. As described in Lecture 2, strategy is a plan or method for achieving a specific goal, and usually involves developing a competitive advantage so that the business can succeed in the current or anticipated market. For both for-profit and not-for-profit organizations, the purpose of strategic planning is to develop a plan (strategy) that includes the steps necessary to achieve their missions.

But all forms of business planning (or organizational planning), whether they entail developing a plan for a new enterprise or evaluating and directing an existing operation, involve a similar process. A new or proposed business has an initial *business plan* to guide its activities. Once it is up and running, however, the business leaders will need to reevaluate the plan through the development of a *strategic plan*. Subsequently, periodic strategic plans consider where the business has been and describe where it is going. The idea behind both a business plan and a strategic plan is the same (i.e., achieving a goal), as are some of the development and presentation tools and processes. Some businesses even label their strategic plan a business plan. Since there are some differences, however, and since a formal business plan for a new enterprise was discussed in the previous chapter (Lecture 9), this chapter will focus on strategic planning—the process of developing a plan for an existing business, such as a medical practice.

Why Plan?

Organizations plan for at least three reasons: to assess their current position, to anticipate the future, and to coordinate and control organizational activities. One cannot plan a trip without knowing its starting point. Performance measures provide a means to evaluate the success of the current plan. They also serve as objective criteria on which to base future action. Anticipating the future means addressing both current problems and opportunities. The extent to which an organization initiates changes based on forecasting varies considerably. Venture capitalists make their living predicting and investing in the next profitable boom. For them, the risk is often quite high, but the reward can be, too.

Medical practices, however, like most small businesses, cannot afford to make risky bets on the future. This is where performance measures can be helpful. By examining them, one can discern trends that suggest a course of action or strategy. For example, Dr. Christopher (who developed a fee-schedule model in Case 3) and Dr. Gersoff (who determined the cost of preauthorization in Case 1) used the performance measures of payers to develop strategies for their practices. By collecting and reviewing data, they were able to make fairly objective predictions about the future and plan accordingly.

Finally, organizations plan in order to coordinate and control their activities. In a very simple medical practice (e.g., a solo practitioner with a single employee), the duties of each member of the organization are clear. But in organizations with more than a handful of employees, developing a plan and communicating it is essential. If the goals, actions, and performance measures of an organization are clearly articulated and widely distributed, all members of a practice—from the managing partner to the temporary receptionist—can know what is expected of them. A plan gives the group a template for action. It has the added benefit of enabling the group's leadership to align rewards (financial or otherwise) with performance.

Dr. Phillip Harvey, by designing a structure for his practice, which expanded from one office to three, was in fact developing a strategic plan (Case 2). He configured a formal reporting structure and defined performance measures by which to assess its effectiveness. This would be the first in a series of steps designed to coordinate and control the activities in his practice.

Tools

One common tool used in the development of a strategic plan is a SWOT analysis (strengths, weaknesses, opportunities, and threats). This simple technique is based on the concept that a successful plan for a business requires a connection between its internal capabilities (strengths and weaknesses) and external circumstances (opportunities and threats). The planning group incorporates performance measures, projections, and opinion—even hearsay—into a list that addresses each SWOT component. The SWOT analysis enables the group to consider all relevant data, arrange it in categories, and use the resulting information as a road map for developing a plan. Assigning a given piece of data to a specific category depends on such factors as the nature and situation of the organization. For example, among the strengths or opportunities on the list of a medical group with the capacity to expand might be the growing number of patient visits. This would be labeled a weakness or threat for a practice that already has more patients than it can handle.

A SWOT analysis is ideal for establishing the plan's foundation. Once the organization evaluates its internal capabilities and external influences, it develops a specific plan to achieve goals derived from its mission. One popular method of developing an organizational plan is the balanced scorecard.

The balanced scorecard model was developed in 1990 by Robert Kaplan and David Norton.[1] It examines an organization from four perspectives by answering the key question suggested by each perspective:

- The *financial* perspective: How do we look to our shareholders, board of directors, partners, or investors?
- The *customer* perspective: How do our customers (patients, referring physicians) perceive us?
- The *internal business* perspective: What in our product or service must we excel at?
- *Learning and growth* perspective: What must we do to continue to improve?

The answers lead to the development of a set of goals for each perspective. By assigning performance measures for each goal (i.e., financial, customer, etc.), and by determining the action steps necessary to achieve the goals, the organization has a complete strategic plan.

Proactive or Reactive?

Unfortunately, many businesses plan only in response to a threat, rather than as part of routine operations. For example, Dr. Harvey never considered evaluating his office procedures until the prospect of managing three offices overwhelmed him (Case 2). It was only when Dr. O'Connor's practice faced danger of collapse that the in-house lab operation was reevaluated (Case 3). But successful businesses plan proactively; it is an integral part of their business operation. Dr. Lustig was proactive in developing a marketing plan to attract new patients at a time when his practice was doing well financially and didn't need them (Case 8).

Each year, Dr. Michael O'Hara and his cardiology group reviewed the preceding year's performance and developed a plan for the new year. The result of the latest session was a *strategic plan* that actually called for the development of a *business plan* for a new venture. His case illustrates the similarities, differences, and relationships between these two types of plans.

Move Ahead or Fall Behind

Dr. O'Hara was the founder of a large cardiology group associated with an academic medical center. The group offered a full array of diagnostic and therapeutic services, including interventional cardiology, and it was the local market leader in providing referral cardiology services. Each spring, on the first Saturday of April, Dr. O'Hara's group held a day-long planning retreat to develop a balanced scorecard for the practice. The day began with a review of the previous year's performance. They inspected a large amount of data compiled by their practice manager, including a financial statement and other data related to billings, collections, accounts receivable, and expenses. Operational data such as the number of new and return patients, visit volume, service mix (CPT codes billed), number of procedures, number of referrals by location (i.e., by zip code and referring physician), and quality of customer service data (e.g., patient satisfaction survey and comments) were studied. Next they did a SWOT analysis of the practice. Using the results of the analysis along with the performance data, they reevaluated their previous year's balanced scorecard objectives and their accompanying measures. This particular year they were pleased with every aspect of the practice except one, and they left the scorecard unchanged except for it. By the end of the day, they reaffirmed their plans, which included a significant new goal.

Dr. O'Hara's group received a steady flow of referrals for cardiac catheterizations from Western Hospital, a community hospital located in the fastest growing area of the state. Western Hospital had no catheterization laboratory and split referrals between Dr. O'Hara's group and one of its competitors, which was equidistant from Western in the opposite direction. As part of the group's annual planning retreat, their review of patient data revealed that the number of referrals from Western decreased significantly. The group became concerned that patients were increasingly being referred to the competition. They feared this loss of business would not only hurt their interventional business, but also other cardiology-related businesses in that part of the state.

Dr. O'Hara and his colleagues considered a plan to open a cardiac catheterization laboratory at Western Hospital and to staff it with a member of their group. If successful, the plan would provide an opportunity for the group to capture every catheterization in the area and firmly establish market dominance for referral cardiology services. With the help of his partners, Dr. O'Hara wrote a business plan to submit to Western Hospital executives. The plan began with the following executive summary.

Proposal for a Cardiac Catheterization Laboratory at Western Hospital

Executive Summary

This business plan has been prepared to obtain $1,500,000 financing for establishment of a cardiac catheterization laboratory in Western Hospital, a 125-bed community hospital in the fastest growing area of the state. The primary diagnoses of patients admitted to the hospital are related to cardiac disease, and more than 80 percent of the hospital's transfers come from this group. The closest cardiac catheterization labs are 50 and 60 miles from Western, and the nearest tertiary care center is 100 miles away. Creating a catheterization lab benefits the hospital in four major ways. First, it minimizes the transfer and, thus, loss of patients and associated revenue. Second, it decreases unnecessary use of resources; currently, elective catheterization cases remain in-house at Western until other hospitals can accept them. Third, it enhances Western's ability to compete successfully for capitated managed-care contracts. And finally, establishing a cardiac catheterization laboratory will increase patients' general confidence in Western's ability to meet its healthcare needs.

   Dr. Steven Banyas, a cardiologist who trained in interventional cardiology at the tertiary care center affiliated with Western Hospital, will direct the laboratory. Procedures will be limited to elective catheterizations in stable patients. It is anticipated that the laboratory will perform 400 procedures during its first year of operation, increase its volume by 100 cases per year, and reach a steady state of 700 catheterizations per year by the end of its fourth year. Revenues are expected to exceed operating expenses from the first year, with the initial investment recovered within five years.

How to Do It

1. *Base planning on performance.* A business plan for a new enterprise can only project market, operational, and financial performance based on data that it assumes is relevant. An ongoing business, however, has the advantage of access to its actual performance for use in planning. As stated repeatedly in this book, the more objective the data, the more useful it is in tracking progress, and the more valuable it is during efforts to gain support. Each step that arises from a strategic plan requires time, money, or both. The more certain one is about the need for action (as evidenced by objective measures), the easier it is for an organization to justify its cost. Dr. O'Hara based his decision to develop a business plan for the new catheterization lab at Western Hospital on a critical performance measure—the number of patients referred out by the hospital. The objective data convinced him of the importance and viability of his plan.

2. *Start with a threat or opportunity.* What is the biggest problem facing your practice? What about the practice would you like to improve? Answering these questions is the start of strategic planning. Ideally the plan should identify the undertaking that, if successfully completed, will provide the most value to your enterprise. Remember that successful business plans eliminate existing threats or take advantage of emerging opportunities.

Dr. O'Hara's group came upon a threat to their practice—losing referrals from Western Hospital—during their annual review. Dr. Harvey (Case 2) had an opportunity to expand his practice to include three offices but was simultaneously faced with the challenge of streamlining and centralizing operations. It is not uncommon during strategic planning to address threats and opportunities concurrently.

In healthcare, routine operations almost always need adjustment. Review all aspects of your practice regularly in meeting with staff. Avoid the temptation to examine only short-term operational issues (e.g., billings, collections, patient data) and reflect on longer-term strategic issues (e.g., competitive threats, market positioning) as well. Use these meetings as a means of identifying problems and opportunities and a mechanism to address them.

3. *Take advantage of your strengths.* The most successful plans are developed from a position of strength. Even if your practice is losing in a competitive struggle, include in your strategic plan a goal based on *something* you do well. Building even a piece of a plan on strengths has several benefits. First, it's a form of positive reinforcement for those who work hard. Second, emphasizing what can be done, and done well, makes planning easier and far more enjoyable than focusing on a negative. And planning activity that is enjoyable is more likely to result in creative and profitable ideas. Finally, a practice's strengths are the invariable basis for new opportunities, possibly even those that will be crucial to future success.

Dr. O'Hara knew that his interventional partners were a strength he could leverage to gain market share in the Western Hospital area. He built on this strength and developed a plan that went beyond solving the problem of decreasing referrals. Business plans are about business opportunities as well as business problems. But it's extremely difficult to take advantage of an opportunity from a position of weakness.

4. *Keep it off the shelf.* A strategic plan is not a book report. To be of any value, it must be a living plan, one that is reflected in the daily activities of every member of the organization. For this to happen, it must be communicated to everyone. Some organizations do this by publishing a yearly statement of goals. Others review goals and performance measures as part of regularly scheduled management meetings. The more savvy organizations find ways to incorporate their strategic plan into multiple communications (e.g., job descriptions and performance reviews, newsletters, recognition activities) with staff at all levels of the organization. And they are wise enough to avoid using the label strategic plan when it is prudent to do so.

Another way to make the plan a reality is to offer staff incentives based on accomplishing its goals, or better yet, exceeding them (based on performance measures). Nothing motivates like money, but other incentives and forms of recognition can induce superior performance. To communicate your strategic plan and spur achievement, you should use as many mechanisms as are reasonable for your organization. Remember, the goal is to get everyone functioning as a single organization with common goals.

5. *Keep it simple.* Keeping the message simple is always good advice in communications. This is true for both the actual business or strategic plan and the dissemination of information about the plan. Enough said.

Note

1. Kaplan, R. S., and D. P. Norton. "The Balanced Scorecard—Measures That Drive Performance." *Harvard Business Review* (1992): 71–79; Rimar, S., and S. J. Garstka. "The Balanced Scorecard: Development and Implementation in an Academic Clinical Department." *Academic Medicine* 74 (1999): 114–122; Rimar, S. "Strategic Planning and the Balanced Scorecard for Faculty Practice Plans." *Academic Medicine* 75 (2000): 1186–1188.

Selling an Idea

Stephen Rimar

Why Selling Is Important

James MacGregor Burns, in his classic volume about leadership, states that the two essentials of power are motive and resource.[1] Without motive (a reason to do something), resources are of no value; without resources, motives remain unfulfilled. Without either, there can be no power for leaders. And because both are in short supply, power is elusive and limited.

The Yale Management Guide for Physicians is written for physicians with motive. Whether it's taking back control of healthcare or simply keeping a practice afloat, these motives involve leading and managing the practice of medicine. The book's purpose is to introduce physicians to the means used to secure resources that can support motive and create power. The resources may be large or small, financial or nonfinancial, short-term or long-term—whatever is required to match the motive.

Much of the book is devoted to ideas: developing, organizing, and articulating them as a means of defining motive. This chapter discusses selling ideas in order to obtain resources. This concept—selling an idea—is both foreign and intrinsic to the practice of medicine. It is also a notion that medical leadership must embrace if they wish to achieve the power to change things.

The Handicaps of Medical Training

A recurring theme of this book is the difficulty physicians have with management because of the nature of medical training and practice. There can be no doubt that the American medical educational system is successful at training skillful practitioners. Certain assumptions, dogma, and traditions, however, in both the profession and its training grounds, handicap physicians when it comes to management of people and resources. Acknowledging these limitations is the first step to overcoming them.

Physicians Believe the Facts Speak for Themselves

Physicians believe the answer is in the data. They are taught to use data to build a case to support diagnosis and therapy. The scientific foundation of medical practice is built on the principle that, sooner or later, data points to the right decisions. In fact, a differential diagnosis is simply a list of potential diagnoses based on the preliminary data. As additional data is received, the list is refined, until the evidence converts a working diagnosis to the real one.

In business, however, individuals often propose ideas based on limited data or data obtained by methods that fall short of meeting scientific standards. Even market data and financial projections, the most quantifiable forms of business information, are different from data used in medicine. They are collected, organized, analyzed, and reported with varying attention to procedures and circumstances that would make their interpretation indisputable. It is not surprising, therefore, that investors often find data alone to be insufficient to convince them to support an idea. While medicine uses data to find the truth, management uses data to advance an idea. Learning how to use data to sell an idea is therefore an essential skill in the business of healthcare.

Physicians Speak Only to Each Other

Physicians are trained to communicate with other healthcare professionals. In fact, the language of medicine allows for very precise communication within the profession and with nurses, pharmacists, and the like. Often, though, it is a barrier to communicating with others, particularly patients. The language of medicine is foreign to most people, including physicians in training. Consider that one of the first books medical students purchase is a medical dictionary. Once learned, these students speak this foreign language for the rest of their careers.

The problem is not that physicians acquire another language—it is essential to their trade—but that they use it as their exclusive form of communication. Medical schools, having recognized this problem, have introduced patient communication courses. But their success to date is limited. Astute patients understand that in order to effectively communicate in the medical world, they, too, must learn the doctors' language rather than relying on them to translate.

If physicians have difficulty communicating with patients, how can they expect to sell an idea to people, many of whom have their own professional language? The answer is with great difficulty. Spending the time necessary to polish general communication skills and learning some new vocabulary will make the job much easier.

Physicians Order Rather than Persuade

Except for the military, no profession accomplishes as much of its work through commands as medicine. Even the phrase "doctor's orders" found its way into our everyday language. But a physician can't order people to support an idea. Instead, he must persuade them of its value. Physicians receive little training in this, perhaps because they believe (erroneously, some would suggest) it is not essential to their practice. In business and management, however, mastering the art of persuasion is often the difference between success and failure.

Physicians Do Not Compete for Resources

Their inexperience with competing for resources may be physicians' greatest obstacle to achieving success in management. It's not that they're unfamiliar with competition. Indeed, physicians are some of the most competitive people on earth. But the means of achieving competitive success in medical training, mostly by knowing more information than one's peers, has nothing to do with competing for resources in the real world.

When a physician attempts to convince a managed-care company to cover services for a patient, he is competing for resources. If the request is granted for his patient, money is shunted from some other source meant to help patients (directly or indirectly). Physicians rarely appreciate or even care about this. But the financing of health services, even through public sources, is a business and as such is subject to the rules of a competitive market.

Until recently, physicians were free to do whatever was necessary to provide care for their patients, regardless of the cost. As a result, they expect effortless access to the resources needed to carry out their plans. This was never the case in the business world. Now healthcare is becoming like every other business, in which competition for resources is a fact of life. Learning how to compete for these resources, therefore, is essential for success in healthcare management.

Sales Strategies

The cases in this book were inspired by actual projects conducted by physicians attending the Yale Management Program for Physicians. As they demonstrate, physicians overcame the handicaps of medical training to achieve some level of management success. They all were motivated to change something in their practice, but it was their ability to obtain resources—which was a direct function of their ability to sell an idea—that gave them the power to succeed. While there are many ways to sell an idea, these cases highlight some of the most successful strategies.

Do Your Homework

You must know a product before you sell it. This includes being able to successfully anticipate and address buyers' questions and criticisms. Each time an answer satisfies a potential buyer's needs, the sale comes closer to reality. Informed buyers know when a sales pitch is bull. Selling an idea is often more difficult than selling a product because of its complexity and innate uncertainty. The more background information and credible data you offer, the more plausible the argument, and the more likely the sale.

Dr. Lustig wanted to increase his business through marketing (Case 8). Before he began selling his practice to patients and referring physicians, however, he spent a considerable amount of time uncovering their perceptions of it. This information was critical to developing his sales approach. Successful advertisers embark on a campaign only after fully understanding both their product and its market. So it is with selling an idea.

Dr. Gersoff's study of preauthorization costs was all about doing homework (Case 1). It was, in fact, only after he completed an analysis that he was convinced he had an issue worth addressing with his payers. The same was true for Dr. Christopher, who had no idea whether his practice stood to benefit or lose if he signed a managed-care contract (Case 3). In these two cases, the physicians initially had no idea to sell; rather, they had a question to answer. The results of their investigations produced answers to their questions and also led them to develop a plan. For these physicians, the decision to continue with specific payers depended on the payers' response to their concerns. The background research sold *them* on an idea, and provided the basis for them to argue their cases.

In other cases, however, the physicians began with an idea they believed would solve a problem. Their background research was necessary to collect data that would convince others their idea was worth supporting. Dr. O'Connor believed reinstituting in-house laboratory testing would benefit the practice (Case 3). Before she could convince her colleagues, however, she needed more convincing evidence. Dr. Beecher saw that her practice was in severe jeopardy unless she could convince the hospital to support a plan for more ICU beds (Case 4). Her analysis supported the financial feasibility of her proposal, lending credibility to a plan that others were willing to support only if the financials were favorable.

Finally, Dr. O'Hara began his sales pitch with a business plan for a new cardiac catheterization center (Case 9). A formal business plan is the epitome of a well-researched and carefully considered proposal. While Dr. O'Hara's special case required submission of a formal plan, physicians in each of these cases had to develop some kind of business plan, no matter how informal, before selling their idea. And the good business plans clearly captured what was for sale and why it should be purchased.

Choose the Right Thing to Sell

There are too many problems in medicine and not enough time or resources to solve them all. In the cases throughout this book, the physicians carefully chose what ideas to sell and understood they were competing for resources that could help solve any number of problems. There are a multitude of things to consider when selecting the right idea to sell. Among the most important is the amount of data available that supports the idea, its potential cost vs. benefit, the likelihood that it will succeed in solving the problem, and the potential time frame (long or short) for implementation. In an environment like healthcare with its host of problems, spending time on an idea with little chance of success can be frustrating, even demoralizing, not to mention financially irresponsible. However, even small successes can be a powerful impetus to solve bigger problems.

Dr. Barry Davids quickly realized his idea for emergency department staffing could not succeed because it was completely unacceptable to his group (Case 7). He therefore modified it to something that had a chance of acceptance—to an easier sell. Although it would not solve his real problem (how to provide 24-hour coverage by specialty trained physicians), it brought him a step closer to realizing this goal.

Dr. David Gersoff was unwilling to fight managed care's preauthorization policies until he had data to support his office staff's notion that the cost of adhering to the policies was excessive (Case 1). He firmly opposed the preauthorization policies, but larger and more politically influential practice groups in the area were unsuccessful at changing them. He therefore approached the issue cautiously, conducting a small, short-term, simple study in his office, knowing that unless the results were striking, there was little he could do. Because the results were so powerful, he had a good chance to impact the policies, or at least improve service on the part of the payer that would result in decreased practice costs. By choosing an issue supported with convincing data, he optimized his chances of selling the idea that a problem existed and needed to be addressed.

Finally, Dr. Lauren O'Connor's practice faced financial trouble that would take several years to correct, if it could be done at all (Case 3). Understanding that long-term recovery was dependent on small, short-term successes, she developed the idea to reinstate in-house laboratory services to increase practice revenue and quality.

Restoring her practice's financial health depended on many factors, but she knew that improving customer service and office morale were also essential to recovery. After a careful financial analysis, she chose to sell her idea by explaining that the group made a mistake when it eliminated the lab, from both a service and financial perspective. Her group was particularly ripe for her idea because they were willing to do anything, even overturn a previous decision, in order to save the practice.

Each physician's idea was specifically intended to address only a small piece of a larger problem. The physicians chose these pieces because each involved an area over which they had control. But what if you don't control any piece of the problem? Even worse, how do you sell an idea if you can't get an audience?

Get Your Foot in the Door

Decision makers have ideas pitched to them nearly every day. Sometimes the trick to winning their support involves getting their attention. If you're proposing a solution to a problem at the top of an organization's priority list, it should be easy to attract interest. If it's for a problem not on the list, however, one must use creative ways to draw attention to the idea. Entrepreneurs talk about the elevator pitch. It is a two-minute description of an idea that could be presented to someone riding an elevator with you (or otherwise next to you for a brief time). This can work to attract attention if the right person is in the elevator and can be quickly engaged. But elevator pitches, like any other sales presentation, should be carefully developed and rehearsed. Confusing, or even worse, boring a potential supporter could spell disaster for an idea.

Dr. Sally Beecher needed to get on her organization's radar screen before she could sell her idea to increase the number of ICU beds (Case 4). The hospital administration understood the problem, but because it was intermittent and did not fit into their strategic plan, Dr. Beecher needed a way to get attention for her idea. She conducted a feasibility study, a financial and operational analysis designed to evaluate a what-if scenario. She asked, "What if we had additional beds—would their use result in a profit?" By calculating the potential profit, her selling strategy changed dramatically. Her elevator pitch changed from "We had to refuse two patients this week, we need more beds," to "I have a financial feasibility analysis that shows if we had two more beds in the ICU, we'd be making money from them. Can I set up a meeting to show you?" Dr. Beecher found a way to get her foot in the door.

Taking time to get a foot in the door is difficult for physicians to accept. Again, doctors are accustomed to people listening to them, following their orders. The notion that they must compete for such a little thing as someone's attention is difficult to understand. But as Dr. Beecher found, there are times when it simply must be done. Once you've gotten the attention of the appropriate people, however, you need something to hold it. Money usually does the trick.

Pick the Right Numbers to Speak for You

People support an idea if there is something in it for them or their constituency. It is not a matter of selfishness, it is just that when it comes to business, people must chose wisely in distributing their support because its supply is not unlimited. So if you can use data to make a case for cost savings or profit, the chances of making a sale improve. But physicians are unaccustomed to presenting only the data that advances their case. They understand the value of presenting contrary data. And while there is a place in sales for mentioning risks, what needs to be done in the name of medical science and what normally promotes a sale should not be confused.

Selling an idea is not the same as proving a theory. The scientific foundation of medical practice is based on rigorous experimentation. A new therapy must meet specific criteria during an extensive and exacting process before it can be labeled effective, and the process involves time and resources. Even after the experimental process is complete, a peer review process that consumes additional time and resources is required before the results are deemed scientifically valid. In the case of a new therapy, this means it is proven clinically effective.

The physicians in the cases presented in this book had neither the time nor resources to approach problem solving as they would scientific research. They needed to act quickly and, in most cases, had limited means of data collection. Rather than attempt to prove their point scientifically, they collected data that would advance their argument. In each case, they conceded each study had methodological flaws as a result of practical limitations. By carefully choosing the kind of information they needed, however, each was able to obtain data to suggest, rather than prove, that their proposed solution was the answer to an important problem. And in each case, the data was powerful in selling the idea.

Dr. Gersoff's study of preauthorization costs incurred by his office (Case 1) lacked the statistical power (a large enough sample) for a scientific conclusion. His comparative analysis did not involve statistical significance. His findings, however, had meaning—they were the real costs to his practice. Scientists would want to know if these costs were representative of all practices and would suggest the use of scientific techniques to determine this. But Dr. Gersoff didn't particularly care about other practices. Even so, the simple study he developed for his practice could be replicated by any practice. If he were so inclined, he could enlist other practices to obtain similar data and make an even stronger argument to the managed-care payers of the need to change their preauthorization requirements.

Dr. Beecher lacked the data necessary to prove the profitability of additional ICU beds (Case 4). Instead, she used surrogate data (physician rather than hospital revenue) to build her case effectively. Dr. O'Hara's information about the catheterization laboratory was based on very limited data (Case 9). In each of these cases, the studies would have been severely criticized by scientific reviewers, with good reason, *if* they were meant to be scientific studies. Their purpose, however, was to support an argument, to sell an idea. The physicians only needed to determine which information (from which data) would help the most and then obtain it. This data, for the most part, involved money. But money is not the only force that motivates people.

Money Isn't Everything

While money is frequently the key to realizing an idea, it is not the only valuable commodity. Sometimes, for example, an endorsement is all that is required. Dr. Davids needed to sell his emergency medicine colleagues a plan that would be acceptable to the hospital and medical school administration (Case 7). He knew the physicians were dedicated to forming an all-specialist group. The creation of such an exclusive group would validate each member's decision to seek specialty training and provide the prestige and professional cohesiveness they sought. Dr. Davids used this knowledge to motivate the physicians to support a compromise staffing solution that, while costing the group in the short term, would bring them closer to their goal. Dr. Treadwell, however, had a more difficult time finding a motivator in the laboratory he managed (Case 6). Each staff member wanted something different. In the end, the common desire for a more pleasant workplace set the stage for progress.

Give Something to Get Something

Finding a motivator strong enough to sell an idea at first presentation is often difficult. Most sales involve negotiation. In a successful negotiation, one must focus on each party's interests and strive to invent options for mutual gain (see Lecture 7). After investing much time and effort in developing and articulating an idea and getting an audience for it, people may find it difficult to compromise on the specifics of a proposal. The key to a successful sale, though, is frequently more a matter of what you are willing to give, rather than receive.

Dr. Barry Davids started on the road to a successful sale only after realizing that negotiation was essential to selling his approach to his emergency physician group (Case 7). As the leader of a group of professional peers, he knew he was powerless to force a plan on the group. The only way to resolve the staffing issue was to find a working solution through negotiation.

Dr. Phillip Harvey, however, was in a different position. As principal partner in an expanding practice, he had the authority to implement changes in his offices through a simple decree (Case 2). The employees of his practice had no choice but to agree to his plans or resign. He knew he could easily find replacements for those unwilling to agree to the changes. His practice was successful, however, and he preferred to implement the changes without disrupting the quality of service. In order to win the support of his staff (and successfully sell his idea) he involved them in the decision-making process. Decisions about dress code, hours of operation, and the décor of the individual offices were placed in the hands of the staff at each office. So while they underwent a series of prescribed changes designed to standardize and centralize the practice, each individual office had control over many of the day-to-day aspects of their jobs and workplace. By relinquishing some of the decisions to his staff (and somewhat compromising his plan for standardization and centralization), he hoped to retain the support and excellent performance of his employees.

What if the idea you have to sell is that someone else's idea should be rejected? Dr. Gulisano found himself in that position when a proposal for a new dental clinic was presented (Case 5). His analysis of the situation uncovered strong evidence to suggest the clinic was a bad idea. But support for the clinic was strong and widespread. He knew the energy and enthusiasm for this proposal was a good thing and wanted to encourage the development of other ideas. So in his presentation outlining why the dental clinic proposal should not be supported, he was careful to describe the conditions under which it might be more desirable. Rather than criticize and deny their plan, he gave a little, recognizing their concerns and needs. Because Dr. Gulisano understood the elements of the dental clinic proposal that appealed to its proponents, he could have gone a step further and proposed an alternative idea—either one in development or in implementation that would appeal to them and could use their support and participation.

Other cases were more obvious in their need to negotiate in order to sell. Dr. Gersoff based a formal negotiation process with his payers on the preauthorization data he obtained (Case 1). Dr. Beecher got her proposal on the table and then needed to convince the hospital to support a plan to create more ICU beds (Case 4). Dr. Davids, having negotiated a workable solution for his own emergency medicine physician group, had to negotiate with the dean and hospital CEO for acceptance of his proposal (Case 7). Finally, Dr. O'Hara attempted to sell a new catheterization facility to a hospital (Case 9). His business plan was only the start of a negotiated sale.

Summary

Despite the handicaps of training that they must overcome, physicians are not completely unfamiliar with selling an idea, although they may think so. Many doctors negotiate for their patients, arguing with payers, suppliers, hospitals, and even colleagues to obtain what they believe is best for them. Each has sold the idea that a specific patient needs a specific resource many times during his or her career. Selling an idea that is not patient care–related is not very different. The skills needed are similar. Only the language and methods are different. By recognizing the similarities and adding some new knowledge and skills, physicians can obtain the power necessary to secure the resources they need to implement their ideas. The only other requirement is that they try.

Note

1. Burns, J. M. *Leadership*. New York: Harper & Row, 1978, p. 12.

How to Make an Oral Presentation

Stephen Rimar

This book is filled with tools and strategies for bringing an idea to fruition. It presents the case that written documents brimming with detail and logic are essential to gain support for a well-conceived plan. And that is true. But it is often an oral presentation that provides the enthusiasm and spark to trigger acceptance.

Why an Oral Pitch?

Clever investors know that when they provide support for an idea they actually declare support for the person behind it. They understand that the leader of a new business is just as important as the business idea itself, if not more important (see Lecture 9). He or she is often the key to a successful enterprise. So investors want to know as much about that person as they do about the plan. An efficient and effective way to know a person is to watch him, hear him speak, and see if there is that spark in his eyes that says, "This idea is a winner, and so am I."

For those who will decide the fate of a proposal, there are several advantages to attending an oral presentation in addition to, or even instead of a written presentation. First, it is considerably easier and usually more pleasant to sit back and listen to an oral presentation than to study a written proposal. Second, since a limited amount of information can be delivered during an oral presentation, the content presented is more likely to be succinct; there is less fluff than in a written presentation. For an audience that might be overwhelmed by the data presented in a written proposal, the oral presentation is much easier to digest, particularly if it is their introduction to the material. Finally, no matter how controlled an oral presentation is, the audience has the ability to interrupt the speaker with questions and create an interactive discussion about the proposal. This is, of course, impossible with a written presentation, which requires additional meetings or correspondence to address questions.

Presenters can use oral presentations to supplement the strengths of their written plans or to enhance the chances of having their written proposals considered in the first place. Oral presentations often serve as the vehicle for the initial pitch of an idea—a chance to grab the decision makers' attention. Or a presentation can satisfy the need for a detailed question and answer session following study of a written proposal by reviewers. In either event, oral presentations may be integral for translating an idea into reality, and their mastery represents an essential management skill for physicians.

Structure Is Important

Physicians are not strangers to oral presentations. Medical students are taught to present to patients on the very first day of clinical training. Indeed, virtually all medical training exercises, including case conferences, grand rounds, and even most board examinations, require an oral presentation of pertinent facts, case analysis, and recommendations. And practicing physicians rely on oral presentations daily for communication with clinical colleagues about patient care.

What kind of structure is necessary for a business presentation? Physicians are familiar with the structure of medical and scientific presentations. This structure (background, hypothesis, methods, etc.) works primarily because the audience is familiar with it and accepts it as standard operating procedure. Business presentations, unfortunately, have neither a common format nor audience.

Audience members approach a presentation unsure of the structure that best suits the content presented. Those who are knowledgeable of a presentation's content may expect some specific organization of the material to be covered, but most attendees likely have no more than a vague notion of how things will or should unfold. Since the presenter wants the audience to understand, accept, and commit to his ideas, it is necessary to structure the presentation in a way that promotes this. He needs to decide such things as the content to be presented and what can be omitted, the order of the content, what information will receive the most emphasis, and when and if questions will be entertained. The role of a presenter is much like that of a film director or editor. Each is challenged to provide a structure that satisfies multiple audience members, some of whom arrive with assumptions about what they will see and others with no such preconceptions, willing to have a structure imposed on them. Most audiences respond well to a structure that is compatible with what is being presented.

How to Structure an Oral Presentation

Physicians have a wide variety of experience with oral presentations. Some deliver talks frequently while others prefer never to speak in public. Whether an experienced expert or a hesitant novice, however, physicians can benefit from reconsidering the structure they use in their oral presentations.

Establish the Main Point

There is no better way to capture an audience than to go straight to the heart of the matter. And because there is no other time in a presentation when the speaker holds an audience's full attention without exerting any effort, the beginning of a presentation is the time to get the message out. One common reason why presentations fail is because the purpose of the presentation—what the presenter is selling—is unclear. For every minute that passes without an audience knowing what a presenter wants, some amount of interest in the speaker's message is lost.

Build a Platform for the Main Point

As soon as an audience knows the point of a presentation (the idea being put forth), the speaker needs to explain why the point is important. In other words, who cares? This can be done very briefly by restating the main point in the following sequence: (1) present a situation that highlights the area of concern; (2) state a complication to reinforce the need for action; (3) anticipate a question from the audience, the answer to which is the main point; and (4) state the main point as the answer to the question. This approach frames the speaker's idea and structures how the audience thinks about it. Framing an idea or position properly is vital to a successful presentation, just as it is in a successful negotiation (see Case 7).

Anticipate the Audience's Primary Question

If the main point of a presentation is properly framed and clearly articulated, the natural response to it will be a question—usually Why? but occasionally How? The question will be voiced by audience members, even if they do so only silently in their heads. For example, if the main point of the presentation is, "We must open a new office," the initial question of the audience will likely be, "Why?" Answering the question is an extremely important aspect of the presentation because, if done successfully, it engages the audience from the start. Without making a sound, the audience interacts with the presenter.

Use Audience Question/Speaker Answer Cycle

The audience/speaker interaction established in the first minute can be used throughout a presentation to lead listeners to an understanding and acceptance of an idea. It is a powerful tool to convince an audience of the speaker's point of view.

The concept is simple. The main point in the presentation is followed by an answer to the audience's anticipated question. For example, the main point is "We should open a new office." The anticipated question is, "Why?" Therefore, the next point of the presentation should be, "Because we have an opportunity to increase our business as never before." The anticipated response of the audience to this statement will likely be the question, "What do you mean?" or "How?" Each subsequent statement then becomes an answer to an anticipated question by the audience, which prompts another question (usually how, why, where, or what). One can see that this technique enables the speaker to direct the audience, to steer its thinking and reasoning in the desired direction.

Close the Loop at the End of the Presentation

While a successful oral presentation leads an audience to understand an idea, accept it, and commit to action, it also discusses the steps that must be taken. The final moments of a presentation are the speaker's last chance to ensure the commitment of the audience, and the close must be prepared with this in mind. This is the time for more than a mere summary of the presentation—it is the time for the final sales pitch and a call to action. It is the speaker's opportunity to direct those committed to the cause.

Stay within the Presentation's Time Limit

One sure way to antagonize potential supporters is to take advantage of them. And that is exactly what a presenter does by exceeding the time limit for his talk. Any presenter looking for more than hostile stares from his audience needs to plan his presentation to end on time (or earlier). Timing a presentation (and adding time if the potential for audience interaction exists), therefore, is an important aspect of preparation.

How to Say No

In Case 5, Dr. Vincent Gulisano found himself in the unenviable position of having to recommend against implementing a popular proposal—the establishment of a new dental clinic. Although the reasons for his decision were compelling, he was sure his advice would not be well received. His presentation to the CEO and hospital board had to be convincing, because he knew they expected him to endorse, not veto, the proposal. Using the presentation structure outlined above, he developed the following slides to accompany his oral presentation.

The presentation begins with a simple opening. It builds to the main point (Slide #4) by framing the situation (Slide #2) and raising a complication (Slide #3). The main point then addresses this complication. The situation (the hospital clinics cover all other areas of care, serve the community, and provide clinical experiences for trainees) frames the area of concern for the audience. The complication (no dental clinic at present, an underserved population, deficiency in training programs, and the potential for more patients) is

**A new dental clinic
for our hospital**

Current situation

- Hospital primary-care clinics
  - Include all areas except dental
  - Major provider for local population
  - Site of professional training programs

What's the problem?

- No dental clinic
- Population underserved
- Training program deficient in dentistry
- More patients needed for other clinics

**Should we establish a
dental clinic?**

NO

Why not?

- Population not underserved
- Too expensive
- Several dental training pro-grams nearby
- Will not draw patients to other clinics
- Many competitors

Population not underserved

- Medicaid managed care pro-vides wide coverage and choice
- In immediate area:
  - Two city clinics with dental service
  - Eight school-based dental clinics
  - Ten private dental offices

Too expensive

- Will operate at a loss
  - Even with optimistic revenue projection
- No available space
  - Would take space from existing clinics
- Start-up costs not recoverable

Nearby training programs

- Six dental residency programs within driving distance

Will not bring new patients

- Unlikely to capture new busi-ness
  - Patients unwilling to switch dentists
  - Saturated local Medicaid dental market

No dental clinic: Why?

- Our population is not under-served
- It's too expensive
- Several dental training pro-grams nearby
- It will not draw patients to other clinics
- There are too many competitors

Answer is NO: Unless

- Higher Medicaid fees
- Fewer dental providers
- Start-up and supporting grants

a statement that highlights the circumstances forcing action. This leads to a question (Should we establish a dental clinic?), which the leads to an answer—the main point of the presentation (in this case, no).

The presentation then focuses on each reason for rejecting the idea; there is some elaboration, but it is succinct. The presentation assumes that the full set of data will be reviewed at another time. After all, this is a summary. The close of the presentation is likewise brief and to the point. The presenter summarizes by restating the main point (rejection of a new dental clinic) and why it is so. He finishes, however, by stating future steps. For many proposals, steps listed at the presentation's close would be actions necessary to start implementing the proposal. In this case, they include steps that could be taken if changes occurred to make the proposal more attractive.

How to Do It

The ability to deliver a good oral presentation is a critical management skill. For physicians interested in management, it is an art worth mastering. Whatever the content or structure, consider the following points when making any presentation.

1. *Decide on your message.* Decide what your message is and state it clearly. Both the speaker and, if asked, the audience, should be able to state the main point of the presentation in a single sentence, preferably a short one. If the main point is not simple, rethink it. If it requires more than 10 words to state the main point, it likely has not been reduced to its core. In the previous presentation, the message was clear: "We should not build a dental clinic." Once you have articulated your message, be sure that every part of the presentation echoes it. As a final check, ask someone to listen to the presentation and repeat the main point to you. You will know right away if you have successfully communicated your message.

2. *Target the audience.* There are three questions to ask yourself about any audience: How much does it know about the topic?, How interested is it in the topic?, and What do I want the audience to do with the message? The answers will differ depending on the audience, suggesting that different audiences require different approaches. For example, a presentation to a finance group will not be the same as a presentation to clinical staff. The finance group, for example, may know little about dental clinics; nor might they care. Conversely, clinical staff may have no concept of the costs associated with establishing an outpatient service, and perhaps could not care less. The content of the presentation, therefore, would need to be different for each of these groups because of their varying education, experience, and interest. Many speakers ignore this fundamental principle and make the same presentation regardless of the audience. A successful presentation, however, is designed for the audience, not the speaker. Indeed, one may need to develop several presentations—one for each audience.

3. *Don't let technology confuse the message.* Speakers made successful presentations long before computers, overhead projectors, and even color charts were invented. Use these technologies to enhance, not hinder a presentation. Fancy overheads, video clips, and imaginative sound bites can help tremendously, but they can also kill a presentation. For the most part, the more dependent a presentation is on technology, the less dependent it is on the presenter. How often have you seen a presentation come to a standstill because a laptop failed to function properly or a slide projector bulb burned out? Use technology wisely and be ready for it to fail completely.

Experienced speakers have a backup plan (or two) in case technology fails. For example, if a computer is needed for a presentation, consider bringing your own rather than relying on the house computer. Also, put your presentation on a floppy disk (or two) as well as the hard drive. Some speakers bring overheads in case the computer projection equipment doesn't work, since most organizations own standard overhead projectors. As a fail-safe backup, consider bringing hard copies of your presentation (on paper) and be ready to distribute them to the audience. Finally, arrive early enough to test all the equipment and make sure you know how to use it. Be sure to have a tech failure sequence rehearsed.

4. *Keep the house lights on.* Left alone, many of us are prone to daydream or sleep during a presentation. A dark room encourages this. Except in the rare case in which a projected image needs perfect resolution, sacrifice the projected image for the live image of the presenter. Demand the attention of the audience by keeping the lights on; force them to look at you. This will not only help you control the presentation, but also reinforce your role as leader.

5. *Look at people.* If you want to engage an audience, you must look at them. Too many speakers focus on the overheads, either reading directly from them, or pointing with a laser dot at words on a screen. The problem with presentation materials, particularly overheads or written handouts, is that an audience has a natural tendency to read them as soon as they're presented. The only way to get peoples' attention is to look into their eyes and engage them. Try making eye contact with every person in the room at least once during the presentation. Stepping away from a podium can also draw attention to you.

6. *Graphs and pictures are better than words, sometimes.* Sharing data with your audience may help you get the main point of your presentation across. But if you spend too much time discussing data, you will have little time to put it in context. Use graphs to summarize pertinent data and make them simple and self-explanatory; simple illustrations minimize the time the audience spends deciphering rather than listening to you.

Pictures can help presentations, but they often require that the room be darkened for viewing. Be aware of this potential interruption to the flow of a presentation and plan accordingly. Remember, too, that any and all material can be reviewed in as much detail as needed *after* a presentation.

7. *Keep your points short and your bullet points shorter.* When you project a slide, people will read it, so make it brief. Understand that an audience will not give you attention until after they read the slide. Some presenters control the audience's focus by covering up any bullet points not being discussed, or by using computer technology to show only one point at a time. Any technique can be helpful, as long as it doesn't interfere with the flow of the presentation. To be easily read, bullet points on slides should be large and simple—use fancy fonts and busy slide backgrounds sparingly.

8. *Practice.* Presentations are performances and should be practiced. The purpose of the practice is to polish the public-speaking skills of the presenter and test the effectiveness of the presentation on a trial audience. Not everyone is a showman or an orator, but good presentation skills can be learned. If you must, write a script for your presentation and memorize it. Avoid reading from a paper or slides; it prevents you from engaging the audience and makes for a boring presentation. Finally, if the idea presented is the brainchild of several people, choose the person most talented at presenting to talk about it, even if he or she is not the leader of the effort. If possible, however, have the entire group attend the presentation and rehearse the method the group will use to field questions (i.e., who will answer questions on which topics).

9. *Watch other speakers and learn.* The best way to learn about presenting is to watch the pros. Pay attention to presentations at work or even on television. Think about presentations that have convinced you to support an idea, and characteristics and behaviors of speakers who have held your attention. Ask yourself what made them effective and then emulate them.

INDEX